THEOLOGY AND THE ARTS

D1350558

THEOLOGY AND THE ARTS

Encountering God through Music, Art and Rhetoric

Richard Viladesau

Paulist Press
New York / Mahwah, N.J.

Cover design by James Brisson

Type Design by Casa Petta

Library of Congress Cataloging-in-Publication Data

Viladesau, Richard.
    Theology and the arts: encountering God through music, art, and rhetoric / by Richard Viladesau.
        p. cm.
    Includes bibliographical references and index.
    ISBN 0-8091-3927-8 (alk. paper)
    1. Aesthetics—Religious aspects—Christianity. 2. Christianity and the arts. I. Title
BR115.A8 V56 2000
261.5'7—dc21   00-026145

Published by Paulist Press
997 Macarthur Boulevard
Mahwah, New Jersey 07430

www.paulistpress.com

Printed and bound in the
United States of America

CONTENTS

To the memory of my father
Richard Viladesau, Sr.
1921–1999

Introduction

"Beauty is back."

So proclaims a large, bold-print headline on the front page of a recent issue of *The Chronicle of Higher Education*. The feature article to which it refers details how aesthetic criteria have once again become an important part of contemporary cultural and literary studies.[1] The same declaration might be made of other fields as well—including religious studies and theology. The relation of beauty to the gospel message has received increasing attention in recent years. A half century ago, author Dorothy Sayers made her much-quoted remark:

> In such things as politics, finance, sociology, and so on, there really are a philosophy and a Christian tradition; we do know more or less what the Church has said and thought about them, how they are related to Christian dogma, and what they are supposed to do in a Christian country.
>
> But oddly enough, we have no Christian esthetic—no Christian philosophy of the arts.[2]

On closer examination, one finds that Sayers's complaint was perhaps not entirely well founded: Christian philosophy and theology in the Middle Ages produced a profound metaphysical theory of beauty (although, it is true, without a great deal of attention to the arts). In addition, some early twentieth-century neo-Scholastics (in particular, Jacques Maritain) gave a prominent place to the theological consideration of art. Nevertheless, it is clear that for a long time aesthetics was located more or less at the periphery of Christian thought and that in recent years it has moved into a much more central position of theological prominence.

The motives for this renewed interest are perhaps most notable on the pastoral level. In the Roman Catholic Church, the *aggiornamento* of the Second Vatican Council represented a renewed emphasis on making the Word of God intelligible to contemporary people. The reform of the liturgy was one major step in this direction. At the same time, it posed significant challenges on the aesthetic level. It quickly became apparent that the aesthetic qualities of the Latin liturgy—especially its music, but also the entire ambience of mystery that arose from celebration in an ancient language, with age-old symbols and rituals—could not simply be passed over into the vernacular. The reformed liturgy created new opportunities but also placed more demands on both ministers and congregations. Despite the proliferation of new music and experimentation with different styles of celebration, in general there has not been sufficient time for the development of musical, architectural, and visual forms that preserve the intentions of the liturgy, with its strong emphasis on theological meaning, and at the same time attain a high level of beauty.

This situation has made it apparent to many ministers how important the aesthetic dimension—which for so long could be taken for granted—has actually become in concrete pastoral practice. Many religious experiences are inextricably aesthetic—few, indeed, could be called purely spiritual or intellectually theological. The times when people meet their own or the community's Christian faith most profoundly—one thinks, for example, of such family occasions as baptisms, weddings, and funerals or such feasts as Christmas and Easter—are also occasions when they are seeking for a dimension of beauty. From the liturgical point of view as well, this is important: However crucial the verbal dimensions of celebration, including catechesis, instruction, and reflection, there is also need for a rich symbolic communication to bring people emotionally and intellectually into a mystery in which words are inadequate.

Probably many parish ministers would agree that the most significant issues in ministry today (and the cause of most conflicts and disaffection) are frequently less directly theological than aesthetic. Concrete religious decisions often have more to do with taste and with styles of spirituality than with conceptual theology. On the global level, the legitimate differences among the Christian churches, once historical misunderstandings have been overcome, frequently consist largely in matters of style: as Frank Burch Brown puts it, the denominations represent different "performances" of the same Christian classic.[3] On a more local level, commitment to or alienation from a particular church, way of worship, or liturgy can often be based on matters of aesthetic comfort or discomfort. And within parish communities practical questions arise that raise the question of the relation of the aesthetic to other values: Is it right to spend money on renovating a church in the light of the always pressing needs of the poor and the demands of Christian witness? Should one tear down and replace a beautiful old church that has many sentimental associations but is architecturally unsuitable to contemporary celebration or provides inadequate space for the congregation? Where aesthetic decisions are to be made, whose criteria of beauty should be determinative? How does one deal with pluralism and diversity of taste?

If it is clear, at least upon reflection, that aesthetics has a great deal to do with concrete religious life and that its study should claim the attention of both pastoral ministers and their congregations, it is less immediately evident that beauty and art have to do with theology—or vice-versa—except perhaps insofar as "pastoral" theology enters into the study of the communication of the message. Theology is classically conceived as "faith seeking understanding," and is therefore frequently taken to be the specifically conceptual, intellectual aspect of Christian life.[4] In this view, theology may provide material for artists, as it frequently has done in Western literature, painting, and music; but the reverse movement is barely conceivable. (Obviously, the scriptures would be a large exception to this; but the classical view of theology, although it recognized the metaphorical character of much of scripture, tended nevertheless to abstract from its artistry as such and to treat it more or less as a compendium of propositional revelation, sometimes expressed poetically as an accommodation to the weakness of the human intellect.[5]) Theology itself was to be a science (in the Aristotelian sense),[6] not an art.

There is, however, another way of conceiving theology, one that forms the basis for this book: not simply as a separate sphere, separate from and complementary to the aesthetic domain of Christian existence, but as one that overlaps with the latter substantially, both in content and in form.

The commonality between theology and the aesthetic may be seen first of all in terms of theology's object. The first chapter of this book explores this connection: the intrinsic relationship of God with beauty. Using music as an example, this chapter enunciates the book's underlying theme: artistic beauty as a means of the mind's "ascent" to God—or, from another point of view, as a medium of divine self-revelation. On the basis of this insight, the two central chapters turn from the object of faith (and hence of theology) to a more focused concern for theology as a reflection on faith and attempt to establish its methodological connections with art. Chapter 2 explores the thesis that the history of art (in particular, painting) manifests paradigm changes that parallel those in other areas of Western intellectual history, including theology. This parallel history suggests a movement toward a convergence between art and theology in the emerging contemporary theological paradigm. Chapter 3 builds on this idea, exploring ways in which art can serve as a theological "text" or source.

The last chapter moves from theological aesthetics in general (the study of beauty and art in the light of God and revelation) to the consideration of what may be called "aesthetic theology": theology itself exercised in the realm of art, in particular as a form of rhetoric. Chapter 4 focuses on what is arguably the primary creative act of theological artistry in Christian ministry, namely, the art of preaching: the place where word, theological reflection, and art come together in the symbolic context of liturgy.[7] Here the more philosophical and methodological reflections of the middle chapters rejoin the pastoral-aesthetic concerns of the first.

The unifying motif of the book is beauty as revelation, and art as the human mediation that both enables and limits its revelatory power. It is my contention, then, that art enters into theology not merely in those areas of pastoral practice that have a clearly aesthetic dimension (for example the use of liturgical music or preaching), but also in the realm of reflection, not only in pastoral or practical theology, but also in the divisions traditionally called fundamental and systematic. This claim is not intended in any way to deny or to minimize theology's need for intellectual rigor and conceptual abstraction (which have their own form of beauty). Nor is it to reduce all theology to a purely "intratextual" aesthetic enterprise. The notion of theology as rhetoric—a systematic artistic construct of a "way of seeing" the world based on a presumed revelation—has received much attention in contemporary religious thought, sometimes indeed being regarded by "postmodern" thinkers as the only viable contemporary model of theology. It will be seen, however, that in my view "rhetorical theology"—or better, "aesthetic theology," of which the rhetorical is only one subdivision— need not be regarded as an alternative to a transcendental/metaphysical form of theologizing; rather, the two may be seen as equally necessary, complementary, and mutually corrective modes of thinking, each of which has a place in both theoretical study and pastoral practice.

This book makes no pretense to completeness. I have elsewhere attempted to give a more fundamental account of the relation between theology and the various aspects of aesthetics: imagination, beauty, and art.[8] Here I have chosen several significant subthemes, and their treatment is aimed more at illustration and enticement than at systematic explanation. I have purposely mixed theoretical concerns with more pastoral ones and have used different forms of art to illustrate my theses: in the first chapter, music; in the second and third, pictorial art; in the fourth, rhetoric. Although the book has a thematic unity and a logical progression, the four chapters can also be read independently or in different order according to the reader's interests (the first and fourth chapters are particularly related to each other, as are the second and third).

The Book and the Virtual Museum

The author of a book like this is posed with a difficult dilemma. On the one hand, it cries out for illustrations; on the other hand, the cost of publishing reproductions is so high (even for black-and-white plates—color being completely out of the question) that the book would be placed out of the reach of most of its intended readers. Fortunately, contemporary technology offers a possible solution: Many university art history departments, as well as other organizations, offer extensive on-line illustrations of the great works of Western art; in addition, many of the world's great museums have web sites that give access to substantial portions of their collections. Presuming that most of the readers of this book will be computer literate, in place of costly reproductions, I have included the Internet addresses of sites where appropriate illustrations of the text may be found. I believe that the advantages of this method will outweigh the additional burden it places on the reader. The web gives access to excellent reproductions, usually in color, of large size, and frequently with the possibility of multiple and/or detailed views. In addition, the reader can usually find further examples at the same sites.

The interested reader may also explore further through the many art history links that exist on the web—each of which will give access to others. A few of the major ones may be found at:

•**www.arts.mcgill.ca/programs/art_history/arthistlinks.htm**

•**www.umich.edu/~hartspc/histart/mother**

•**witcombe.bcpw.sbc.edu/ARTHLinks.htm**

The day has not yet come (although it may not be far in the future) for the virtual concert hall. I have, however, provided a basic CD discography for musical works referred to in the text. Notes giving academic sources or expansions on the text are indicated by superscript Arabic numerals, and the notes are placed at the end of the book. References to works of art or music are indicated in the text by superscript letters. These notes to illustrations or musical performances will be found at the end of each chapter.

I wish to express my thanks to all those who have aided in the inspiration and production of this book: to Dr. Mary Callaway, for her encouragement of my research in this field; to the Rev. Nicholas Lombardi, S.J., of the Faculty Resource

Center at Fordham University, for his expert assistance with computer images; to the Rev. Joseph Scott, C.S.P., of Paulist Press, for his editorial assistance; and especially to David Gides, both for his aid in preparing the text and for giving me the freedom to work on it through his tireless, cheerful, and efficient performance as my graduate assistant. I also wish to thank all my colleagues—fellow faculty members and students—in the Department of Theology at Fordham University for the generous, dedicated, and genial community of scholarship they have created.

Abbreviations •

AAS   *Acta Apostolicae Sedis.*

DS   *Enchyridion Symbolorum Definitionum et Declarationum de Rebus Fidei et Morum*, ed. by H. Denzinger and A. Schonmetzer, S.J., XXXIII edition (Freiburg im Breisgau, 1965).

Inst.   John Calvin, *Institutes of the Christian Religion.*

PG   *Patrologia Graeca*, ed. by J. P. Migne (Paris, 1857ss).

PL   *Patrologia Latina*, ed. by J. P. Migne (Paris, 1878ss).

ST   Thomas Aquinas, *Summa Theologiae*, Leonine edition (Rome, 1952).

TDNT   *Theological Dictionary of the New Testament*, ed. by G. Kittel and G. Friedrich (Grand Rapids, Mich., 1964–76).

Chapter 1
God and the Beautiful: Art as a Way to God

Recent years have seen a remarkable renewal of interest in sacred music. The extraordinary phenomenon of a recording of Gregorian chant ascending to a position in the best-seller charts has spawned a host of imitations. A number of the best-known and most widely respected composers of contemporary music are renowned largely for their explicitly religious works. Henryk Górecki notes that only a few years ago, no one paid any attention to his work;[1] now, following the enormous success of his "Symphony of Sorrowful Songs" (*Third Symphony for Soprano and Orchestra*), whose lyrics include a prayer and a meditation on the sorrows of the Virgin Mary, he joins such other religiously inspired composers as Geoffrey Burgon, James MacMillan, John Tavener, and Arvo Pärt in forming one of the most important creative forces of the late twentieth century.[a] At the same time, the "ancient music" movement has not only sparked revivals of the sacred music of such giants as Bach, Handel, Vivaldi, Telemann, Haydn, and Mozart, but has uncovered long-lost sacred master-pieces from virtually every period of Christian history; the "world music" scene is enriched by performances and recordings of sacred music ranging from Maronite hymns to Sufi chant and Hindu *bhajans*.

It is difficult to discern the causes of this renewed interest. Is it perhaps a sign of the spiritual hunger of an essentially materialistic culture? An evidence of religious revival? Is it nostalgia for tradition, for a bygone and simpler world, or is it perhaps merely aesthetic curiosity—a transient phase in public taste? Is it possible that sacred music is able to become popular because for most people it is no longer genuinely sacred? That, having lost its religious function, it can be appreciated for its charm or its sense of mystery precisely because it has lost the ability to carry an existential challenge? Is religious sentiment attractive simply as an aesthetic object: one that people like to look at but do not share, just as adults delight in childrens' belief in Santa Claus or as modern people appreciate the myths of the Greeks as literature and art because of, not despite, their lack of existential religious meaning?

Should we perhaps take the appreciation of religiously oriented beauty as a last remnant of a declining sense of the sacred: the degeneration of religion into art? To paraphrase an observation of Alfred North Whitehead: Just as art—in the form of ritual and emotion—marks the emergence of the life of spirit to a level above that of mere physical subsistence, so conversely religion in its decline sinks back to the merely aesthetic level.[2] Author and moral philosopher Iris Murdoch seems to be looking at the same phenomenon, but from its more positive side, when she writes that:

> Good art, thought of as symbolic force rather than statement, provides a stirring image of a pure transcendent value, a steady visible enduring higher good, and perhaps provides for many people, in an unreligious age without prayer or sacraments, their clearest experience of something grasped as separate and precious and beneficial and held quietly and unpossessively in the attention.[3]

In that case, should theology and religion be looking with particular attention to the arts as the most effective remaining point of contact between the secular mind and the sacred?

Probably there is no single cause and no single meaning to the recent spate of popularity for sacred music. Whatever we may make of it, it is, in any case, a reminder of the intimate connection of music—from its very earliest times and in its very highest moments—with religion. The same may be said of the other arts as well. It will be the purpose of this chapter to look at the most fundamental aspect of this connection: the relation of artistic beauty to the human spirit's "ascent" to God. Rather than approach the topic in the abstract, I will take the example of music as a paradigm and ask in what ways it can serve in the apprehension and service of the sacred.

Before doing so, however, we must note the existence of certain tensions between the aesthetic and religious sphere—tensions especially apparent in the history of Western religious music. Having examined these tensions, and recognized the legitimacy of the reasons behind them, we will nevertheless argue that beauty has an intrinsic relation to the sacred and that art can therefore be a means of the mind's apprehension of God—or, from another point of view, of God's self-revelation through creation. Once again, music will serve as the paradigmatic example. Finally, I will briefly consider some of the concrete implications of such insights for liturgical praxis.

A. Historical Tensions Between Music and the Sacred

The association of music with the sacred is taken for granted in the religious sense of most Christians. Who can imagine church celebration without Christmas carols, without psalms and hymns, without the organ? The haunting monody of Gregorian chant; the almost unearthly beauty of the choral motets of Palestrina or Victoria; the solid unison of congregational hymns; the mystical harmonies of Byzantine choirs; the dramatic grandeur of the symphonic masses of Mozart, Haydn, and Beethoven; the infectious intensity of gospel singing—all have formed Christian religious consciousness to such a degree that they now seem inextricably bound with the message itself. Music has flourished in myriad forms in its connection with Christian worship. Different as those forms may be, they share a common element of devotion to beauty of expression that it is difficult to imagine Christianity without.

Nevertheless, just as the association of music with worship has a long tradition, so does a nagging suspicion about it. A certain "musical puritanism"[4] raises its head periodically in the church, leading to varying degrees of tension between art and spirituality. These points of apparent conflict challenge the seemingly obvious connection between artistic beauty and God. Indeed, they introduce an element of suspicion: Is it possible that, even for the believer, there is a danger of the "degeneration" Whitehead spoke of? Might the beautiful not be a distraction, an escape—a way of deflecting the religious imperative and taming it by making it an aesthetic object? Do art and music remove the aspect of "holy fear" from the numinous *mysterium tremendum et fascinans*? As Iris Murdoch says, we may ultimately want to defend music and artistic beauty in general against these charges, but we should also recognize how worthy of consideration some of the charges are.[5] It will be instructive to look more closely at these tensions and their reasons, focusing specifically on the place of music in the church. We will find that the objections are of several different kinds and have different causes, but underlying all is the fundamental question of the relationship of God to beauty. Hence a brief historical overview of these conflicts will shed light on our more ultimate goal of understanding the positive role of beauty as a way to God.

The patrologist Johannes Quasten, in his magistral study of music in antiquity,[6] documents the extent to which the early church placed severe strictures on the use of music in worship. A Christian polemic against music appears already in Tatian, late in the second century; it grows more explicit and intense through the third century and is commonplace in the fourth. There were two interconnected reasons for this. First, certain forms of music were associated with superstitious and sensual pagan worship. (Early Christians inherited this critique not only from Judaism but also from the pagan philosophers.) Second, music was suspect for moral reasons; it appeared to favor the wrong side in the conflict of spirit against the flesh—a dichotomy that owed its prominence in the Christian community largely from the reinterpretation of St. Paul in the light of Platonic thought.[7]

The association of music with the vices of pagandom was apparent to Hellenistic Christians and was determinative of their attitudes. Music not only permeated pagan cultic acts, but was in general considered consecrated to the divine powers. Furthermore, the ancients took seriously the idea that music reaches to the heart and affects one's life. Among the ancient Greeks, as among the Chinese, some musical modes and instruments were considered to be intrinsically sensual and leading to the excitement of the lower passions. John Chrysostom condemned musical instruments, along with dancing and obscene songs, as being the "devil's garbage."[8] Moreover, some instruments, like the flute (*aulos*) were associated with the orgiastic frenzy incited in the Dionysian rites (Aristotle in the *Politics* explains that the flute is an immoral instrument, opposed to reason, and should be prohibited to young people;[9] St. Jerome later would say that a good Christian girl should not even know what a flute is). Female choirs who performed at the rituals were considered the "harem" of the gods, and female singers (like actresses in later times) were suspected of loose morals (a reason why male church choirs, using boys' voices for the soprano parts, have prevailed in some Christian traditions until modern times).

The fathers of the church taught that in contrast to pagan cult, which was sensual and irrational, Christian worship should aspire to the philosophical ideal of "spiritual sacrifice," identified by them with the Johannine "worship in spirit and truth."[10] They held that this kind of worship takes place interiorly and should avoid the trappings associated with the external and bloody sacrifices of the pagan and Jewish temples–including the kinds of music that were an intrinsic part of those rites.

It was of course recognized that the Old Testament not only spoke approvingly of the use of music (including instruments) in worship, but even commanded it. However, in the Hellenistic church, derived principally from Gentile roots, the music prescribed by the Torah for Jewish ritual was thought to be an accommodation by God to the weakness of the covenanted people—much like the permission of divorce in the Law of Moses.[11] The fathers supported their position by quoting out of context such passages as Amos 5:23—"Away from me with the noise of your songs; the playing of your harps I do not wish to hear"——and Isaiah 5:12— "they have lyre and harp, timbrel and flute and wine at their feasts; but they do not regard the deeds of the Lord."[12] As far as Christian worship is concerned, they interpreted the instruments allegorically as representing powers of the soul and mind. Thus, for example, Pseudo-Origen writes that when the psalm says, "Praise him in the sound of the trumpet," the "trumpet" is to be understood as the contemplative mind.[13]

These philosophical considerations did not lead to the total exclusion of music; after all, St. Paul had exhorted the community to "address one another with psalms, hymns, and spiritual songs, singing and making melody to the Lord." (Some patristic commentators, however, saw Paul's addition of "in your hearts" as a confirmation of their spiritualizing interpretation.[14]) Simple monophonic singing was permitted in worship, as long as the text was not lost in elaborate melody. According to St. Augustine, Athanasius insisted on a form of "chant" that was "nearer to speaking than to singing," and Augustine himself was sometimes inclined in the same way.[15] Instrumental music, even to accompany song, was generally forbidden. (Quasten notes that the *Canons of Basil* of the fourth century prescribe that a lector who insists upon accompanying the chant with a stringed instrument should be excommunicated!)

Nevertheless, the Platonic philosophical currents that were adopted by the church did not oppose the idea of music per se. Indeed, the objections against "earthly" music in the early church were frequently based on the notion that music in itself is a *heavenly* reality. "Real" music is celestial, spiritual, and therefore inaudible; as Philo of Alexandria wrote in *De Plantatione*, the songs that truly praise God are "not such as the audible voice sings, but such as are raised and re-echoed by the invisible mind." Even earthly music, after all, is not simply a matter of sound—which can also be mere chaotic noise—but depends on the proper proportion and ordering being present in the sounds. A higher form of music, then, is that in which the proportion is perceived not by the lower senses, but purely by the heart and intellect, without the distracting sensual quality of audible sound.

(This idea of music as essentially something purely spiritual, whose effect is entirely within the soul, is the basis of the ancient classification of music among the "liberal" arts, along with mathematics and logic, while painting and sculpture, which require an effect in matter, were considered "servile" arts. This distinction was preserved throughout the Middle Ages and was enshrined in the curriculum of the universities. At the same time, the notion that the essence of music is separable from sound allowed the medieval mind to regard all proportion as "musical" and to attempt to structure even the visible world according to its principles. Thus the Gothic cathedrals were conceived as a kind of polyphony in stone, echoing the higher "music" of the mathematical proportions of the universe itself.)

It is both interesting and instructive to read how St. Augustine agonized over the use of music in the church. During his time, the singing of hymns and psalms (already customary in Eastern churches) had only recently been adopted in the church of Milan.[b] The practice had been begun by St. Ambrose to provide an encouraging form of prayer for the increased night vigils during the persecutions fomented by Justina, the Arian-influenced mother of the boy-emperor Valentinian.[16] (Apparently the use of hymns was a response to the practice of the Arians, who attracted the common people and scandalized the orthodox by using popular tunes in the liturgy.)

We see in Augustine a prime example of putting music in the Platonic context of the struggle between spirit and flesh. He is attracted by the usefulness of song for raising the soul to God, but on the other hand he fears that its pleasures will entrap the soul in a lower order of beauty and prevent its ascent to the true Good:

> The delight of the ear drew me and held me more firmly, but you unbound and liberated me. Now I confess that I repose just a little in those sounds to which your words give life, when they are sung by a sweet and skilled voice; not such that I cling to them, but that I can rise out of them when I wish. But it is with the words by which they have life that they gain entry

into me, and seek in my heart a place of some honor, even if I scarcely provide them a fitting one. Sometimes I seem to myself to grant them more respect than is fitting, when I sense that our souls are more piously and earnestly moved to the ardor of devotion by these sacred words when they are thus sung than when not thus sung, and that all the affections of our soul, by their own diversity, have their proper measures (*modos*) in voice and song, which are stimulated by I know not what secret correspondence. But the gratification of my flesh—to which I ought not to surrender my mind to be enervated—frequently leads me astray, as the senses do not accompany reason in such a way as patiently to follow; but having gained admission only because of it, seek even to run ahead and lead it. I sin thus in these things unknowingly, but afterwards I know.

Sometimes, however, in avoiding this deception too vigorously, I err by excessive severity, and sometimes so much so that I wish every melody of the sweet songs to which the Davidic Psalter is usually set, to be banished from my ears and from the church itself. And safer to me seems what I remember was often told me concerning Athanasius, bishop of Alexandria, who required the reader of the psalm to perform it with so little inflection of voice that it was closer to speaking than to singing.

However, when I recall the tears which I shed at the song of the Church in the first days of my recovered faith, and even now as I am moved not by the song but by the things that are sung, when sung with fluent voice and music that is most appropriate, I acknowledge again the great benefit of this practice. Thus I vacillate between the peril of pleasure and the value of the experience, and I am led more—while advocating no irrevocable position—to endorse the custom of singing in church so that by the pleasure of hearing the weaker soul might be elevated to an attitude of devotion. Yet when it happens to me that the song moves me more than the thing that is sung, I confess that I have sinned blamefully and then prefer not to hear the singer.[17]

From the end of antiquity through the Middle Ages, music, in the form of the singing of texts, gradually came to occupy an increasingly important place in the church. The legend of the "invention" of Western chant by St. Gregory the Great (whence "Gregorian" chant) oversimplifies what was actually a long and complex evolution whose intricacies are only now being uncovered by musical historians.[c] But Gregory's compilation of already existing chants and his founding of the Roman Schola Cantorum in A.D. 600 undoubtedly gave a strong impetus to the development of church music. As Christianity adapted to new cultures and established itself as the universal religion of Western Europe, the older scruples arising from the association of music with pagan Roman and Greek worship became less relevant. The loss of Latin as the universal popular language in the Middle Ages no doubt increased the importance of church music, for the beauty of the sound not only glorified God and solemnized the ritual but also provided a substitute form of sacred experience for a general populace that could no longer understand the texts.

In this context it is instructive to read St. Thomas Aquinas and to compare his reflections on music with Augustine's. In the *Summa Theologica* (II II, q. 91 art. 2) he asks the question, "Whether song should be used in prayer of praise (*ad laudem divinam*)."[18] As usual, he first states the objections against the position he will take. In this case, the objections stem from Patristic tradition and echo those cited above. In St. Thomas's answers, we note several things. First of all, he rejects the Platonic division between spirit and flesh: Corporeal song can also be spiritual and can lead to spiritual devotion (*ad 1am*). Second, the fathers (according to Aquinas) did not reject singing as such, but only its abuse; that is, they wished to eliminate only a theatrical kind of singing that was inappropriate to the church (*ad 2am*) because it was aimed toward ostentation and pleasure, not devotion. But, Thomas implies, "*abusus non tolit usum*"—"[the possibility of] abuse does not remove [the legitimacy of] use." Although singing may sometimes be theatrical and hence inappropriate to church, it need not be so. Furthermore, although there is a hierarchy of offices in the church in which the spoken word of preaching predominates, this does not eliminate the use of song in its proper place (*ad 3am*).

However, Aquinas agrees with the fathers concerning the use of instruments in church: Musical instruments were an accommodation to the less spiritually developed stage of Old Testament religion and/or are to be understood allegorically (*ad 4am*). (Note that, unlike some of the fathers, Aquinas had no objection to instrumental music outside the church; he only thought it inappropriate to sacred functions.) But song is different from instrumental music: It is useful in the service of the word to provoke the souls of the weak ("*animi infirmorum*"—quoting Augustine) to devotion (ibid. *corpus*).

Finally, St. Thomas returns to the Platonic objection that pits spirit against body, but now in a more concrete and practical form. The objection reads:

> (Furthermore) praise originating in the mind is higher than praise from the mouth. But mental praise is impeded by singing [for two reasons]: first, because the singers' intention is distracted from the content of the song, since they are concentrating on the singing; second, because what they sing is less understandable to others than if it were spoken without song. Therefore [it seems] songs should not be used in prayer (of praise). (II II, q. 91 art. 2, 5)

Anyone who has sung in a choir knows that the first observation is frequently true, and anyone who has listened to a choir (or an opera) without a text in hand can recognize the second danger. This is especially the case when the music is complex and polyphonic, as it was beginning to be in St. Thomas's time. Thomas answers:

> (To the fifth objection it should be answered that) if one is artfully (*studiose*) using song for the sake of [simply] producing pleasure, then the mind is abstracted from what is being sung. But if someone sings out of devotion, that person is [even] more attentive to the words: first, because one dwells on them longer [in song]; second, because, as Augustine says (in the *Confessions*, bk. X), "all the affections of our soul, by their own diversity, have their proper measures (*modos*) in voice and song, and are stimulated by I know not what secret correspondence." And likewise for those who hear the singing: even if they sometimes do not understand what is being sung, they nevertheless understand the reason for the singing, namely, the praise of God; and this suffices to excite their devotion. (II II, q. 91 art. 2, *ad* 5)

The last sentence is very significant. Even though Thomas cites Augustine as his authority and quotes him several times in the article, he ends up going far beyond Augustine in saying that singing has a valid place in worship, *even if the words cannot be understood.* Augustine certainly says that song can excite a feeling of devotion and a longing for God by the "unknown secret correspondence" of music with our spiritual affects, but he presumes that to dwell in that feeling, without attention to the words, is a distraction from the purpose of prayer. In contrast to Augustine, Aquinas considers "*refectio mentis*" (the "restoring" or "healing" of the mind) as only a tertiary end of prayer; it is "intention" (in the Latin sense: "movement toward," in this case, toward God) that is most important. Such *intention* can be present even without *attention* to words. Indeed, Aquinas comments elsewhere that "sometimes this 'intention,' by which the soul is carried toward God, is so intense that the mind forgets everything else" (II II, q. 83, a. 13, c.).[19]

Augustine also speaks with approval of a kind of nonverbal sung praise—what he calls singing in jubilation, which he describes thus:

> One who jubilates (*iubilat*) does not speak words, but it is rather a sort of sound of joy without words, since it is the voice of a soul poured out in joy and expressing, as best it can, the feeling, though not grasping the sense...between the songs which they express in words, they insert certain sounds without words in the elevation of an exultant spirit, and this is called jubilation. (*In* Ps. XCIX, 4).[20]

And in another passage:

> What is it to sing in jubilation [Ps. 32:3]? To be unable to understand, to express in words, what is sung in the heart. For they who sing, either in the harvest, in the vineyard, or in some other arduous occupation, after beginning to manifest their gladness in the words of songs, are filled with such joy that they cannot express it in words, and turn from the syllables of words and proceed to the sound of jubilation. The *jubilus* is something which signifies that the heart labors with what it cannot utter. And whom does jubilation befit but the ineffable God? For he is ineffable whom you cannot speak. And if you cannot speak him, yet ought not to be silent, what remains but that you jubilate; so that the heart rejoices without words, and the great expanse of joy has not the limits of syllables? 'Sing well unto him in jubilation' (Ps. 32:3). (*In* Ps. XXXII, ii, S. I, 8).[21]

But this is quite different from allowing that hymns themselves may be sung in a way that the words are not attended to—much less in a way that makes them unintelligible. "When you pray to God in psalms and hymns, let what is pronounced by the voice be meditated upon in the heart." (Epist. CCXI, 7. PL XXXIII, 960; CSEL LVII, 361.)[22]

We must of course recognize the great difference in context between the two authors: Augustine is writing at the very beginnings of Western church music and is thinking of the simple, monophonic chant that the early church insisted on—the "one voice" in song that symbolized the unity of the church. The music that Augustine is talking about (with the exception of the wordless *jubilus*) is clearly intended as a medium for the word and not as an end in itself. But by the High Middle Ages, a long process of evolution had produced complex multivoiced singing in which the words are lost completely and the hearer who is not reading or remembering the text is left simply with beautiful sound. Aquinas is in effect giving a seal of approval to quite a different use of church music than Augustine had in mind, one in which the word is not simply momentarily forgotten in a (sinful) lapse of attention, but in which the word is completely subordinated to musical composition. (For examples, listen to polyphonic music of Léonin or Pérotin, masters of the Notre Dame School[d] that flourished in Paris immediately before Aquinas's time there.)

From Aquinas's time onward, church music became increasingly complex and further removed from the word. Restrictions still applied, particularly with regard to the use of instruments in church, but even here more latitude was eventually allowed. Objections reemerged periodically, especially in movements of reform. Pope John XXII, for example, condemned the musical innovations of the Ars Nova[e] of the fourteenth century, thus accidentally contributing to the development of secular

music by driving the best musicians away from the service of the church and into the employment of wealthy
and cultured princes.

The greatest emergence of "musical puritanism" or,
more generally, of consciousness of a conflict between
the beauty of music and the demands of the Word
occurred in the Reformation of the sixteenth century. All
the Reformers were concerned to reestablish the primacy of the Word, not least in the church's liturgy. Their
solutions, however, varied widely. Luther was extremely
positive in his evaluation of music: "except for theology
there is no art that could be put on the same level with
music."[23] "Nothing could be more closely connected with
the Word of God than music."[24] Even apart from the
sacred texts it might accompany, Luther thought that
music is "a wonderful creation and gift of God."[25] He
agreed with the ancient and medieval theory that the
right kinds of music can directly affect the human heart,
disposing it to virtue:

> It is music alone, according to God's word, that should
> rightfully be prized as the queen and ruler over every
> stirring of the human heart....What can be more pow-
> erful than music to raise the spirits of the sad, to
> frighten the happy, to make the despondent valiant, to
> calm those who are enraged, to reconcile those filled
> with hatred...?[26]

A composer and lyricist himself, Luther valued the use of
music in both the secular and sacred spheres. With his col-
laborator Johann Walter, he established the cantorship as a
ministry in the evangelical church;[f] he established congregational singing as an integral part of worship; and he wrote
religious songs for recreational use. In his view, music in the
church served as a *predicatio sonora*—a resounding sermon. It
was to be valued not only as a vehicle for sacred texts, but

also as being in itself a mirror of God's beauty and thus a means for reaching the soul directly with a message about God that is inexpressible in words.

Not all of the Protestant leaders were as positive about musical values as Luther. Konrad Grebel rebuked Thomas Münzer for introducing congregational singing. Ulrich Zwingli—although himself a highly skilled musician, probably the most accomplished of the Reformers— completely eliminated music from the sacred services, replacing it with scripture readings (1525).[27]

John Calvin took a somewhat intermediate position. In his *Institutes of the Christian Religion* he explicitly deals with the question. On the one hand, he affirms the value of music; on the other, he echoes Augustine in insisting on its subordination to the word:

> ...it is fully evident that unless voice and song, if interposed in prayer, spring from deep feeling of heart, neither has any value or profit in the least with God. But they arouse his wrath against us if they come only from the tip of the tongue and from the throat, seeing that this is to abuse his most holy name and to hold his majesty in derision...[Calvin here quotes Is 29:13, cf. Mt 15:8–9: "The people draw near to me with their mouth, and honor me with their lips, but their hearts are far from me...."]
>
> Yet we do not here condemn speaking and singing but rather strongly commend them, provided they are associated with the heart's affection. For thus do they exercise the mind in thinking of God and keep it attentive—unstable and variable as it is, and readily relaxed and diverted in different directions, unless it be supported by various helps. Moreover, since the glory of God ought, in a measure, to shine in the several parts of our bodies, it is especially fitting that the tongue has been assigned and destined for this task, both through singing and through speaking. For it was peculiarly cre-

ated to tell and proclaim the praise of God....[Here Calvin cites Augustine in defense of singing, and also mentions his doubts.]

And surely, if the singing be tempered to that gravity which is fitting in the sight of God and the angels, it both lends dignity and grace to sacred actions and has the greatest value in kindling our hearts to a true zeal and eagerness to pray. Yet we should be very careful that our ears be not more attentive to the melody than our minds to the spiritual meaning of the words.... Therefore, when this moderation is maintained, it is without any doubt a most holy and salutary practice. On the other hand, such songs as have been composed only for sweetness and delight of the ear are unbecoming to the majesty of the church and cannot but displease God in the highest degree.[28]

In line with this reasoning, Calvin objected to instrumental accompaniment and restricted singing to the psalms in the vernacular. (It was not until the seventeenth century that the organ was permitted in Reformed church music.)[g] Note the difference between Calvin's position and that of Aquinas: Both would no doubt agree that "...we must unquestionably feel that, either in public prayer or in private, the tongue without the mind must be highly displeasing to God."[29] But Aquinas is willing to allow a broader meaning to "mind" and therefore can allow a sacred function to music apart from its mediation of the explicit, verbal level of understanding.

The Reformation emphasis on the word also affected the Anglican and Roman Catholic traditions. The Anglican tradition generally shared the moderation of Calvin's approach, valuing music but insisting on the primacy of the word. Compare, for example, Thomas Tallis's early complex polyphonic Latin church music with his later English settings of the divine services, in which the rule of using only one note per syllable of text makes the words much more understandable. The early Catholic Reformation (or Counter-Reformation) included efforts to do away with the "excesses" of Renaissance music,[h] and some fathers of the Council of Trent favored a return to the simplicity of chant alone. But although church music was reformed in the direction of more priority to the clear presentation of the text,[i] the Roman Catholic liturgy remained in Latin. It is understandable, therefore, that through the Baroque and Classical periods, music was once more increasingly liberated from the need to concentrate on communication of the text and became more an end in itself—or, rather, more a separate means of glorifying God.

This brief historical survey has given us some idea of the tensions between music and Christian spirituality, especially in its liturgical forms. We have seen three principal reasons for the ambiguous reactions to music in relation to the sacred: (1) the pagan associations of music in the ancient world; (2) the conflict between spirituality and immersion in sense experience; (3) a certain competition between musical art and the word. In the remainder of this chapter, we will consider these three points in inverse order. The last aspect of the problem will occupy our attention in the next section. The second will be answered in a theological consideration of music and beauty as a positive way for the human spirit to apprehend and approach God. To the first we shall return in the final section of this chapter when we consider the implications of our study for liturgical practice, for although the situations are in many ways radically different, we may find certain analogies to the early church's experience vis-à-vis music in Christianity today as it becomes once again a minority voice in the Western world, competing with the media messages of a consumerist and materialistic society.

B. MUSIC AND THE THEOLOGY OF THE WORD

"...some to church repair,
Not for the doctrine, but the music there."

Alexander Pope's lines[30] wittily summarize a principal issue raised by Augustine and the Reformers regarding the use of music in the sacred realm: the tension between music and word, medium and content. At the extreme point of that tension, we confront a basic divergence on how we are to conceive the primary mode of God's self-revelation and humanity's reception of it: in a verbal and intellectual or in a nonverbal and intuitive form.

These two tendencies may be symbolized by reference to two great myths of creation. Of the great bronze statuary of India, perhaps no figure is better known than that of Śiva Nataraja, Śiva the Lord of the Dance[†]. The infinite God is portrayed surrounded by a ring of fire, engaged in his creative/destructive dance through which the worlds come into being and are annihilated. In one of the hands at the end of his multiple arms, he holds a tiny drum that he beats with his finger: with this rhythmic sound he creates the world. For Hindus, God creates through music, and the cosmic order is his dance. But in his other hand Śiva holds the fire that burns up the universe. Worlds in infinite succession come into being and are destroyed in God's cosmic "play." Creation itself is ultimately an illusion (*maya*), an ephemeral and veiled appearance of the only true reality, the Godhead itself. Broadly speaking, philosophical Hinduism, especially in its classical nondualist form, tends to devalue history and human understanding by placing them within the perspective of an infinite cosmic process. All words are relative and finally futile, for the finite existence to which they are tied is itself ultimately illusory. For such a worldview the aesthetic and intuitive or mystical is the primary religious attitude, while conceptual-intellectual and moral aspects are relativized. Of course, the philosophy of the Advaita Vedanta does not represent all of Hinduism, but even though the notion of *maya* is given a much more positive sense in theistic systems (as God's creative power), there is nevertheless a relativization of the historical and interpersonal sphere because of the doctrine of rebirth; correspondingly, there is a valuation of the mystical and intuitive. "Pure" music is a fitting symbolic expression for such theologies.[31]

By contrast, the creation myth of Genesis portrays God creating not through contentless sound, but through word. Karl Rahner writes in an early essay that

> ...real beauty is the pure appearance of reality as brought about principally in the word. Principally in the word; we have no desire to say anything here against music. It is too full of mystery. Nevertheless, perhaps lovers of music who are at the same time theologians might give a thought to the fact that God revealed himself in word and not in purely tonal music....[32]

Revelation for the "prophetic" religions centers on the intelligible, communicable word and on its correlative, the imperative to moral action in history. The notion of creation through the Word thus symbolizes, first, that for biblical faith the world and its history are God's creatures, with a genuine reality, in some way "distinct" from God's self;[33] second, that they have a purpose and meaning that demand human knowledge and collaboration; and third, that this knowledge and collaboration take place most fully in and through the mediation of symbol or "word." The identification of Christ with God's creative and revelatory Word in the prologue of John's Gospel manifests both the continuity of Christian faith with these ideas and its distinctive difference: the conviction that in Jesus we have God's final "word" and definitive mediation.

The New Testament emphasis on preaching the word (i.e., the message about Jesus) corresponds to the conviction that God is revealed in a final and salvific way in Christ. The knowledge and acceptance of Christ becomes central to our living relation with God. This means that there is a particular emphasis on the intellectual aspect of faith: Faith is "belief," the affirmation of the content of the divine revelation in Christ as real. We can participate in God's salvific action only by accepting it in its saving power for us; but we can only accept it by first receiving the message—hence Paul's insistence that "faith comes through hearing" (Rom 10:14–16), and hence the centrality of communicating the word to bring about the encounter with the Lord. The importance of the intelligible content of faith—the "word"—corresponds to the Christian insistence on the reality of God's salvific activity in Christ. (Of course, the center of the Christian message is not a purely intellectual faith but a life of love. But what love *is* is defined by Christ; God reveals the nature of love and gives us its pattern.)

Hence from the New Testament viewpoint, the criterion of genuine faith is not an elevated state of feeling but an encounter with God's historical revelation in Christ and a response to it in concrete action. In this perspective one can understand the recurrent Christian suspicion of any form of piety that distracts from the mediation of the word or threatens to replace it with merely aesthetic experience or with a purely individual relation to God that bypasses the community of faith. The strictures placed on sacred music by evangelical movements that stress God's word, like the Protestant Reformation, signify the attempt to assure that music serves as a vehicle for the word rather than constituting an end in itself; for music is a language of its own and can overpower the words it carries, making them into mere sounds to carry its notes. The medium can in truth become the message—a potentially different message from that embodied in word.

We have made a contrast between Hinduism, representing a mystical and intuitive type of religion, and Christianity as a religion of the Word. But the contrast between an intellectual/verbal and an intuitive/sensible emphasis can be seen within Christianity itself (just as the same contrast may also be found within Hinduism).

We might exemplify this with reference to two contrasting forms of liturgical practice. Reference has already been made to the more radical Reformed groups who practically eliminated church music altogether. Even the more musically tolerant Calvinist and Lutheran churches aimed at an ideal of congregational singing in which the message clearly predominated. (It is well known that even the sublime music of J. S. Bach was severely criticized by his more pietistic contemporaries for being too ornate and distracting from the Word.) The other end of the spectrum may be exemplified by the Russian Orthodox service, with its nearly totally sung and chanted liturgy and its magnificent choral tradition. Here, the verbal element is subsumed into a grand sacred performance integrating all the senses through architecture, icons, candles, light, incense, gesture, chant, and harmony. The unaccompanied and often repetitive vocal music serves as the force that brings all together in a profound sensation of the sacred. Although there can be no doubt of the power of such a service to move the heart, it can also happen that the meaning of the words is neglected or even lost in the vast sweep of the ritual. Boris Pasternak in the novel *Doctor Zhivago* describes a Russian liturgy in which in a short span of time the cantor "sang nine of the Beatitudes, rattling them off like a list of things already well enough known to everyone without him."[34] The emphasis on sensible manifestation rather than word and concept carries the danger of sacrificing reflection and moral challenge to comforting feelings or (at worst) pure ritualism.

As we have seen, both Thomas Aquinas and Luther represent a commonsense solution to this problem. We are not
necessarily faced with an either/or choice between word and
music: Christian liturgy can utilize music well in the service
of the word. Naturally, there is a need for reflection on what
kind of music is appropriate to the mediation of verbal
meaning. To this issue we shall return in the last section of
the chapter. More immediately, however, a different aspect of
music's mediation of the sacred remains to be examined.

We noted above Aquinas's opinion that even when vocal
music is not acting in direct service to the word (i.e., when
the words are not understood), it can still perform a legitimate function in mediating an "intentionality" toward God.
He states that those who do not understand the words nevertheless understand why they are being sung and can thus
enter into an act of worship. Moreover, when speaking of the
singers, he cites Augustine's phrase about how the affects
are stimulated by music through some "secret correspondence." Presumably this applies as well to those who hear
the music without knowing the words.[35] But if this is the case,
then those who repair to the church "not for the doctrine but
the music there" are not necessarily seeking "worldly" aesthetic enjoyment only. Is it not possible that they may be
engaged with the sacred—albeit in a way that bypasses the
church's mediation of God's "external" word?

In a passage from *Doctor Zhivago*, Pasternak says of his heroine, Lara:

> Lara was not religious. She did not believe in ritual.
> But sometimes, to be able to bear life, she needed the
> accompaniment of an inner music. She could not
> always compose such a music for herself. That music
> was God's word of life, and it was to weep over it that
> she went to church.[36]

Lara's experience of the liturgy still mediates the dimension of "the holy," although she does not believe in what the ritual signifies for the church. Naturally, this kind of purely individual and interior religion is far from the Christian ideal of explicit communion and action mediated by the "dangerous memory" of Christ. Nevertheless, this aesthetic approach to Christianity—an appreciation of its beauty, without commitment to its meaning—is a phenomenon that is frequently encountered not only in the secularized culture outside the church, but even among many of its nominal members. How many Christians "use" the church's liturgy and sacraments on particular occasions, but essentially on their own terms without wishing further involvement? How many even of those who practice their religion regularly are engaged by it primarily on an "aesthetic" level—by the music, rather than the doctrine? And even for those who are committed to explicit communitarian faith, is there not a legitimate and valid approach to God through music and art as well as through the proclaimed word? If so, how are we to understand this approach? Once again, we shall ask this question using music as our point of reference, with the understanding that what is said here of it may be applied, *mutatis mutandis*, to the arts in general.

C. MUSIC AS AN APPROACH TO GOD

We have seen that Luther strongly articulated the view that music in the church serves as a *predicatio sonora*—a resounding sermon. It was to be valued not only as a vehicle for sacred texts, but also as being in itself a mirror of God's beauty and thus a means of reaching the soul directly with a message about God that is inexpressible in words.

Although Luther greatly expanded the use of music in the church by the introduction of congregational singing in the vernacular, his essential ideas on music stem directly from the medieval Catholic tradition that he inherited. Once the associations of music with pagan worship were overcome or forgotten, the "mainstream" of Christian thought and culture virtually universally embraced music not only as an embellishment of liturgical life, but as a symbol of the divine itself and hence as a means of mediating consciousness of God.

From the time of Boethius, earthly music had been regarded as an imperfect reflection of the "music of the spheres," the celestial harmony of the heavenly bodies moved in their orbits by the "prime Mover," God. When Dante proclaims in the last lines of his *Paradiso* that his "mind and will have been moved by the same love that moves the sun and all the heavenly bodies"—

> *ma già volgeva il mio disiro e il velle . . .*
> *L'amor che move il sole e l'altre stelle*[37]

—he is expressing the commonly accepted theory of Aristotle, mediated to the West especially by Boethius: God moves the universe "as its beloved," that is, as what all things desire, the world's reason for being or final cause. The stars and planets are moved in their spheres by heavenly intelligences which are caught up in the love of God.[38] Dante's lines in the *Paradiso* closely echo the sense of the verses of Boethius in *The Consolation of Philosophy*:

> Love binds together the multiplicity of things,
>> Ruling the earth and sea,
>> And governing the heavens . . .
>> O happy human race
>> If the Love that rules the heavens
>> Should also rule your souls![39]

From this Christianized Aristotelian idea, both ancient and medieval thinkers developed the notion that the beautiful and harmonious motion of creation, inspired by love, is the "music" with which it praises its maker and goal. Nicholas Brady's ode, "Hail! Bright Cecilia," set to music by Henry Purcell as the "Ode on St. Cecilia's Day, 1692,"[i] gives poetic expression to the idea that music is the "soul" of the world, since it gives form and unity to the whole creation:

> Soul of the World! inspir'd by thee,
> The jarring Seeds of Matter did agree,
> Thou didst the scatter'd Atoms bind,
> Which, by thy laws of true proportion join'd,
> Made up of various Parts one perfect Harmony.
> Thou tun'st this World below, the Spheres above,
> Which in the Heavenly Round to their own music move.

Likewise it is music that will bring the world finally to its ordained end in God, as John Dryden proclaims in his "Song for St. Cecilia's Day," set to music by G. F. Handel:[k]

> As from the pow'r of sacred lays
> The spheres began to move,
> And sung the great Creator's praise
> To all the bless'd above;
> So when the last and dreadful hour
> This crumbling pageant shall devour,
> The trumpet shall be heard on high,
> The dead shall live, the living die,
> And music shall untune the sky.

Thus the positive evaluation of music in the church was founded on the idea that the music we hear on earth gives us a sensible taste of the spiritual order and finality of all being and, in its truest nature, expresses the praise of and desire for God. Luther's hearty congregational singing and the ethereal choral music of the masses of Palestrina or Victoria are based upon the same idea: that music raises the mind to God because it reflects and expresses the beautiful order and intelligibility of creation itself.

For most modern people, a cosmology based upon the "music of the spheres" belongs to a worldview that is irretrievably mythological and that has been definitively surpassed by modern science. Yet even for us the medieval idea seems to give poetic form to a valid intuition. Music seems to have a spiritual dimension that goes beyond merely sensual pleasure and that somehow reflects a deeper reality. Anthropology makes it clear that primitive religion is inseparable from music and dance; even for the most modern of cultures, music retains a mystical fascination, not only when heard in church, but also in the concert hall. What is it that gives to music this spiritual quality? What allows it to convey meaning? What accounts for its continual association with the sacred, so much as to make it, in Luther's words, a "sonorous preaching?"

As we have seen, on one level music is "spiritual" as the bearer of sacred words and texts: It is used to solemnize, ritualize, make these words "sacred" in the etymological sense of separate, apart from the normal mode of communication. But this function would hardly be possible if there were not something in music itself that makes it an apt medium for sacred word and gesture, and both history and experience testify that wordless music (or music whose text is in a dead or unknown language, as with the Latin Mass or the Sanskrit chants of Hindu priests) can often be equally effective in conveying a sense of spiritual reality. The key to music's possibility for sacred meaning, therefore, must first be sought in asking what makes it possible for musical sound to convey meaning at all.

On this question Nicholas Brady's verses may once again give us poetic insight:

'Tis Nature's Voice; thro' all the moving Wood
Of Creatures understood:
The Universal Tongue to none
Of all her num'rous Race unknown!
From her it learn'd the mighty Art
To court the Ear and strike the Heart:
At once the passions to express and move;
We hear, and straight to grieve or hate, rejoice or love:
In unseen Chains it does the Fancy bind:
At once it charms the Sense and captivates the
Mind.

Music, in short, is a kind of symbolic language: not merely
sound, but also "voice." It does not merely "charm the sense,"
but also "captivates the mind" and "strikes the heart." Brady's
words evoke a "naturalistic" theory of music; unlike our spoken languages, music is a universal tongue, based not on
conventions that arbitrarily attach meaning to certain
sounds, but on a kind of natural symbolism inherent in the
sounds themselves. Music is "a tonal analogue of emotive
life."[40] That is, it *directly* symbolizes certain feelings: "We hear,
and straight we grieve or hate, rejoice or love." This symbolism seems to be governed by a complex series of associations of sounds and rhythms with our natural bodily
functions (e.g., faster or slower heartbeat), the intrinsic limitations of our hearing (loud and soft, or frequencies that are
easy or difficult to hear together) as well as a certain degree
of association with human sounds (weeping, sighing, laugh-
ing) or those of nature (the waters, the wind, etc.).[41] Added
to this "natural language" would be certain culturally determined conventions of meaning or association. Musical
sounds are thus associated with certain basic human feelings, and these feelings, in turn, evoke the contents or situations that produce them. Music therefore is able not only to
charm the sense by pleasurable experience, but also to
engage the heart by analogously representing emotional

states, and to engage the mind by evoking the meanings associated with those states in the human mind.

A similar theory is used by Rudolf Otto in his classic work *The Idea of the Holy*[42] to explain the specific connection of music and art with the experience of the sacred. Otto speaks of this connection as a "law of associations." The experience that grounds religion—the experience of the holy, the *mysterium tremendum et fascinans* (the awesome and attractive mystery)—is for Otto *sui generis*: It cannot be reduced to moral or aesthetic or any other kind of experience. Nevertheless, the feelings produced by encounter with the holy have analogies with similar feelings produced in other areas of human life by beauty, moral goodness, or truth. The presence of one set of feelings can stimulate the appearance in consciousness of its analogues. Thus music properly constitutes a world and language unto itself; the feelings and moods it produces are simply "musical" and should not be confused with any nonmusical experiences. At the same time, some of these feelings afford analogies to the ordinary emotions of life and, by association, can call those emotions into the hearer's mind. (Thus, for example, the canons and fugues of J. S. Bach almost invariably evoke the analogy of logic or of mathematics; to hear them is to have an inner experience somehow similar to that of proceeding step by step through an elegant geometrical demonstration and feeling the satisfaction of arriving at an inescapable conclusion. How is this similarity to be explained? One might seek a cultural explanation in the undoubted association of music with rhetoric in Bach's time. At the same time, there seems to be some evidence pointing to the use of certain common patterns of neural impulses in the brain in both music and mathematics.)

Likewise, on Otto's theory, some properly musical "vibrations of mood" are similar and analogous to those aroused by the encounter with the holy and can by association produce the latter in the hearer's consciousness. It is for this reason that some forms of music are more intrinsically suited to serve as the medium and expression of religious content than others and why some styles or techniques in music are peculiarly apt to express sacred meaning. (So, for example, the supreme moment of transcendence is frequently expressed by extreme softness of sound or even stillness: the analogue of the silent awe experienced before the Transcendent.)

Otto's theory throws a great deal of light on the relation of music to spirituality. It accounts for the difference between what is called serious and what is called light music, and shows why there is some sense to the idea of a sacred "style": those forms of music that have emotional and intellectual associations of sufficient "depth" to be appropriate carriers of sacred words or themes (while light or frivolous forms of music, although perhaps pleasant in themselves, may betray a sacred message by inappropriate associations that trivialize it). It also explains why music can be seen in religion as the height of spiritual expression or, alternatively, as the epitome of sensual depravity.

At the same time, Otto's position raises a further question: Is musical experience merely the emotional *analogue* of sacred experience so that it works exclusively by association, or can music and art *in themselves* be an experience of the sacred? The question leads to a reexamination of Otto's basic premise: Is the human encounter with the Holy a separate experience, *alongside* those of the beautiful, the good, and so on, or is it rather *identical* with those experiences when seen in their deepest reality, as their ground?

Without denying the essential validity of Otto's notion of associations of feelings, operating on many different levels, it is perhaps possible nevertheless to regard the experience of the holy (as distinguished from the contents of explicit religions) not simply as a parallel experience, but more as a kind of *meta*experience (in a way parallel to the experience of being in metaphysics). Otto's theory is based on the perception of a sacred "object" in religious experience; this in turn presupposes an explicitly religious consciousness. My proposal is based on the conviction that there is also an underlying implicit or transcendental dimension of religious experience. Its object—the *mysterium tremendum et fascinans*, the numinous—would then be ontologically identical with the ultimate object of aesthetic or moral or intellectual experience (as in the medieval theory of the "transcendentals"); it would never be experienced simply in itself as a categorical object but would always be "coexperienced" as the dimension of mystery implicit in all human knowing and loving; and it would ground the analogies that are in fact found in the human reaction to the beautiful, the good, the true, and the holy.

In this perspective, the ultimate reason for music's ability to mediate the spiritual is not merely that it echoes emotions that are felt in religious experience, but also and more profoundly that its object is the beautiful, which itself is godly and thus leads toward God. There are, of course, different kinds of beauty, and these can ground the multiple and diverse associations with the feelings connected with spirituality. Music that represents and/or produces feelings of peace, contentment, joy, unity, harmony—or, on the other hand, of striving, power, majesty, awe—may call to mind similar feelings that occur in nonmusical religious states of mind. There are also different levels of beauty: from mere prettiness or sensual enjoyment to the deepest and most mysterious attraction, in which there may be experienced a painful tension in the call to self-transcendence. Beauty at its profoundest may call for purification, discipline, and even renunciation: "the beautiful is difficult"![43] What unifies all of these kinds and levels in music is precisely the fact of their being experienced not simply as representations of the feelings of human existence, but as presenting these feelings as in some way *beautiful*—and, as such, revelatory of the transcendent.

Why, then, is the beautiful a revelation of God? An answer to this question depends on a recognition of what constitutes the experience of beauty and makes it possible. Once again, a passage from the novel *Doctor Zhivago* succinctly summarizes the critical insight. Pasternak writes of his hero:

> ...he made a note reaffirming his belief that art always serves beauty, and beauty is delight in form, and form is the key to organic life, since no living thing can exist without it, so that every work of art, including tragedy, expresses the joy of existence.[44]

The experience of beauty is a kind of delight: a joy in the experience of "form," the organizing principle that gives "shape" to things and to our knowledge of them. What distinguishes music from noise is precisely its patterns, which create a unity out of disparate elements. Analogously, form, or organization, is what makes biological life possible; on yet another level, form is what makes any existing thing into an identity, a whole that is differentiated from others; and form is what corresponds to the mind's quest for intelligibility.[45] In this sense, form is the key to existence itself, and delight in form—what makes existence possible—is an implicit affirmation of the goodness and joy of existence, of being itself.

The affirmation of the joy of existence, however, can only take place in an intelligent and free being if existence is somehow—even if only implicitly—seen as worthwhile, as meaningful, and as having an ultimate intelligibility or purpose. To experience beauty is to experience a deep-seated "yes" to being—even in its finitude and its moments of tragedy; and such an affirmation is possible only if being is grounded, borne by a reality that is absolute in value and meaning. In short, the experience of finite beauty in a spiritual being implies the unavoidable (although perhaps thematically unconscious) coaffirmation of an infinite Beauty: the reality that we call God.

The fact that God is the "horizon" of every experience of beauty explains why even the tragic emotions can be experienced in art as beautiful, and why there is at the heart of every deep aesthetic experience—and perhaps particularly in music—an intense feeling of striving toward something beyond the moment. In Peter Schaffer's *Amadeus* the aged Salieri says of Mozart's music: "This was a music...filled with such longing, such unfulfillable longing, that it seemed to me that I was hearing the voice of God." This longing is intrinsic to the experience of finite beauty, for the joy of existence in any finite being can never be complete or ultimate but must point beyond itself to a final and infinite goal. It is in this sense that philosophers from Plato onward have seen beauty as the manifestation of God to the senses and have claimed that "the beauty of anything created is nothing else than a similitude of divine beauty participated in by things."[46] In music, because it is temporal and therefore intrinsically fleeting, the symbolism of a dynamism toward a whole that is beyond the moment is especially present.

On the basis of the foregoing we may say that music can lead the mind to the sacred in three different but interconnected ways: by being the bearer or accompaniment to sacred words, gestures, or motions; by association with emotions characteristic of religious psychological states; and by the manifestation of beauty as the sign of the transcendental goal of human spirit.

A specific example of great sacred music will perhaps show how the working of these three levels together can create a "sonorous preaching" of faith. The interplay of text, association, and beauty is heard in an elegant way in the opening chorale of J. S. Bach's cantata, "*Liebster Gott, wenn werd' ich sterben?*" (BWV 8).[1] The work begins with the creation of a musical picture: the oboes play a roundlike tune, symbolizing the ceaseless turning of the wheel of time; the pizzicato of the violins reminds us of a clock, ticking away the hours and minutes; at intervals the viola da gamba, joined by the organ, simulates the pealing of a great church bell, while the flute joins on a single repeated high note to imitate the small bell tolling. Then the voices of the choir enter, singing a sober meditation on human mortality:

> Dearest God, when shall I die? My time is constantly running out, and the descendants of ancient Adam—of whom I am one—have this for their inheritance: to be only a short while, poor and miserable, upon the earth, and then to become earth themselves.

Seldom can art have produced a more effective memento mori. Hearing the words, I am explicitly reminded that I must die, while the music, whose very nature is to pass through time and disappear, makes me feel the present experience of time's inexorable passage and, by its imitative allusions, anticipates the inevitable moment when the funeral bells will toll for me. Yet what makes Bach's treatment more than a mere didactic exercise is the spirit in which the whole is presented, for the feeling of the chorale is anything but morbid. Rather, it conveys a sense of peace, joy, comfort, beauty, even in the presence of death. As E. Power Biggs once remarked, Bach looks death in the face and writes cradle songs. Thus for one who hears and understands the text, the music is felt as a profound statement of faith—a positive assertion of hope and joy even in the face of the inevitability of death. The grounds of that hope are made explicit in the remaining sections of the cantata, which meditate on Christ as savior. The believer thus finds here a powerful and moving reminder and reinforcement of the basic attitude of supreme confidence in and abandonment to God.

But what of the nonbeliever? Clearly it is not necessary to have Christian faith to appreciate the skill and beauty of Bach's music, apart from its message, and it would be possible to enjoy such a cantata on one level by consciously abstracting from the text. But to do so would deprive the experience of a major part of its aesthetic power. If one is really to feel the beauty of the emotion Bach evokes, one must attempt to feel, at least for the moment, what he felt, and one must therefore in some sense believe with him in the ultimate beauty he is presenting: the triumph of goodness over death, the existence of a final purpose to life, the comfort of confidence in a loving savior. The unbelieving hearer of Bach's music will not, of course, personally affirm the faith that is presented in it, but he or she must at least vicariously feel the attitude of faith. (Cf. Nietzsche's celebrated remark on Bach's *Matthäuspassion*: "One who has completely forgotten Christianity hears it here truly as a gospel [good news].")[47]

For the act of aesthetic appreciation to take place, there must be a willing, if only momentary, suspension of disbelief: a willingness to see life, at least for this moment, *as if* the hearer shared Bach's faith. This aesthetic act is of course far from real assent; yet it is significant, for it involves a certain openness to faith as a genuine human possibility. If one can feel the human possibility of such an act of confidence in the face of death, even for a moment, even while more or less regretfully denying its truth, then one is at least faced with the further question: How is such an act possible? What is it in the human being—even in the unbeliever—that can not only intellectually acknowledge, but can existentially feel a fundamentally positive stance toward existence, even in the face of death? In this sense Bach's music—like all great religious music—performs a kind of "apologetic" function by evoking in the hearer a belief in the beautiful, a belief in life, and by raising thereby the question of the grounds of such belief.

If what we have said above about the nature of beauty is correct, then this apologetic function is not restricted to music that is explicitly tied to religious texts or even to faith, but occurs wherever the spirit is moved to an affirmation of beauty and the meaningfulness of existence. In this sense even secular music may be a "sonorous preaching," for it leads the spirit—perhaps more effectively than any argument or reasoning—through the experience of beauty and the affirmation of life to an implicit knowledge of its Maker and Goal. Thus music does more than convey a message about God: in its highest forms, it brings the hearer face to face with the reality of God's presence-in-absence and absence-in-presence.

D. CONSIDERATIONS FOR LITURGICAL PRAXIS

This brief overview may give us some insight into factors that must be taken into account in practical considerations of the role of music in church. There are different media or "languages" for symbolizing the sacred, and each is more apt for a different aspect of the expression of our relation to God and to each other in worship.

The unaccompanied spoken word is the normal form of discourse in ordinary life; it therefore has the power of plainness to address us in our everyday reality. It is particularly suited for expressing religion as content, either intellectual or moral: the understanding of a creed or the imparting of an imperative. Although we can be comfortable with the singing of many parts of a liturgy, a sung homily, for example, would probably strike us as anomalous and inappropriate. The spoken word serves well the dimension of faith as prophetic, as direct interlocution demanding the response of critical thought or action. Where the word must be presented in its dimension of *kerygma*, with its specific Christian meaning, the medium of speech seems the most direct and effective form of expression.

Wordless music, on the other hand, is capable of raising the mind to God by means of the senses through the exaltation of feeling. A kind of association of like emotional states allows the experience of the beautiful to serve as an analogy to the awe and desire we feel when confronted with the holy, and hence to call forth a religious attitude. It serves not the intellectual but the affective dimension of faith; it brings the sensible and emotive levels of the person into accord with the mind and spirit. At its best, it is also itself a revelation from God—not in the specificity of the Christian message, but in the universal revelation of beauty. In this way, great music can be sacred and has a place in Christian worship, even if it has no explicit connection with the message.

Vocal music attempts to combine the intelligible revelation of word with that of sensible beauty. The relation of word to music, however, is complex. On the one hand, music may be used as a simple vehicle for the message. The musical form in this case is clearly subordinated to the text, either merely carrying it, as in chant, or attempting to "express" it by musical means. On the other hand, it is possible for the sacred text to be used merely as a vehicle for the music so that the words become secondary and the aesthetic effect the primary message.

When music is used to carry or to express a text, the dimension of conceptual meaning is still present. Skillful music can enhance the meaning by associating appropriate feelings with it; poor music can undermine the meaning by connecting it with trivial sounds or inappropriate associations and emotions. In either case, however, the text takes on a character different from that of the spoken word. Gerardus van der Leeuw gives an example:

Unforgettable to anyone who has heard it is the last word of Bach's Christ: "Eli, Eli, lama sabachtani." But closer to the event, to the desolate victim, comes the simply spoken. "My God, my God, why hast Thou forsaken me?" when it is spoken by a minister who knows the meaning of worship, pronouncing it in the Communion Prayer without music, without even declaiming. Of course, I do not mean that the latter is more beautiful or better; I only assert that the words cannot stand up to the music.[48]

Because singing is not our normal form of address, in it the word is taken out of the "I–Thou" context of speech and placed in the "we" context of shared musical experience. The irregular and personally determined cadences of speech are replaced with the artfully constructed cadences and emphases of rhythm and melody. Music in this way serves a hermeneutical function: It interprets the word by taking it out of the world of interlocution and bestowing upon it an emotive value determined by the composer. (Even the most "neutral" music—e.g., chant—does this, in the case of plain chant, precisely by the omission of an accentuation flowing from the meaning of the words and, hence, the reduction of each word and each repeated phrase to the same level.) Singing enables us to step back from the word's immediacy as communication and to make it an aesthetic object; it allows us to contemplate and to celebrate the word rather than simply hear or speak it. It does not simply convey the word but places it in the context of "something for which there are no words."[49]

At the extreme, it is even possible for the priorities of meaning to be reversed so that the feeling conveyed by the music is the primary value and the sacred words serve as the physical medium for the voice as an instrument.[50] In the best sacred music of this type, the words are allowed to be (to a greater or lesser extent) "suppressed" by the music because word alone is not enough.[51] On the other hand, religious texts may be used simply as the "occasion" for music whose primary goal is aesthetic rather than devotional. (Thus, for example, Rossini freely admitted that he did not pay much attention to the meaning of the words in his setting of the *Stabat Mater*, because he feared such a concern might detract from the music.) The text in this case colors the music by its associations with a religious tradition and/or its place in a liturgical setting.

The musical settings of sacred texts, therefore, can have very varied relations to the attitude of worship, and one must ask whether a particular piece more properly "belongs" to the church or to the concert hall. Scarlatti's *Stabat Mater* is a sacred meditation; Rossini's is opera. Mendelssohn's settings of the psalms, although composed without any liturgical setting in mind, are prayers; Leonard Bernstein's *Chichester Psalms*, although commissioned for church performance, really belong to the genre of musical theater: They portray prayer, rather than engaging in it. Aesthetically, the difference is perhaps insignificant, but religiously it is crucial. Of course, it is by no means clear that concert music, with or without a sacred text, should be excluded from the church; if it genuinely serves beauty and transcendence, it may still lead the spirit to God.[52] But it should be clear that it does so in a way different from the mediation of the word, so that it should not be conceived as a substitute for the latter, but rather as (in the best case) complimentary to it. At the same time, we must keep in mind that the better the music, the more the possibility that its mediation of transcendence may overwhelm that of the religious word and the historical revelation it represents. Alasdair MacIntyre points out the reverse side of the observation made in the last section regarding Bach's music and the unbeliever:

[W]hen we listen to the scripture because of what Bach wrote rather than because of what St. Matthew wrote, then sacred texts are being preserved in a form in which the traditional links with belief have been bro-.ken, even in some measure for those who count themselves believers....[53]

We have seen in our brief historical overview that the early church, existing in the midst of a pagan society, was wary of many kinds of music because of their intimate link with idolatrous worship. Although this kind of explicitly pagan cult no longer exists, we may see some parallels in the contemporary pursuit of materialistic and egotistical values; and it may be well to remember that there is a kind of "law of associations" in the human psyche—so that some forms of art or music might be inappropriate to the church not because of any intrinsic qualities they possess (although this might also sometimes be the case) but because of the moods or contexts associated with them in the secular sphere. Here, of course, there may arise a conflict between the desire for relevance to people's everyday lives, on the one hand, and, on the other, the danger of compromising the challenge of the sacred by too facile an accommodation to tastes formed by the media and entertainment industries. This is not to suggest that one can determine in principle, and in abstraction from concrete circumstances, what musical genres (or other forms of art) are or are not suitable for liturgical use; but only that the category of "suitability" itself has a legitimate place in aesthetic—liturgical considerations.

We have also seen that in the early church practical reservations about music because of its pagan associations were bolstered by a more theoretical consideration, adopted from the philosophers: Audible music is associated with the senses and hence with sensuality; it is unspiritual, a distraction from the true worship that should take place in the mind.

(Interestingly, an ambiguous relation to music is not simply a peculiarity of Christian religious history. Similar reservations about music appear in other religious traditions as well. Despite—or perhaps because of—the pervasive presence of music in primitive religion, the "higher" religions have frequently seen it as a danger. An extreme example is found in classical Jainism, which forbade all instruments and even the use of chanting. But the strongest parallel to the tension in early Christianity is found in Islam. The Qur'an did not definitively settle the issue of the status of music; it required an appearance of Mohammed in a vision to Dīnawarī [died A.D. 896] to establish music as an acceptable art—but only if it was attended by the reading of the Qur'an. Even today, conservative Muslim canonists forbid music of any sort. Others insist that only religious chants are permitted and/or differentiate the vocalization of the Qur'an from "music." The great classical theologian al-Ghazāli, in approving the use of music, nevertheless excludes certain types of instruments and teaches that unless the Muslim truly loves God, he or she must never listen to music at all, lest it endanger the soul.)

In the Christian context, Platonic or dualistic objections against sacred music can in principle be met by an incarnational theology, joined to an integral anthropology: one that holds that the whole of human life, including the bodily and sensible, must form part of spirituality and worship. Such an integral view of human being is based on the conviction that human spirit does not simply "inhabit" an alien body but is intrinsically "spirit in the world." This position is presupposed by St. Thomas in his approval of the use of music to praise God.

Concretely, however, the "integration" of our humanity, that is, of our spiritual/biological personhood, is only partially actual; it remains an ideal and a goal to be attained by a series of conversions. As Lonergan reminds us, human consciousness is polymorphic, and the achievement of authenticity is always a withdrawal from inauthenticity on a number of different levels.[54] The situation theologically named *concupiscence* implies that objects of human desire that are in themselves genuine, God-oriented values may nevertheless become obstacles to human development toward deeper and more ultimate values.[55]

Hence, the Christian lover of art and beauty may be given pause not only by Aristotle's (or Freud's) realistic appraisal of the dangers of pleasure, but also (and perhaps even more) by the scriptural warnings about the peril of riches and the necessity of "taking up" the cross. The prophet Amos portrays artful music making as a part of the lifestyle of the complacent rich, who are condemned because they forget the ills of God's people;[56] on the other hand the church identifies Jesus with the "suffering servant" of Isaiah who "had no beauty in him."[57] In an earlier section of this chapter we have noted Augustine's scruples about taking pleasure in music when it did not serve the divine word. Preoccupied with the journey toward God ("our hearts are restless until they rest in Thee"), like Plato he feared that the pleasures of art might cause us to forget that we are on a pilgrimage and persuade us that we have already arrived.[58]

In short, Christian solidarity with the poor and suffering, symbolized by the spirituality of the cross, introduces a "hermeneutic of suspicion" to our experience of the world and its beauties. (Not surprisingly, such mistrust of the world is strongest in those theological traditions that emphasize human sinfulness and its effects.) For the Christian message is not merely that God is lovely, but that God is love; not merely that God is beautiful and is to be found in the pursuit of what is attractive and desirable in the world, but that God is transcendently and absolutely beautiful and is to be found even in what to the world's eye is ugly and deformed and unworthy.

The last statement means that the Christian vision of beauty and lovability has an eschatological perspective; that is, *beauty*, which we ascribe analogously to creatures and to God, attains its full meaning only in the light of the final, total order and harmony of God's kingdom, the triumph of God's love over the evil, sorrow, and pain, the ugliness and disorder, that we now experience in an incomplete and still evolving world.[59] A similar statement must be made about the Christian vision of the desire and fulfillment to which the idea of *beauty* corresponds. The New Testament insistence that real love of God cannot exist without love of neighbor (1 Jn 4:20–21; cf. Jn 13:34; 15:12f., 17; Mt 25:31–46; Lk 10:25–37) redefines *love* in such a way that it surpasses mere *eros* toward God as the final Good, the attaining of which confers beatitude; it sees human love for God not as a simple drive toward happiness, conceived as self-fulfillment, but as a sharing in the divine way of being, which is self-giving love that is universal in extension. This kind of love demands a certain de-centering of the self that even appears as "loss" of self, "death" to self, in the realization of a higher, more total good. The self and its fulfillment are conceived ecstatically; and so is the beauty by which we are drawn.

Religious experience in this context is not simply elevation of spirit, heightened interiority, and peace, but contains also an element of unrest and incompleteness, as well as a consequent imperative to action. Further, it consists not merely in communion of the individual with God, but also in solidarity with others, including those whose lives are at present not beautiful and full. It would seem, then, that the aesthetics of Christian worship should not only eschew religious *kitsch*, or sentimentally and superficially pious art and music; it should also contain an element of wariness concerning aesthetic satisfaction, even of a deeply religious kind, that would lead simply to spiritual repose, without being joined to a reminder of the anticipatory and world-changing nature of the joy and beauty that are central to our celebrations. In short, the sensible beauty of church music and art should serve and not distract from another and higher form of beauty.

Of course, it is the word that normally mediates the eschatological, agapic, and diaconal dimensions of the Christian message and worldview; our present considerations therefore rejoin our earlier reflections concerning the tensions and complementarity between music and word. At the same time, should there not be some place for witness to solidarity with the poor in a certain simplicity and poverty in the style of liturgical worship itself—even apart from that which may be imposed by a community's priorities in allocating its limited resources?[60] (In this regard it is instructive to recall that the church has traditionally used a kind of fasting from sensible beauty to heighten consciousness of those permanent dimensions of Christian life that are especially brought to the fore in the penitential seasons.)

Having said this, we must nevertheless insist that the way to God through the beauty of music and art should not be the exclusive province of secular humanism; the church above all should honor and cherish the foretaste of God's glory—and its participation by the world. Clearly beauty, like any aspect of the goodness and richness of the world, including religion itself, can be made an idol. This is an argument not for the rejection of music or other forms of art, but for the creation of an explicit and pastorally relevant theological aesthetics.

The Christian narrative and imperative—including the message of the cross (but always in the light of the resurrection)—are and must be presented and celebrated as *good* news. God and the historical impulses and workings of God's love are ultimately beautiful: They connect with the desire of our hearts, even on the sensible level. The desire itself, however, is God's gift that must be freely accepted, discovered, and continually reconfirmed and expanded; this involves a conversion and extension of our sense of beauty, as Christian love converts, subsumes, and extends our personal relations.

In this process, art and music of the right kind can serve as a pedagogue. First of all, the more art serves not merely to please but to present form, beauty, truth, the more it faces us with a transcendent value—with something to be admired and loved in and for itself, rather than for its usefulness or pleasantness to us. It thus already demands a certain level of conversion from our egotism toward a more ultimate good. The interpersonal word of the Christian message directs us to where that good is to be encountered in the world and how it is to be further realized by our acts. (The word itself must, of course, also be presented in such a way as to reach and attract the heart; thus there is need for art in preaching as well as in ritual. This is a theme that will be taken up in the fourth chapter.)

Moreover, the experience of beauty may calm our hearts' fears and allow us to enter with sympathy into worlds that might otherwise be simply alien to us. In addition, artful presentation of the message allows us to see ourselves and our needy and frequently unattractive neighbors in the light of God's love. By the same token, sacred art shows the cross itself—Christ's, and our own—as beautiful, provided it is seen in the light of the resurrection, that is, in the light of God's opposition to and reversal of the evil it represents. (But as with every "theodicy," so also with that contained in sacred art, one must beware the twin dangers of an implicit masochism, on the one hand, and, on the other, a facile acceptance of evil and suffering—especially that of others— as being part of "God's plan.") We have given above a single example of this "evangelical" function of beauty in the music of Bach; it might be multiplied many times by other great and small works of sacred music and art.

Finally, and in connection with symbolizing the "eschatological" nature of beauty for the Christian, a few words must be said regarding sacred silence. The use of silence in worship bespeaks the mystical and contemplative dimension of religion: the depth of God experienced as transcending all categorical mediation, beyond our ability to speak or feel.

Although the potential conflict between word and music is born of the tension between an intellectual/conceptual and an intuitive/sensible approach to religion, yet another factor is introduced by the theological and spiritual insight into the absolute transcendence/immanence of God which cannot be adequately expressed in any objectification, either in word or in contentless sound. Even the New Testament, with all its emphasis on the word of revelation, insists that external preaching and hearing are of no avail without the direct interior "witness" of God, moving the mind and heart (Jn 6:4). It is here that silence becomes an important part of religious expression. Religious silence is not simply the absence of sound but is an active attitude of attending to the encounter with the absolute Mystery in Itself, unmediated by creatures. It is a fitting symbol of the reverential awe with which we seek the utterly Holy: God as the One beyond all our concepts, desires, and feelings. Silence is also a language—that of mysticism and interiority. Both word and music occupy the mind and senses; the purpose of silence is to free them from activity and create the space for contemplation.

Even the sublimest music when it attempts to convey the deepest mysteries tends to fade to softness and silence. Silence also permits or even demands a different kind of personal stance. Singing, speaking, and even listening all imply, to different degrees, a task to be performed: they occupy the mind and sometimes can even distract it from a confrontation with the depths of being by giving it something concrete to do. Silence invites us to contemplation—which is no doubt why reverent silence is difficult to attain, and why so many are uncomfortable with it.

It seems clear that there is a need in Christian worship for a balanced use of these different ways of standing before God, giving attention to the strengths and emphases of each, as well as the needs of specific congregations, occasions, and types of prayer. By the same token, it seems to be impossible to impose a priori norms regarding what ought or ought not to have a musical setting. Tradition, rubrics, and liturgical—theological principles can certainly provide guidelines, but clearly, in their application, practical criteria must be joined to theoretical and liturgical principles (contrary to the well-known clerical joke: "What is the difference between a liturgist and a terrorist? Answer: you can negotiate with a terrorist"). Music can be good or bad, suitable or distracting; the word can be vitally proclaimed or recited in a meaningless, ritual fashion; silence can be reverent and deep, or shallow and uncomfortable. A meaningful recitation of a psalm can be more prayerful than a bad singing of it; a beautiful organ solo can be more sacred than a routinely recited prayer. Word and melody and silence are all crucial aspects of worship; regarding their concrete use and mixture, the virtue of prudence must decide.

In this first chapter we have used music to introduce and exemplify the central thesis of this book: that beauty, specifically in the form of art, can be for the Christian a revelation of God and a way to God. We have noted the reasons for certain historical tensions between the arts and Christianity. Nevertheless, we have argued for a positive and intrinsic connection between God and beauty. At the same time, we have noted that there is a need for the "conversion" of the aesthetic sense for it to enter into the higher integration of human life that is represented by grace. The liturgical use of music and its relation to the proclaimed word illustrates the kind of questions that Christians must face in the practice of such integration.

In the next chapters, we turn from art's relation to faith itself to art's relation to reflection on faith; that is, to theology. How is the mediation of God through humanly created beauty related to God's mediation through humanly conceived truth? We shall first show that there is a factual connection between theology and art—as well as other manifestations of culture, such as natural science and philosophy—insofar as all are historically conditioned expressions of human cultural situations. We shall then explore ways in which art can function as a "text" for theological reflection.

Web sites for viewing illustrations———

† Śiva Nataraja, the Lord of the Dance.
A fine example from South India (Tamil Nadu) from the
Chola period (12 c.) may be found at the web site:

www.upenn.edu/ARG/asian/asian3.html

Other examples:

www.nortonsimon.org/nsmnat.htm

144.16.100/~gopal/arts/dance.html

Discography

a. Some representative sacred works of these composers include:

Geoffrey Burgon. *Cathedral Music*. Choir of Chichester Cathedral; Alan Thurlow, director. Hyperion CDA66123.

———. *The Fall of Lucifer and other works*. The Elysian Singers, conducted by Matthew Greenall. Silvia Classics SILKD 6002.

Henryk Mikolaj Górecki. *Symphony no. 3 for Soprano and Orchestra "Symphony of Sorrowful Songs."* Stefania Woytowicz, soprano; Radio-Symphonie-Orchester Berlin, conducted by Wlodzimierz Kamirski. Schwann CD 311 041 H1.

———. *Beatus Vir; Totus Tuus*. Prague Philharmonic Choir, Czech Philharmonic Orchestra, conducted by John Nelson. Argo 436 835-2.

James MacMillan. *Seven Last Words from the Cross*. London Chamber Orchestra; James MacMillan, conductor; Polyphony, Stephen Layton, director. *Cantos Sagrados*. Christopher Bowers-Broadbent, organist; James MacMillan, conductor; Polyphony, Stephen Layton, director. Catalyst 09026-68125-2.

———. *Visitatio Sepulchri*. Scottish Chamber Orchestra, Ivor Bolton, conductor. *Busqueda*. Scottish Chamber Orchestra, James MacMillan, conductor. Catalyst 09026-62669-2.

Arvo Pärt. *Arbos*. Includes the sacred works, "An den Wassern zu Babel"; "De Profundis"; "Stabat Mater." The Hilliard Ensemble; Gidon Kremer; Vladimir Mendelssohn; Thomas Demnga; Brass Ensemble Staatsorchester Stuttgart. Dennis Russell Davies, conductor. ECM 1325.

———. *De Profundis*. Includes "De Profundis"; "Missa Sillabica"; "And one of the Pharisees"; "Cantate Domino"; "Summa"; "Seven Magnificat Antiphons"; "The Beatitudes"; "Magnificat." Theatre of Voices, conducted by Paul Hillier. Harmonia Mundi HMU 907 182.

———. *Litany*. Includes "Litany"; "Psalom"; "Trisagion." The Hilliard Ensemble, Tallinn Chamber Orchestra, Estonian Philharmonic Chamber Choir, conducted by Tönu Kaljuste. The Lithuanian Chamber Orchestra, conducted by Slulius Sondeckis. ECM 1592.

———. *Miserere*. The Hilliard Ensemble, conducted by Paul Hillier. Orechester der Beethovenhalle Bonn, conducted by Dennis Russell Davies. ECM 1430.

———. *Passio Domini Nostri Jesu Christi Secundum Joannem*. The Hilliard Ensemble. Paul Hillier, conductor. ECM 1370.

———. *Te Deum*. Includes "Te Deum"; "Magnificat"; "Berliner Messe." Estonian Phiharmonic Chamber Choir, Tallinn Chamber Orchestra, conducted by Tönu Kaljuste. ECM 1505.

John Tavener. *Akathist of Thanksgiving*. James Bowman and Timothy Wilson, countertenors; Martin Baker, organ; BBC Symphony Orchestra; Westminster Abbey Choir and BBC Singers. Marin Neary, conductor. Sony Classical SK 64446.

———. *Sacred Music by John Tavener*. Choir of St. George's Chapel. Christopher Robinson, conductor. Hyperion CDA66464.

———. *Svyati*. Steven Isserlis, cello. BMG Classics 09026-68761-2.

———. *The Protecting Veil*. Steven Isserlis, cello; the London Symphony Orchestra. Gennadi Rozhdestvensky, conductor. Virgin Classics VC 7 91474-2.

———. *We Shall See Him As He Is*. BBC Welsh Symphony Orchestra and Chorus; the Britten Singers; Chester

Festival Chorus. Richard Hickox, conductor. Chandos CHAN 9128.

b. Marcel Pérès has attempted a reconstruction of the manner of Milanese "Ambrosian" chant as it might have been sung during this early period. *Chants de l'église milanaise.* Ensemble Organum, directed by Marcel Pérès. Harmonia Mundi HMC 901295.

c. For an attempted reconstruction of the music of the earlier period: *Chants de l'église de Rome des VIIe et VIIIe siècles. Période Byzantine.* Ensemble Organum, directed by Marcel Pérès. Harmonia Mundi. HMC 901218. (Compare much of the same music sung with less stress on similarity to Byzantine chant: *Old Roman Liturgical Chants.* Schola Hungarica, conducted by Lászlo Dobszay and Janka Szendrei. Hungaroton. HDC 12741-2.) The Lombard (Ambrosian) tradition is represented by *Chants de la cathédrale de Benevento (VIIe–XIe siècles).* Ensemble Organum, directed by Marcel Pérès. Harmonia Mundi. HMC 901476.

d. Two examples may be found on the CD *Music of the Gothic Era,* which also contains music of the Ars Antiqua (ca. 1250–ca. 1320) and Ars Nova (ca. 1320–ca 1380). Performed by the Early Music Consort of London, directed by David Munrow. Archiv. 415 292-2.

For the Notre Dame School in general: *École de Notre Dame de Paris 1163–1245. Monodies et Polyphonies vocales.* Ensemble Gilles Binchois, directed by Dominique Vellard. Harmonic Records. H/CD 8611.

For the music of Léonin and Pérotin: *Magister Leoninus.* Capella Amsterdam. Hyperion 66944. *Pérotin.* The Hilliard Ensemble. ECM 1385.

e. In addition to selections on *Music of the Gothic Era* (cited above), the Ars Nova period is well represented by the recording, *Musique liturgique et profane du XIVe siècle,* containing the "Messe de Barcelone" and "Messe de

Toulouse," as well as selections from the Monserrat manuscript and a number of secular works. Performed by the Ensemble Mediéval de Toulouse, conducted by Pierre Hudrisier. Ariane ARI/148.

Among the most celebrated liturgical products of the period is Guillaume de Machaut's *Messe de Notre Dame*, available in a recording by the Taverner Consort and Choir, directed by Andrew Parrott. EMI CDC 7 47949.

f. For examples of Luther's and Walther's music, as well as selections from other Reformation composers: *Ein feste Burg ist unser Gott. Musik der Reformation*. Members of the Dresdner Kreuzchor, Capella Fidicinia, conducted by Hans Grüß. Berlin Classics. 0091192BC.

Also: *Songs of the Reformation*. Peter Schreier, tenor, Capella Fidicinia Leipzig, conducted by Hans Grüß. Capriccio. 10089.

Martin Luther und die Musik. (Works by early Protestant composers.) Musica Antiqua Wien, directed by Bernhard Klebel. Christophorus. CHE 0025-2.

g. Different styles of singing the vernacular psalms of the influential Geneva psalter, intended for both church and family gatherings, are exemplified in the collection *Pseaumes de David*. Ensemble Claude Goudimel, directed by Christine Morel. Champeaux. CSM 0008. The collection is devoted primarily to the contrapuntal settings by the composers Claude Goudimel (1520–1572) and Jan Pieterszoon Sweelinck (1562–1621); but it also gives examples of the anonymous unison melodies that appeared in the 1562 edition of the Psalter.

h. The masses of Josquin des Prez (ca. 1440–1521), for example, frequently attain great musical beauty through a polyphonic complexity that obscures the clear presentation of the liturgical texts. At times the melodic basis is taken from a secular tune, as in the *"l'homme armé"*

masses. Des Prez's music is well represented in recordings. For example:

Josquin. *L'homme armé Masses*. The Tallis Scholars, directed by
Peter Phillips. Gimell. CDGIM 019.

Josquin des Prez. *Missa "Hercules Dux Ferrariae."* The Hilliard
Ensemble, directed by Paul Hillier. EMI Records. CDC 7
49960 2.

i. The great example of "reformed" Catholic Church music is
that of Palestrina. According to legend (which some
think is perhaps not without factual basis), his *Missa
Papae Marcelli* was composed precisely to demonstrate
that polyphonic music could conform to the directives
of the Council of Trent; the legend thus credits it with
"saving" church music from the more radical solution
of permitting chant alone. Recordings of this work
abound.

Giovanni Pierluigi da Palestrina, *Missa Papae Marcelli.
Motets*. Regensburger Domspatzen, directed by
Georg Ratzinger. Deutsche Harmonia Mundi. 05472
774182.

_____. *Missa Papae Marcelli. Tu es Petrus*. Choir of
Westminster Abbey, directed by Simon Preston.
Archiv. 415 517–2.

j. Henry Purcell, *Ode on St. Cecilia's Day* ("Hail, Bright Cecilia!").
Taverner Consort, Choir, and Players, directed by
Andrew Parrott. EMI Records. CDC 7 47490 2.

k. George Frideric Handel, *Ode for St. Cecilia's Day*. The English
Concert and Choir, directed by Trevor Pinnock. Archiv.
419 220–2.

l. A recording using authentic instruments and a boy treble
for the soprano part is found in the second volume of the
Teldec series of the complete cantatas of Bach:

Johann Sebastian Bach, *Cantata BWV 8 "Liebster Gott,
wann werd'ich sterben?"* in *Das Kantatenwerk*, vol. 2.
Leonhardt–Consort, King's College Choir Cambridge,

led by Gustav Leonhardt. Teldec. CD 8.35028 ZL.
(Contains also Cantatas BWV 5, 6, and 7.)

Likewise with authentic instruments, but using a female
soprano, is the recording of the same cantata by the
Bach Ensemble under Joshua Rifkin. L'Oiseau–Lyre. CD
421 728–2. (Contains also Cantatas BWV 78 and 99.)

Chapter 2
Paradigms in Theology and in Art

PRELUDE: TWO VISIONS OF DAVID: MICHELANGELO AND BERNINI

In September of 1504, the Republic of Florence officially unveiled in front of the Palazzo della Signoria one of its greatest commissioned artistic projects: the gigantic statue of David by Michelangelo Buonarroti.[1] Destined to become one of the world's best known sculptures, the David[a] was immediately recognized as a work of surpassing genius. Vasari, writing in the mid-1500s, rhapsodized: "this work eclipsed all other statues, both modern and ancient...anyone who sees this statue need not be concerned with seeing any other piece of sculpture done in our times or in any other period by any other artist."[2]

It was nearly a century and a quarter later (1624) that Gian Lorenzo Bernini completed another David,[b] intended for the decoration of his patron Cardinal Scipione Borghese's suburban villa outside Rome.

The differences between the two works are striking even at a glance and are accentuated when they are placed in their respective historical contexts in relation to art, society, and ideas.[3]

The monumental size (more than 16 feet high) and towering position of Michelangelo's David determine its relation to the viewer. To see it as a whole and in proportion, one must maintain a certain physical distance. This establishes a certain aesthetic and psychological distance as well. The form exists in its own space/time, which is not that of the viewer. Moreover, although the frontal perspective of the statue is dominant, the work is executed "in the round": it presents an aesthetically satisfying (although incomplete) form from every side. (There is a well-known drawing by Raphael of the statue seen from the back.) The work invites the viewer to walk around it, observing it in various perspectives.

In style, the David represents the epitome of the Renaissance revival of the ancient tradition of the male nude. The figure adopts the classical contraposto stance—an artificial but graceful position that combines balance with visual interest. The figure is consciously and artistically posed: It stands this way precisely to be looked at. Michelangelo disposes us to make his David an object of contemplation, to admire its beauty from multiple complementary points of view.

The statue also presents several complementary levels of meaning. First of all, of course, it evokes the biblical story of the encounter of the young David with the giant Goliath (1 Sm 17:32–51). Second, the figure has an "iconic" function. It is frequently pointed out that although earlier portrayals of David (notably those of Donatello and Verocchio)[4] had shown the youth after his victory, with the head of Goliath at his feet, Michelangelo has instead chosen to depict "a psychologically charged pause of apprehension"[5] before the battle. This is no doubt true. But we would miss a great deal of the figure's meaning if we simply interpreted its purpose (in the light of the function of later art works) in terms of the realistic portrayal of a discrete moment in time. Like medieval paintings and statues, the David serves also as an icon: It goes beyond the particular narrative moment and recalls the person of David as a symbolic figure. It therefore evokes not only the fortitude and courage of the youthful warrior, but also the wisdom of the mature ruler. Thus Vasari saw the statue as a symbol of the Florentine republic, whose seat of government it was to adorn: "for just as David had defended his people and governed them with justice, so, too, those who governed this city should courageously defend it and govern it with justice."[6]

On yet another level, the David transcends its narrative and iconic functions to become a more universal symbol. Iconographic conventions—the sling over the left shoulder and (perhaps) the oversized right hand[7]—identify the person of David. But on a different plane, the unbiblically nude figure, like that of newly created Adam in the Sistine Chapel, refers us not to a historical person or event but to a different sphere of reality. It represents or symbolizes an idea: that of perfect humanity—its Platonic "form."[8] The intent gaze evokes the identifying mark of the human being: mind, consciousness, elevating its material sign, the body, to the level of spiritual beauty.

With Bernini's statue of David we enter into another world, with a new artistic language—of which Bernini is one of the principal inventors. We can see already in this early work many of the characteristics of the Baroque spirit that contrast sharply with the Renaissance style of Michelangelo.[9]

We are first of all presented with an entirely different relation of the work to the viewer. Unlike Michelangelo, Bernini imposes a single point of view. (The statue was in fact originally intended to stand against a wall.) Moreover, this life-size David does not create a separate, aesthetically distanced space/time; it occupies the same real space as the viewer and invites us to participate in the dramatic moment in time that it makes present. As Howard Hibbard comments, Bernini has created a new kind of sculptural art:

> His revolution was manifold: he tried to tie sculpture to the mass of its architectural surroundings and he began to relate it to the space enclosed by that architecture— the area in which we ourselves live and move. To do this he smashed the proud isolation of art as an object or entity on its own and made it participate in a larger conception, spatial and psychological; Bernini's sculpture charges the atmosphere of the room and even discourses with its inhabitants...The "David" takes up a new and fascinating problem...the communication of the spirit of the subject by including spectators in the action.[10]

Bernini accomplishes this by portraying David in motion, in the very act of pulling back his sling for the throw. The twisting figure is visually dynamic; the tense muscles of David's limbs and the contortion of his face (Bernini's self-portrait) create a maximum of psychological tension.

> Feet wide apart, he twists to gain the maximum swing for his shot while his head remains fixed in his concentration on the gigantic adversary. The unruly hair, the knitted brow, and above all the clenched mouth indicate one of those moments when the complete physical and psychic resources of the will are summoned to superhuman effort.[11]

The tense facial expression here evokes not thought or consciousness but total concentration on activity. Moreover, the viewer is directly in the path of the impending action:

> As spectators we must imagine a Goliath towering somewhere behind us; we too become physically

involved with the action of the statue. David's eyes sight past us: our space is his and will soon be the stone's; we are in an activated space embracing a statue, real spectators, and an unseen adversary who cannot be far away—three levels of existence fused into one.[12]

David's right toes curl over the edge of the original plinth, so that the statue seems to be stepping out of the boundaries of its aesthetically defined space—a technique that Bernini would later use frequently and with great impact. The tight flesh of the figure's musculature is cunningly contrasted with varied textures (the rope sling, the fur pouch, the metal of Saul's discarded armor, etc.) to produce an effect of color in the white marble.[13]

Through its physical and psychological realism, Bernini's *David* connects us to the biblical narrative in a way that Michelangelo's does not.[14] It captures a single compelling moment and draws the viewer into the action of the story. By the same token, however, the "iconic" and symbolic levels of meaning are totally subordinated to the dramatic.[15] Hence Bernini's statue is beautiful in a different way from Michelangelo's: It is a superb example of the sculptor's craft and of dramatic skill, and in this way it is a beautiful work of art, but it is not concerned to *represent* beauty itself (bodily and spiritual) in the way Michelangelo's *David* does.

In confronting these two works, we are faced not simply with alternate portrayals of the same subject but (to a certain extent) with different conceptions of the function of art. Michelangelo invites us to contemplation from multiple perspectives, Bernini to dynamic emotional engagement from a single point of view. Michelangelo's *David* evokes a Platonic vision of ideal forms; Bernini's recalls the use of imagination in the Ignatian *Exercises* (which he is known to have practiced): One makes the object of meditation "pres-

ent" by placing oneself at the scene. Michelangelo's intellec-
tualism is replaced by direct communication through feeling. Platonic idealism is replaced by a new form of realism,
one that aims not at historical or natural but at dramatic
verisimilitude.[16] In fact, the effect of Bernini's David is theatrical. (When we look at his sculpture, we realize that it is
surely no accident that Bernini lived in the age when opera
was invented, and we are not surprised to learn that he
engaged in the production of stage spectacles, working not
only as sculptor but also as architect, painter, playwright,
and designer.)[17]

We are perhaps not going too far if we take these differences as being in some sense emblematic of two distinctive
worldviews. It is perhaps permissible, for example, to see
Michelangelo's David, in its Platonic aesthetic function, as an
incarnation of the questioning and idealistic spirit of the
early Renaissance—soon to be broken by world events; and
to see in Bernini's imposition of a definite dramatic point of
view an expression of combative Counter-Reformation spirituality and doctrine.[18] Hence, the examination of such works
should be of interest to the history of ideas—and in a special
way to the history of Christian religion and theology, which
are so intimately involved in Western culture.

In making such statements we must of course exercise
all due caution regarding the individuality of artists, the
plurality within every age, and accidents of circumstance
that cannot be reduced to systematic understanding.
Nevertheless, it may be admitted that art in general reveals a
great deal of the spirit or temper of its epoch. This is not to
say that the history of art should be used as the illustration
of conceptual history as such—although such a relation
does at times exist. But art frequently provides us with
encapsulations of an era's "view" of the world: its unspoken
presuppositions, attitudes, stances, and biases—the "situatedness" and symbolic imaginative matrix in which concepts

occur.[19] This should be all the more true in the case of such creative geniuses as Michelangelo and Bernini, who did not merely passively receive but in large measure invented the artistic languages of their eras.

Is it possible to find a further relationship, beyond the "correlation" of art works to the ideas and culture of their times? Gadamer remarks that in Hegel's lectures on aesthetics, aesthetics becomes the history of changing worldviews[20] and adds that art is indeed the primary example of such shifts because its historical multiplicity cannot be understood in terms of a progression toward a definitively "true" art.[21] Is there nevertheless some kind of pattern to be discerned in the history of art, ideas, and religion? Can the paradigm shifts that each has undergone provide some insight into the others? And, if so, can such insights give us a better understanding of the present and indication of the future for Christian faith and theology?

In the previous chapter I argued for an intrinsic relation between artistic beauty (represented by music) and the human apprehension of God. This chapter will proceed a step further by exploring the question of historical relationship between art and theology as parallel expressions of the more general human culture of particular eras. To do so, I will first examine the idea of *paradigm changes*, derived from contemporary philosophy of science, as it has been applied to the history of theology. In the brief reflections that follow, I hope to expand the discussion by suggesting that the history of art adds a fruitful dimension to the understanding of theological change. I shall first discuss the idea of *paradigm change* as it has been applied in science and theology (section A). Then I shall expand on José Ortega y Gasset's analysis of the moving "point of view" in Western art—this time using the visual arts as our example (section B)—and will apply this analysis to parallel movements in philosophy and theology.

This will result in the outline of an understanding of the parallels in art, philosophy, and theology as expressions of a "moving point of view" in Western culture (section C). Finally, I shall conclude by attempting to discern some of the features of the current theological and cultural paradigm shift and speculate on its trajectory into the future (section D).

A. THE NOTION OF PARADIGM CHANGE IN SCIENCE AND THEOLOGY

When professor Thomas Kuhn's book *The Structure of Scientific Revolutions*[22] appeared in 1962, the author could hardly have had an inkling of the enormous influence his work would eventually have. This technical and specialized treatise on the philosophy of science would eventually not only become a seminal reference work in his own field, but also would have significant repercussions for reflection on rational method in general, reaching even into the realm of theology.

What made Kuhn's treatment significant is his notion of *paradigm change*. Modern science has long used models as a means of understanding the physical world. Kuhn expanded this use in two ways. First, he applied the idea of models not only to science's objects, but to the performance of science itself, showing that the positivist model of science as objective knowledge is only one possible paradigm for understanding science, and one that is inadequate to the facts. (In this revision of the positivist idea of scientific progress, Kuhn was anticipated by others, for example, Karl Popper.) Second, and more important, for the wider import of Kuhn's work, he presented an analysis of how paradigm changes take place.

This analysis has been adapted by a number of theologians as a useful tool for understanding theology and its development.[23] As in science, the application of idea of *models* within theology is not new; it has long since been adopted from positive and sociological studies. Avery Dulles, for example, has used the notion widely as a dialectical tool to explore different approaches to understanding such topics as revelation, the church, and the uses of scripture in theology; and Sallie McFague (among others) has applied the notion to understandings of God.[24] What is more significant is the adaptation to theology of Kuhn's specific innovations by (1) the application of paradigms or models not merely to objects of theology, but to the understanding of theology itself as a science,[25] and (2) the adoption of Kuhn's thesis on how changes in such paradigms come about.[26]

Hans Küng applies Kuhn's thesis to theology in an explicit way. A "paradigm" for Küng is the equivalent of a model—"an entire constellation of beliefs, values, techniques, and so on shared by members of a given community."[27] Küng further distinguishes three main levels at which such models may be operative and gives examples of each.[28] *Microparadigms* are systematic approaches to individual questions: in science, for example, the theory of X-rays; in theology, the doctrines of original sin or of the hypostatic union. *Mesoparadigms* are models that govern larger systematizations: for example, in science, the wave theory of light, or electromagnetic theory; in theology, the Anselmian "satisfaction" model of salvation, or the doctrines of creation, grace, or the sacraments. Finally, what Küng calls macroparadigms are basic and overarching models of interpretation, explanation, or understanding that predominate throughout an entire epoch. In science such macroparadigms might be represented by the Ptolemaic, Copernican, Newtonian, and Einsteinian models of the physical universe; in theology, by the Alexandrine, Augustinian, Thomist, or Reformation models of thinking about God and the world.

Sallie McFague's somewhat different terminology allows for more differentiation between types and levels of thought. *Metaphors*, based on analogies between ordinary experience and our relation to God, constitute for McFague the basic structure of theological and religious thought. *Models* are the dominant metaphors in a particular way of thinking. Metaphors and models, which arise in the imaginative/symbolic mode of thinking, give rise respectively to *concepts* and *theories*. Concepts are abstract notions; theories are a speculative systematic statement of relationships among those notions. There is a possibility of complex interaction between all these modes of thinking; and all of them together constitute an overall theological paradigm.[29] Hence McFague's paradigms are equivalent to Küng's macroparadigms; models and theories are respectively the imaginative and the abstract forms taken by meso- or microparadigms, and all of these are systematizations of basic metaphors and their derived concepts. The following diagram represents the correlation of the two terminologies.

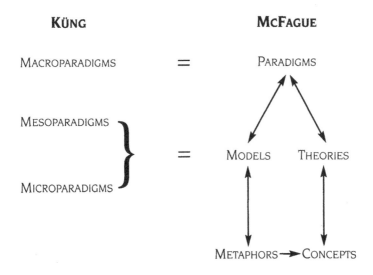

Küng's essential concern is with the most general level of paradigms, where they represent an overarching framework, a set of accepted thought patterns, rather than individual thoughts or theories. A paradigm in this sense designates fundamental notions or ways of thinking that are common to various schools of thought within an epoch, despite their differences on particular subjects. As C. S. Lewis remarks in his essay, "On the Reading of Old Books": "Every age has its own outlook… Nothing strikes me more when I read the controversies of past ages than the fact that both sides were usually assuming without question a good deal which we should now absolutely deny. They thought that they were as completely opposed as two sides could be, but in fact they were all the time secretly united—united *with* each other and *against* earlier and later ages—by a great mass of common assumptions."[30] Thus, for example, although St. Thomas and St. Bonaventure disagree fundamentally on many issues, we can correctly understand them together in a "medieval paradigm" that is essentially different from the apocalyptic paradigm of the early church or the Hellenistic one of the early fathers. A paradigm does not consist so much in answers given to particular problems as in a set of questions and heuristic structures (i.e., means of working out problems and anticipating answers). These provide the presuppositions that guide the method, organizational structures, language, point of view, and goals for thought within a particular horizon.

Crucial to Kuhn's theory is his explanation of how changes in these large paradigmatic complexes take place. The process, according to Kuhn, is not one of organic development nor of piecemeal improvement but rather one of crises that lead to the replacement of the paradigm as a whole. There is in each era its "normal science," characterized by the growth of knowledge, dedicated to solving the remaining problems, and resisting alteration. Eventually, however, the very successes of the normal science reveal its inadequacy. There arise data that cannot easily be fit within the paradigm. These new data cumulatively call for a new perspective that can deal with them more adequately. This leads to a crisis in which the presuppositions of the normal science are challenged. The challenge is radical in that it questions not only the answers given by the normal science, but also its way of dealing with the data and indeed its conception of the problem itself. An example of the process might be found in the replacement of the Ptolemaic with the Copernican astronomical system. As astronomical measurements became more precise, it was observed that movements of the planets did not in fact fit the circular orbits around the Earth ascribed to them by the Ptolemaic theory. Astronomers took account of the new data by modifying the system, adding epicycles to the supposed orbits. More precise observations called for epicycles to be added to the epicycles. The entire system became enormously complex and unwieldy. The solution was finally found not in further modifications but in the replacement of the entire Earth-centered system with the simpler explanation provided by Copernican heliocentrism. A similar process might be observed in the replacement of a biblically literal creationist view of human origins with an evolutionary paradigm because of the discovery of increasing fossil evidence.

In Kuhn's view, then, paradigm changes come about not as an integral process of evolution but as a series of crises and revolutions in which basic perspectives are changed. An old model adapts as long as possible and is dropped only when a new one is ready to replace it.

Hans Küng's adaptation of Kuhn's thesis accepts the basic notion of paradigm changes but both expands and modifies it in several regards. Küng emphasizes that nonscientific factors are significant in the process of accepting (or rejecting) paradigm changes in any particular field.[31] One inevitable factor is how the presuppositions of the model in question fit with the rest of experience and with the whole human situation of those involved, for paradigm change in one area foments change in others, as the interrelations of different areas of life come into play.

Küng also points out that the relationship between an older paradigm and its successor may not necessarily be so simple as Kuhn's schema seems to suggest.[32] A new model may simply replace the old on a wholesale basis, as Kuhn's thesis holds (a theological example might be found in the theologies that stemmed from the Protestant and Catholic reformations, supplanting the earlier medieval paradigm). Even in this case, Küng suggests that there is frequently more continuity than might immediately be apparent. On the other hand, the new paradigm does not always simply prevail. It may be absorbed into the old (Küng gives as examples the survival of an adapted Augustinianism after Aquinas, and Thomism's perdurance in the Roman Catholic Church well into the modern era;[33] in a non-Christian context, one might point to Hindu Vedanta theology's remarkable capacity to co-opt old and new insights and viewpoints into its systems), or the new model may be resisted, and the problems that call for its adoption may be shelved for the moment.[34] At the limit, the new paradigm may be persecuted and destroyed (as occurred for example in twelfth-century Islam's rejection of the innovative philosophical theology that had developed in dialogue with Greek thought, especially Aristotelianism).

With these reservations, Küng finds the ideas of *paradigms* and *paradigm changes* fruitful for an understanding of the development of theology. He discerns six major periods characterized by particular theological paradigms, with significant shifts from one to the next:[35]

1. The first century was dominated by an apocalyptic paradigm inherited by Jewish Christianity from the worldview of late Judaism. The reigning theological framework was the imminent arrival of the eschaton: the "last times," to be brought about by divine intervention with the coming of Christ as judge of the world.

2. With the delay of the eschaton and the entry of the Gentiles into the church, apocalypticism quickly gave way to the Hellenistic paradigm of the early Greek and Latin fathers. Greek philosophy—especially Stoicism and Platonism—provided a model for theological thinking. This patristic paradigm provides the basis for Orthodox traditionalism.

3. Through the mediation of Augustine, by the eleventh century there emerged the medieval Catholic paradigm, centered on Scholasticism and the papal organization of the church.

4. The crises precipitated by the Renaissance beginning in the fifteenth century set the background for the sixteenth century beginnings of the Reformation Protestant paradigm and the Counter-Reformation Catholic paradigm. These continue as thought forms in Protestant and Catholic traditionalism.

5. The turn to independent reason in the seventeenth and eighteenth centuries, the advance of natural science, the shift to historical consciousness, the philosophy of subjectivity, and the growth of political movements toward democracy, gave rise to the Modern Enlightenment paradigm. It continues today in liberal traditionalism.

6. In our time there survive the theological descendants of previously dominant paradigms: Orthodox traditionalism representing the ancient ecclesiastical-Hellenistic model of the fathers; Roman Catholic traditionalism upholding a neo-Scholastic model stemming from the medieval synthesis, via the Counter-Reformation; Protestant fundamentalism adhering to a Lutheran or Calvinist orthodoxy, based on

the inerrancy of the scriptures; and a liberal traditionalism defending the Enlightenment claims for reason without yet having made the shift to the postmodern context. Alongside these, as a result of the explosive events of the twentieth century, a contemporary postmodern theological paradigm is in the process of formation. It is characterized by ecumenism, critical thought, and a stress on praxis toward human liberation. Within this large model coexist many types of theology: dialectical, existential, hermeneutical, political, liberationist.[36]

To this contemporary paradigm and the prospects for the future, we shall return in our concluding section.

B. PARADIGM CHANGES IN THE HISTORY OF ART: THE MOVING POINT OF VIEW

Long before the appearance of Kuhn's hypothesis on scientific paradigm changes, the Spanish philosopher and aesthetician José Ortega y Gasset proposed a model for understanding the major shifts in style in European painting. Just as, according to Küng, there are unspoken presuppositions that unite differing theological theories within a particular epochal paradigm, so we may discern in the history of art recognizable styles that characterize periods, despite differences between individual artists. The style of a period includes such elements as technique, materials, genres, and so on, but above all, it consists of the schemata of representation that characterize a period— the conventions by which visual reality is represented, that form the "basic grammar" of the symbolic language of painting.[37] In this sense, I will suggest, the major changes in style that are observable in Western painting are in some way parallel to the conceptual paradigm shifts that have taken place in various areas of thought.

According to Ortega, the history of Western art from Giotto to the contemporary period can be seen as a single simple movement; and he finds that, curiously and disturbingly, this movement is the same as that which has ruled European philosophy in the same period.[38] Ortega asks: "What moves in the history of painting?" He believes that the answer is clear: what moves is the point of view of the painter. It shifts from what Ortega calls close-up vision to a long-distance view.

As Ortega uses these terms, they do not simply refer to proximity or distance from the object of sight; they represent rather two different ways of seeing.[39] Physically, proximate vision organizes what is seen in an optical hierarchy: There is a central nucleus that is clear and perfectly defined, and a peripheral vision of what we are not looking at, but see indistinctly. Distant vision, by contrast, provides us with a homogeneous field of vision; it presents an "optic democracy" in which the entire field is seen in the same way.[40] In proximate vision, objects are solid, corporeal, and tactile; in distant vision, things lose their solidity. Vision surrenders its tactile quality and becomes "pure" vision: a surface composed of light.

Ortega notes that the characteristics of proximate and distant vision can be separated from the degree of physical separation from objects and can refer instead to the way we look at them. In this sense, *proximate vision* means focusing on an object; *distant vision* means that we do not look at any point but take in a total visual field, including its borders.[41] Distant vision is the vision of space as such. This space is concave and begins with the eye itself. Hence, there arises the paradox that what we see in "distant" vision is not farther away than what we see in proximate vision; on the contrary, it is closer, because it begins with our eyes.[42]

Having established this distinction, Ortega is able to enunciate his thesis: The progression of European art since Giotto can be understood in terms of a shift in the point of view of the painter from proximate to distant vision, from the painting of mass to the painting of space, and finally to the representation of the act of seeing itself. The evolution of Western painting is thus a progressive withdrawal from objects to the subjectivity of the painter.[43]

Ortega gives a number of examples of this progression, beginning with the Renaissance and ending with the styles contemporary with his writing in the 1920s. In what follows, I shall use his exposition as a basic framework, expanding on his essay in several ways. Most significantly, I shall extrapolate from Ortega's analysis in two directions: backward to cover the ancient and medieval periods, and forward to the contemporary context. Thus I will attempt to see in what sense Ortega's insight can be applied to art throughout the whole period covered by Christian history and theology. In doing so, I shall follow the widely accepted observation that Western painting moves increasingly from the exposition of "knowledge" to the representation of perception; that is, that its general movement is in the direction of Naturalism.[44] I shall also expand on Ortega's treatment by referring to concrete instances. Ortega's examples are general, referring to the style of an artist or period as a whole; I, however, shall cite particular works as illustrations of each shift. Although Ortega limits his thesis to the history of painting, I shall occasionally use examples from other parallel forms of graphic art—for example, mosaic—where they exhibit the same visual characteristics. To provide a basis for comparison with Küng's analysis of paradigm changes in theology, I shall when possible (especially, that is, for the premodern period) refer to sacred works of art. It is not possible to draw examples of the shifts Ortega refers to exclusively from sacred art, for two related reasons: (1) since the Renaissance, the prime subjects of art have been secular; and (2) sacred art since that period has tended to be traditional and imitative, clinging to older styles even when newer ones were predominant in the secular sphere. For the premodern period, then, I shall refer to artworks that are similar in theme in that they have a eucharistic referent: scenes of the "breaking of the bread," the Last Supper, the Eucharist, or the supper at Emmaus.

When Christianity appeared on the scene, Hellenistic painting had already attained significant achievements. In some ways, in particular with regard to the representation of three-dimensional space, its techniques surpassed what would succeed it in medieval art; hence it stands outside the parameters of Ortega's analysis of the shifting point of view. With the Christian adoption and adaptation of Hellenistic painting, however, the movement Ortega refers to can be said to begin.

An example from Christian catacomb art may serve to illustrate. In the famous fresco known as the *fractio panis* (third [?] century) from the catacombs of Priscilla in Rome, we are presented with a stylized but basically realistic representation of a Roman meal. It is uncertain exactly what kind of gathering the painting represents. In the past, it was frequently assumed that it was a eucharistic celebration; but it may be an agape, or love-feast, or—given the catacomb setting—a commemorative meal at the tomb of the deceased. Although the picture is reduced to essentials, as befits the demands of the fresco style and the difficult conditions for painting in the underground location, there is sufficient detail to bring the subject to life for the viewer. The participants recline on a large cushion in front of a table, obviously engaging in conversation. One member of the group is clearly discernible as a woman by the style in which she wears her hair. One, clad in a short tunic, has arms extended and hands joined—possibly in the act of breaking bread that has given the picture its traditional title. On the table in front of the participants are two plates, each holding a fish.

At this point, for the viewer acquainted with Christian iconography the genre of the painting is clarified. We recognize that it is not simply a visual portrayal but a symbolic statement. The fish is a frequent ancient Christian symbol of Christ, the Greek word ιχθυς being read as an acronym for Ἰησοῦς Χριστὸς Θεοῦ Ὑιὸς Σωτήρ ("Jesus Christ, Son of God, Savior").[c] Two fish are typical of Roman Christian images and recall the first miracle of the loaves and fishes (Mt 14:17ff.; Mk 6:38ff.; Lk 9:13ff.; Jn 6:9ff.). The painting is then telling us that Christ is present in the midst of his followers in their *koinonia* (Mt 18:20). It is realistic not in the ordinary visual sense but in a Platonic sense: Its purpose is to portray not what is seen but what is known by faith; not the world of physical appearances but the world of religious truths; not material objects but spiritual reality.

The shift from Hellenistic realism to a symbolic, iconic style sets the agenda for painting in the Middle Ages. It is only with the era of Leonardo da Vinci that painting will be defined as the "imitation of nature"; for the medieval world, it is the "imitation of Christ" that is primary. Thus there is no effort at representing the visual field; in general, each thing is painted independently, without relation to an overall perspective. This means that there is no peripheral vision, only a series of direct, up-close views of individual objects. The unity of the picture is not visual but intellectual: It resides in the message being communicated. The relation among the objects presented—including even their size, shape, and position—is a function of their place in the narrative or doctrine presented and the conventions used to symbolize ideas. Because of its intellectual rather than visual focus, painting is essentially two dimensional. Objects are sometimes shown from more than one side or in more than one perspective; the purpose is not to capture their volume but to indicate their properties or their place in the narrative.

A manuscript illustration of the Last Supper from the Rossano gospel (sixth [?] century) shows these features clearly.[d] Christ and the disciples are portrayed reclining in the Roman style in a semicircle around a table. The sides of the couches and of the table are perfect rectangles, as though they are seen directly ahead of the viewer. Christ on the extreme left and one apostle on the extreme right are also drawn from this perspective, seen full length in reclining position. But the top of the table is presented as a full semicircle, as though seen from above, and eleven other apostles are fully visible around it, seen from the chest up. Here there is no consistent point of view; figures on all sides of the table are seen nearly frontally, and there is no indication of their reclining. A large bowl is shown on the table. Its baseline is straight, as though seen at eye level; but the top is shown as below eye level so that one can see the hand of Judas dipping into it. Perhaps the most strikingly symbolic features are seen in the portrayals of Christ and the apostles. The latter are all dressed in formal Roman togas and tunics, with the broad purple stripes (*clavi*) indicating the senatorial class. Jesus is shown dressed in the imperial purple, with a gold toga and stripe. His head is encircled by a round gold halo, partially truncated at one side to provide a view of the apostle next to him. The bowl on the table and the sides of the couches and table are also gold.

We find a very similar picture in the mosaic of the Last Supper in the sixth century church (at this period in Arian hands) of St. Apollinare Nuovo in Ravenna.[e] The disposition of Christ and the apostles reclining around a semicircular table is nearly the same, except that, despite the semicircular arrangement, the artist has preserved the isocephalism (heads all at the same level) typical of Byzantine style and has placed Judas directly opposite Jesus, hence with his back to the viewer. The falling part of the tablecloth is treated naturalistically, with realistic folds; but on its surface are the symbolic two fish and seven loaves. Jesus is clothed completely in imperial purple; his halo contains a gold and jeweled cross. The whole is placed in a gold background: its setting is not the physical space of the upper room, but the glory in which faith sees the entire Christ event.

The same kind of treatment dominates the graphic art of the Middle Ages. Although there is development in style and content, art remains essentially intellectual and symbolic. Medieval representations of the Last Supper significantly rearrange the figures of the scene, usually showing them seated (instead of reclining) around a rectangular table and putting Christ in the center. But the figures are still stylized and iconic, and there is no effort at presenting a unitary perspective or point of view. This remains true even in late medieval paintings like Lorenzetti's fresco of the Last Supper in the basilica of St. Francis in Assisi or the Last Supper panel in Duccio's *Maestà*.[f] In these, especially the latter, the introduction of architectural elements is a step toward visual perspective. However, we are still presented not with a replica of what the eye might have seen but with the narration of an event or the teaching of an idea and a reflection on its meaning in faith. Art is determined theologically, not visually. The "point of view" is not physical but mental; knowledge, not sensation, determines the mode of representation.

It is with Giotto, according to Ortega, that modern Western painting begins. In many ways, Giotto is still medieval; if we compare his Last Supper fresco in the Capella degli Scrovegni in Padova with the works of Lorenzetti and Duccio mentioned above, we find them for the most part similar in style; for example, there is still no difference in the manner of painting objects in different planes—the farthest is treated in the same way as the nearest. Each thing is seen separately and is depicted in "close-up" vision. Hence, there are as many points of view as there are objects in the picture.[45] But with Giotto there is the beginning of a successful treatment of perspective and, hence, a move toward long-range vision and a particular point of view. In Duccio's or Lorenzetti's "Last Supper" the fanciful architecture is essentially a frame for the event portrayed; it is painted with perspective but without depth and without relation to the figures within it. In Giotto's painting,[g] the room of the Last Supper is actually seen to contain the figures of Christ and the disciples; those on the far side of the table actually seem farther away than those on the near side. In Duccio's picture, however, Christ, on the far side of the table, is visually "closer" to the viewer than the apostles in the foreground. To oversimplify somewhat, we may say that Duccio still represents the medieval idea of painting, telling us about what the subject *is*, while Giotto anticipates the Renaissance idea of showing us what the subject *looks like*. Of course, both painters still depict their main figures in an iconic rather than a naturalistic way; the gold background is now replaced with a room, but the gold halos and hieratic postures remind us that a truth of faith is being portrayed, not a moment of natural vision.

In the quattrocento the painting of nature—that is, what is seen—begins to predominate. Leon Battista Alberti in his book *Della Pittura (On Painting)* gives theoretical expression to what has begun to happen in art: Painting tries to represent what we see, and the surface of the painting is like a transparent pane of glass through which we observe objects.[46] There is generally still no single point of view, in Ortega's sense; the same essential method of portraying individual objects in "near" vision perdures. But an abstract element of unity is introduced: composition, frequently organized through architecture.[47] Art begins to portray physical space as the ordering framework of what is por-

trayed. This is still a rational rather than purely visual principle of unity; but it is a step toward a different way of seeing.
Two very different quattrocento paintings of the Last Supper
illustrate the point.

In the representation of the Last Supper ("the communion
of the apostles") in a series of six scenes from the life of
Christ, from the workshop of Fra Angelico,[h] we find a bold
use of perspective within an architectural framework. The
narrative is set within a large vaulted room. The scene is
divided into three parts by two pillars in the foreground. Six
apostles are seated at a table in the background; however,
communion takes place not at the table, in the context of
the meal, but rather according to the ritual of the medieval
church. Christ is located in the center of the picture, distrib-
uting communion, under the form of a white wafer, to three
kneeling apostles. Three more await in the left foreground. A
sense of boxlike depth is created by the standard technique
of converging lines (the borders of the ceiling and floor), by
the difference in size between the figures in the three planes
of the picture, and by the portrayal of empty space, occupied
only by two low stools, between the figure of Christ and the
frame of the picture. Despite the "illusionistic" representation of space, it is notable that even though the clear visual
and theological center of the picture is the figure of Christ,
each of the other figures may be looked at separately and
made a center of vision. None is portrayed in peripheral
vision: The eye may roam from one to the other.

Cosimo Rosselli's painting in the Sistine Chapel[i] con-
trasts with Fra Angelico's in its more naturalistic portrayal of
the figures and the accoutrements in the room. But here
again it is space—defined in this case by a fanciful architectural schema—that gives unity and order to the picture. The
figures are related to the viewer and to each other through
their relation to the empty space that the viewer imagines in
front of the table and that the portrayal of space defines as

nearly semicircular. The drama of Christ instituting the Eucharist and confronting Judas is made the center of attention, despite the placement of the figures at the farthest distance from the viewer. This is achieved by virtue of their location immediately behind the focal point of the concave imaginary space created by the use of perspective. It is notable that this painting still retains the medieval characteristic of an essentially narrative rather than visual purpose; it does not portray a distinct moment but illustrates the entire Last Supper in its theologically significant moments through the stylized symbolic language of the gestures of the principal figures. Through the windows of the room, one looks out onto naturalistically portrayed scenes, in realistic perspective from the point of view of the room, but with each object still represented in "close-up" vision. Moreover, what one sees is not a coherent landscape but three separate scenes of the Passion that are related to the Eucharist: the agony in the garden, with the "cup" that Christ must drink; the betrayal by Judas; and the crucifixion.

A further advance toward "distant vision" is made by the technique of chiaroscuro. Painting still concentrates on the body of things, their mass. The relation of the figures is still "feudal," with each element demanding its own exclusive and privileged point of view. But now a new element is added: light. It pervades the whole picture and imposes a principle of unity that is no longer abstract or schematic but is real. The single source of light imposes a single point of view.[48] It also imposes a dramatic unity, for the chiaroscurist's subjects are lit not naturally but as they would be on a stage. (The age of the chiaroscuro is also, not coincidentally, important for the development of theater and opera.) The dramatic highlighting of the action also encourages the artist to portray a single dramatic *moment* that evokes the point of the story, instead of representing symbolically the whole narration.

These characteristics are evident in Caravaggio's two paintings of *The Supper at Emmaus*.ʲ Each thing in the picture is solid and visually independent; the eye can rest on each individually and find a complete, self-standing, three-dimensional object. Each person is an individual self-standing portrait. Yet together they form a visual whole because of the play of light and shadow that shows them to be in spatial relation to each other and in dramatic relation to the revelatory event of the painting.

It is Velázquez, according to Ortega, who makes the final step to distant vision. He invents a new way of painting by the simple expedient of holding his eye still. Ortega's words on Velázquez's "revolution" are worth quoting: "Up to this time the pupil of the painter's eye had circled Ptolemaically around each object in a servile orbit. Velázquez decides to fix despotically the point of view. The whole canvas is born of a single act of vision, and the things in it must try to reach the line of sight however they can. We are speaking, then, of a Copernican revolution, similar to that accomplished by Descartes, Hume, and Kant in philosophy."[49] The pupil of the artist's eye now becomes the center of the visual cosmos; objects are portrayed according to their relation to its single line of vision. The whole painting can be seen in its totality, all at once, because a point of view is introduced that is subjective: individual and relative to the viewer.

The Supper at Emmaus by Velázquez,ᵏ although it clearly retains features of the Renaissance and chiaroscuro manners of painting, is already an example of distant vision. Christ is the center of the painting, not by position on the canvas—he is in fact on the extreme left—but simply by virtue of the fact that the painter is "looking" at him. The other two figures—despite the fact that one occupies nearly the middle of the picture—are seen in peripheral vision. The viewer may indeed inspect them individually, but there is nothing to keep the eye: It is drawn irresistibly to the one object on which the artist has trained his vision. Moreover, if one compares these figures with those of Caravaggio discussed above, one immediately notes their comparative lack of "roundness" or mass. This illustrates a second observation made by Ortega concerning the shift to distant vision: It deemphasizes the mass or dimensionality of objects. Figures are now merely molecules of light in the concave visual field that is portrayed;[50] they no longer have the nearly tactile solidity of earlier representations.

These characteristics are seen even more clearly in one of Velázquez's most famous paintings of figures, Los borrachos, or The feast of Bacchus.[1] Here one immediately notes the difference in treatment of foreground and background—or rather, of the subject on which the eye is trained and its periphery. The trees, foliage, and landscape, and even the seated figure in the left foreground are all perfectly realistic as long as one is looking at the main figures; but they are out of focus— mere impressions—as soon as one looks at them directly. The viewer is forced to adopt the single point of view of the artist's eye and, from it, sees a single dramatic moment rather than a whole story.

The full and radical implications of Velázquez's move only become apparent in the next stage of development, which breaks finally with Renaissance realism: impressionism. The artist increasingly retreats within the self. Painting becomes a plane; instead of painting objects as they are known to be, solid and substantial, artists paint the act of seeing itself: not an object, but an impression, a collection of sensations. Art begins to attend not to the outside world but to the activity of the subject.[51] This is already apparent in such diverse artists as Renoir or van Gogh, who are essentially painters of light. In the pointilists, like Seurat, the act of seeing is analyzed into its components: dots of colored light, to be recomposed in the eye of the painting's viewer. In the celebrated painting A Sunday Afternoon in Summer on the Island of

La Grande Jatte,[m] Ortega's point about distant vision is illustrated in act, for the viewer must him- or herself take a distant view of the painting for the scene to become real. Once one does this, the dots coalesce into a single vibrant image.

With Cézanne, says Ortega, painting rediscovers volume; once again artists begins to attend to shapes.[n] But these are not natural shapes; they have little to do with the tangible masses of Giotto. They are rather ideal shapes from the artist's mind. Cézanne himself often spoke of showing the "structure" of the world.[52] Instead of absorbing things from without, the artist now projects landscapes from the interior. The Impressionists, influenced by the science of optics, had attempted to paint the way we see. They self-consciously restricted themselves to the world perceived by the senses: the surfaces of things as reflected to the eye. In this sense, their painting displays a kind of objectivity. The painting of Cézanne and Gauguin represents a rebellion, based on the conviction that art must somehow be revelatory.[53] From Cézanne onward, says Ortega, painting only paints ideas.[54] This explains the dynamism of cubism and abstractionism. (It is by no means coincidental that such movements in art occur just as photography and the moving picture enter into Western culture. As James Martin points out, these new means—especially the cinema—can realize the artistic goal of mimesis, the "imitation" of nature, in a way impossible for painting. Not surprisingly, the latter turns to expressive theories of art: The emphasis is on the affects or thoughts of the artist and/or on the experience of the viewer of the art, which is now an "event."[55])

The movement to progressive interiorization continues beyond the period marking the end of Ortega's essay. With the movement of abstract modern art, the intention of painting the artist's interiority becomes explicit. The manifesto of the new art was Wassily Kandinsky's 1911 essay *Concerning the Spiritual in Art*.[56] Against "the nightmare of materialism, which has turned the life of the universe into an evil, useless game,"[57] Kandinsky proposed an artistic revolution. "When religion, science and morality are shaken, the two last by the strong hand of Nietzsche, and when the outer supports threaten to fall, man turns his gaze from externals in onto himself. Literature, music and art are the first and most sensitive spheres in which this spiritual revolution makes itself felt."[58] Kandinsky's turn to abstraction was directly influenced by modern science, specifically by Rutherford's discoveries about the atom. Kandinsky thought that atomic science showed that the material world is not made up of the objects we see and feel: these are "unreal." The "real" world is invisible, inaccessible to experience. The consequence for art is a turn to purely internal form. "When we remember, however, that spiritual experience is quickening, that positive science, the firmest basis of human thought, is tottering, that dissolution of matter is imminent, we have reason to hope that the hour of pure composition is not far away."[59]

Art's purpose, then, should be to convey lofty emotions, spirit, by the means proper to art, that is, by a direct appeal to the subject's interiority. This means that pictorial art should appeal to inner beauty (which may appear as ugliness to those who are not accustomed to it) rather than to external form.[60] It should seek to express direct spiritual impressions, as music does.[61] Painting, like music, should devote itself "not to the reproduction of natural phenomena, but to the expression of the artist's soul."[62] "Natural forms make boundaries which often are impediments to this expression," Kandinsky writes. "Thus they must be set aside and the freed space be used for the objective side of the form—construction for the sake of composition."[63]

Painting will communicate directly to spirit by means of colors and forms, which have natural psychic effects apart from their embodiment in objects (an idea connected with the teachings of theosophy and of Rudolph Steiner). "Form is the external expression of inner meaning;"[64] while "colour is a power which directly influences the soul. Colour is the keyboard, the eyes are the hammers, the soul is the piano with many strings. The artist's is the hand which plays, touching one key or another, to cause vibrations in the soul."[65] Art then will operate not by pure inspiration but by conscious construction,[66] utilizing the infinite variety of combinations of color and form and exploiting the ways they influence one another by juxtaposition. Kandinsky's fully abstract canvases—his *Composition* VIII of 1923 is a good example—manifest the conviction that form and color of themselves express the artist's spiritual interior state and are capable of producing a corresponding "vibration" in the viewer's soul.[67]

An explicit concern for the spiritual was characteristic not only of Kandinsky, but also of other pioneers of twentieth-century art: Piet Mondrian, Kazimir Malevich, František Kupka. Their reaction against materialism frequently led them into the realms of spiritualism and the occult. Such movements as theosophy, anthroposophy, and Rosicrucianism, as well as Eastern philosophy and religion, were major sources of inspiration. Kupka was a practicing medium at spiritualist seances; Kandinsky took part in black masses, magic, and pagan rituals. Mondrian belonged to the Dutch Theosophical Society and explicitly attributed his inspiration to its esoteric doctrines. (In this light much of his painting can be seen as symbolic in nature: the frequent occurrence of vertical and horizontal lines, for example, represents the theosophical doctrine of ascending stages in the spiritual journey.)[68] For all of these, the turn to abstract art was consciously connected with an effort to recover the spiritual dimension of human existence, which was threatened by modern materialism, positivism, technology, and rationalism. Realism in painting was associated with these dehumanizing forces. Art had lost its soul; a new form of art and music was needed. Truly spiritual art had to be concerned not with the external world, which no longer had anything to say to humanity, but rather with the internal world of the mind and spirit, expressed in composition. Hence the representation of things must give way to free expression in form and color.

Surrealism adopts a different technique for conveying interiority. Its concern is the dream world, the preconscious psyche, or, at times, the mystical. The objects in its paintings may be represented realistically—indeed, with "super" realism; however, their connections with each other and with the viewer are not dependent on an act of seeing but on a mental or spiritual "vision" that goes beyond the conditions of time and space. In Dali's painting *The Sacrament of the Last Supper* (1955)[p] realistic and transcendent elements mingle in a mystical-theological apparition. The table with the bread and wine and the kneeling figures of the apostles are photographically real; but the figure of Christ in the center, although also realistic in form, is transparent and casts no shadow. The whole scene is set within the frame of a partly solid and partly transparent geometrical figure whose shape, dimensions, and spatial orientation are ambiguous. Through it is seen a landscape in which the sun rises behind fantastic mountains surrounding a glass-smooth lake, and at the top of the picture is an incomplete transparent torso that intersects with the geometrical and landscape elements and repeats in itself the overall shape of the figures around the table "below" it.

After the Second World War, abstract impressionism and later minimalism continue the nonrepresentational line of painting, but the emphasis shifts from the expression of the artist's inner state to a concentration on the production of the work. The subject matter of painting becomes painting itself: either the process of creating it, or the event of viewing it, or its very methods and materials—canvas and paint, color and form, and their manners of application.[69]

Art here is more an event than a conveyor of meaning. Jackson Pollock in many of his paintings (see for example *Number* 1A of 1948)[q] evokes Kandinsky's metaphor of painting as music. At the same time, the intersecting splattered and dribbled blots and lines of paint draw attention to themselves and the painter's technique. Mark Rothko's classic paintings[r] typically consist of large bands of color of different intensity, with irregular borders, to which the viewer's feeling is invited to respond directly.

We may now summarize what we have noted in this brief overview based on Ortega's insight and expanding from it. We have seen that the history of Western painting may be seen as a progressively "inward" movement: first from the symbolic representation of spiritual realities to the portrayal of substantial corporeal objects in "close up" vision; next from close-up to distant vision, concentrating not on things, but on the visual field of the subject. Then we move to the mind of the subject him-/herself, and finally from the subject to the act of seeing. Of course there is no claim implied that this is the only way of analyzing the history of Western art or that all painting fits into this general schema. The point is merely that there is on the whole a certain discernible pattern that may be seen to have parallels in other spheres. It remains now to be seen how this movement parallels the shift in paradigms in philosophy and theology.

C. THE MOVING POINT OF VIEW:
PARALLELS IN ART, PHILOSOPHY, AND THEOLOGY

We have seen that Western painting's treatment of objects suggests an overall movement. Philosophy, Ortega notes, follows an analogous route: If we ask what class of things is of most fundamental concern for a particular

7.00pm, Friday 15 December 2017
ST. PETER'S CHURCH, WINCHESTER

Christmas Concert *in aid of Nightshelter*
including excerpts from Handel's Messiah and carols for all

Claire Williams *soprano*   Jamal Sutton *organ*

WMC *Chorus*   David Thomas *conductor*

Winchester Churches Nightshelter is open 365 days a year offering an essential lifeline and first port of call for those in crisis. They provide high quality accommodation and food, a safe and caring temporary home, and specialist support to restore self-esteem, develop skills, and support people back into long-term accommodation and independent living. Their aim is to enable people to rebuild their lives and escape homelessness for good.

Tickets £10 (under 18s £5)

www.winchestermusicclub.org.uk/buy-tickets

Registered charity no 1095619

period of philosophy, we find a movement from ideal spiritual realities to solid corporeal things, then to sensations, to ideas, and finally to events—or from metaphysical reality to external physical reality, to the subject, to the intrasubjective, and finally to the occurrence.[70] I suggest that we may also extend this analogy to the paradigm shifts in theology.

In the Hellenistic period a generally Platonic worldview prevails. The "really real" is transcendental; things of the material world are shadows or images that refer to and to some degree participate in the ideal reality in the divine Mind. Painting is two dimensional: Its objects symbolize rather than represent, and they are concerned with transsensible reality rather than with physical vision. The theology of the fathers, especially in the East, presents a parallel theological vision: The entire sensible world and all of sacred history present a series of symbols and analogies for the spiritual.

In the time of Giotto, the painter of solid, independent bodies, philosophy thinks of the ultimate and definitive reality as "substance": what has existence in itself, independent of other things and of the mind that knows it.[71] In the theology of high scholasticism, God is the supreme Substance, total aseity, whose essence is its existence. The world consists of created substances and accidents, including the substantial "souls" of humans; the essences of things are objectively "real" (although not independently existent) and are knowable by a process of abstraction from the concrete sensible things of which they are the "form." As late scholastic philosophy and theology becomes dominated by nominalism, art turns its attention increasingly to the individual and particular; as metaphysics is cast into doubt, observation of the physical world increasingly occupies the attention of both the scholar and the artist.

When artists like Velázquez present physical reality as extension or geometric space, the reigning philosophy is that of Descartes.[72] But even more significant than Descartes's physical theories is his turn to the knowing subject as the starting point of philosophical reflection. The authority of the past, and particularly of Scholasticism, is rejected—as it had already been in the Protestant Reformation—and thinking takes as its basis the experience of the self. This represents the beginning of a shift of emphasis in philosophy from substances to the subject, from the known to the knower, reflected in art by the introduction of distant vision and the single point of view. Moreover, this turn to the subject also involves a shift in the notion of the subject itself: It begins to be conceived less as a transcendent reality, capable of metaphysical knowledge of objects, and more as a sensible, psychological, feeling self.

The implications of this move in philosophy and theology, as in art, evolve in the succeeding centuries. The Enlightenment pursues the ideal of the independent rational subject and criticizes the accepted authorities of the past. Correlatively, art is secularized, freed from its previous primary role as the servant of religion. By the late eighteenth century, profane subjects dominate painting; religious painting in the traditional Christian style is confined to a cultural ghetto and is practiced almost exclusively by second-rate artists.[73]

Romanticism develops the role of individual feeling and the self, as well as an appreciation of nature. Landscape, as an evocation of the encounter with the sublime, becomes the principal visual medium for representing transcendence. Günter Rombold notes that Kant's distinction of the sublime (das Erhabene) from the beautiful in his Critique of Judgment was anticipated by Edmund Burke, who in 1757 defined the sublime as a quality that evokes fear and awe, as opposed to the love and desire produced by beauty; it is also notable that the concept of the sublime plays a major role in the art theory of the great English land- and seascape artist William Turner. As Rombold also points out, there is a clear parallel between the Romantic experience of the sublime and the religious "feeling of absolute dependence" spoken of by Schleiermacher.[74]

With the passage of time, subjectivism becomes more intense: As impressionists paint pure sensations, positivists reduce knowledge to sensation.[75] The pursuit of the transcendent in art is not totally abandoned: In van Gogh even landscape becomes "the mirror of the human soul," and the empirical world is translated into the visionary.[76] This tradition is continued by the "classical" modern painters in the romantic tradition—for example the circle of the Blue Rider (*Der Blaue Reiter*)[77]—and in various forms of "expressionism."[78] But in the face of the advances of science, a "liberal" paradigm increasingly relegates faith to a purely internal realm of subjective feeling and its assertions to symbolic expressions of that interiority.

In the contemporary period, there is a continuation of the move from the substantial metaphysical subject to the existential subject and finally to the events of sensing, thinking, and communicating. This "turn to the subject," implying the adoption of an existential, historical mode of thinking, profoundly influenced the method of both philosophy and theology. The classical distinction between these two disciplines, which was based on an essentialist separation of the natural and supernatural realms, became questionable once the existential subject was taken as the methodological point of reference. Similarly, art after the Second World War reflected an existentialist tinge that affected its methods. Painting was no longer "about" the visible world, which was no longer seen to convey objective meaning or value; rather, art creates and is its own act of meaning. "Instead of making *cathedrals* out of Christ, man, or 'life,' we are making it out of ourselves, out of our own feelings," declared painter Barnett

Newman.[79] The "death of art," according to Newman, precedes
and presages the "death of God." As science, philosophy, and
theology ask about their own methods, so art's subject
moves from the artist's feelings to its own techniques,
materials, and processes. When the starting point for discourse is event or performance—what one does, rather
than a subject or object of the doing—the project becomes
self-referential, and one arrives at language about language, philosophy about philosophy, painting about
painting. (Is this perhaps the reason why much contemporary art has never found a great popular audience but
appeals primarily to artists themselves?)

Finally, cultural life at the end of the millennium included
a reaction against the allegedly totalizing pretensions of
modernity, a term used to describe the scientific and objectifying intellectual ethos prevailing in the West since the
Enlightenment. The term *postmodern* (with or without a
hyphen) gained currency in the contemporary context in discussions of architecture, where it describes the rejection of
the simple forms and pragmatic functionalism of the modern period in favor of a return to visual aesthetics.[80]
Postmodern constructions often include an eclectic and
ironic approach that juxtaposes elements from different
styles and periods. Similarly, postmodern art emphasizes
appearance and feeling, embraces a plurality of styles, and
is frequently self-consciously unsettling.[81]

Philosophically, consciousness of the historical conditioning of thinking[82]—the awareness that all knowledge is
"perspectival," and (like realistic painting since Velázquez)
represents a particular point of view—leads to a critique of
the classical ontological mode of thinking and its universal
categories. Philosophical/theological reactions to the challenge to Enlightenment modernity move in several different
directions:[83] to a conception of reality as process; or to a
retrieval of premodern thinking enshrined in cultural and

linguistic traditions; or to a renewed appreciation of mysticism; or to a search for the transcendental conditions of subjectivity and a critical "retrieval" of metaphysics, but with an explicit consciousness of the "situatedness" of the subject; or to an investigation and critique of the sociological or linguistic or ideological preconditions of thinking; or to the adoption of praxis as the ultimate norm; or, most radically, to the complete deconstruction of the subject. Some theologians continue and revise the turn to subjectivity of the modern period, attempting to arrive not at universal objective truths, but at basic and universal patterns in the knowing process;[84] others emphasize conversation between irreducibly different but analogous viewpoints;[85] others adopt the privileged perspective of the oppressed;[86] yet others, abandoning hope of any epistemological absolutes, take refuge in a "Wittgensteinian fideism" and emphasize the formative power of a particular tradition.[87] One may be led to complete relativism or nihilism or, on the contrary, to openness to a quasi-mystical apprehension of reality in the "Other."[88] But all these very different movements have in common with contemporary art an awareness of historicity, situatedness, and plurality, as well as a self-conscious concern for performance.

A generally parallel analysis is given by Bernard Lonergan, who sees a succession of "stages of meaning" in theological thought, moving through increasing differentiations of consciousness from common sense to theory to interiority. He discusses five basic stages:[89] (1) Symbolic apprehension: Meaning is expressed in myth, legend, typology, symbol, and truth is approached by the reinterpretation of symbolic constructs. This stage is typical of the scriptures. (2) Philosophical purification: in the fathers there is demythologization and the rejection of anthropomorphic conceptions of God. (3) Occasional systematic meaning: The early councils develop an incipiently theoretical and metaphysical context for understanding faith. (4) Systematic theology: In the Middle Ages a fully self-conscious metaphysical context emerges. Theoretical categories replace descriptive ones; lived faith is organized and explained. There is an interaction between theology and church doctrine, which, although using the language of systematics, is generally postsystematic in context. (5) Modern developments: These include the shifts from Aristotelian to modern views of science, from classical to historical consciousness, from theory to interiority (Descartes through Kant), and from knowledge to decision (Kierkegaard to the existentialists), and finally a self-conscious apprehension of the basic operations of thinking itself, a shift to "method."[90]

Obviously, such schematic generalizations do not do justice to the whole story, either in its detail or even overall. One might look at the same history of art, philosophy, and theology from different perspectives—the material, technical, or sociological, for example—and find parallel but different correlations.[91] Moreover, the relations between the various components of human culture in any age are much more complex and intricate—and also unsystematic—than could be indicated in the few suggestive parallels indicated here. Furthermore, as already noted, movements between paradigms are not uniform or universal; different directions and paradigms can coexist in a single era. Contemporary with Picasso's cubist *Baigneuses dans une forêt* (1908) is Alma-Tadema's classicist *A favorite custom* (1909).[s] Likewise in philosophy and theology, as Küng notes, classical modes of thinking perdure in the contemporary world in the form of various "traditionalisms."

However, without claiming that this schema is without exceptions or that it is the only way in which the history of art or the other disciplines can be viewed, we may nevertheless state that *one* legitimate way to understand that history is as a progressive series of steps in a particular direction and that this understanding, despite its limitations, provides genuine insight.

Moreover, there seems to be a particular value in the comparison of paradigm shifts in theology with those in art. Parallels in art may in some respects provide closer analogies for theological paradigm shifts than do those of science. Changes in artistic style seem clearly to be more like paradigm changes in *religion* than scientific changes are, and for this reason they may also be more relevant to religion's intellectual and critical expression, theology. Specifically, the history of art shows the possibility of paradigm shifts through gradual and uneven change and partial accommodation, rather than full-blown revolution. There is a greater possibility of older paradigms surviving alongside the new with equal legitimacy. Indeed, both art and theology share the possibility of paradigm change by "retrieval" of the past. The analogy of artistic paradigms also permits us to see the relativity of certain theological issues, especially, for example, in liturgy or pastoral theology, but also in dogmatics. Frequently theological conflicts turn out to be a matter of different styles or points of view where a certain pluralism is possible. (It is remarkable, for example, how many of the theological conflicts that produced bitter divisions in Western Christianity at the time of the Reformation have been quietly overcome in contemporary ecumenical dialogues through the recognition that past linguistic misunderstandings disguised complementary perspectives.)

These comparisons also have the intrinsic merit of giving a fuller historical context to the situation of theology (as well as science) in each age by seeing parallel movements in other areas of human activity. Important in Kuhn's idea of scientific revolution is the influence of nonscientific factors on scientific discovery. The interdependence of various areas of human endeavor is perhaps even more apparent in art, whose changes were affected by socioeconomic factors such as patronage, local factors such as the models available for imitation, and physical and technological factors such as materials and techniques. Similarly, shifts in religious and theological consciousness are partially dependent on available imaginative schemas, social conditions, coherence with other areas of experience, and so on. In short, we are enabled to see paradigm shifts as part of a movement of culture as a whole, not as isolated events in different spheres. Paradigm changes in science are not simply parallel to those in art and theology but all are part of a larger progression that has a certain internal historical logic.

If this is admitted to be true, then the question naturally arises: Does this *progression* also necessarily indicate *progress*? Here again, the consideration of artistic development may introduce useful perspectives.

As noted above, one of the purposes of Kuhn's analysis of paradigm shifts was to break with the inadequate nineteenth-century idea of scientific progress. Nevertheless, the "incommensurability" of paradigms need not lead to total epistemological or evaluative relativism.[92] There can be little doubt that, at least according to particular criteria, the history of science does manifest a certain kind of progress.[93] As A. J. Ayer states: "The speculations, say, of Kepler may still be profitably studied in their historical context, but they do not still stand as rivals to the theories of Einstein."[94] Few would deny that—given a particular definition of the purposes of science—contemporary scientific knowledge is actually more adequate than that of our ancestors.[95] But must the same be true of other areas in which there have been parallel shifts? Ayer continues:

> It is otherwise with philosophy. The historian of philosophy can, indeed, trace the influence of one philosopher upon another, especially within the confines of

what is represented as a particular "school." ...There is, however, no question of one of these philosophers superseding another, except in the sense that his work may enjoy a period of greater popularity. One can still maintain, without forfeiting one's claim to competence in philosophy, that Hume was right and Kant wrong on the point at issue between them, that Locke came nearer to the truth than either Berkeley or Hume, that as against Kant it was Hegel who took the wrong turning. One can still be a Platonist while fully understanding Aristotle's criticism of Plato, and without being ignorant of all the positions that different philosophers have taken in the centuries since Plato lived.[96]

We can affirm progress in science because we can define criteria, largely pragmatic and evidential, for its success or failure; science has certain discernible cognitive ends that are more realized in some paradigms than in others.[97] However, it is not at all clear that such criteria may be easily arrived at or agreed upon for the aesthetic or reflective realms, or, if one can formulate them, that their successful fulfillment can be objectively determined, or that such fulfillment takes place in a "progressive" manner.[98]

Certainly there have been remarkable advances in the technology available to artists—one need only think of the revolution in style made possible by the widespread introduction of oil paints in the sixteenth century, not to mention the changes wrought by such modern devices as the airbrush and the camera.[99] If the purpose of visual art were to be defined narrowly in terms, say, of perfectly realistic reproduction of an instant of physical vision, then one could hold that the photograph and the holograph are clearly superior to Giotto. But such a definition would certainly not be universally acceptable, least of all to artists themselves. If, on the other hand, one were to define the purpose of the aesthetic realm differently—in terms of the realization of beauty, for example, or in terms of the expression of feeling—then the notion of *progress* would seem inapplicable. It would be perfectly possible to feel that Bach had achieved the purposes of music or Michelangelo the purposes of sculpture in a way unequaled before or since, despite (or perhaps even because of) the limitations of their comparatively parochial experience and undeveloped technology.

As Ayer's remarks indicate, the situation is similar with philosophy and, by extension, theology. There is no a priori reason to make the positivist assumption that the criteria for progress in science will be applicable to these areas any more than they are to art. On the other hand, Ayer notes, there is a certain kind of progress in the history of philosophy—not necessarily in the attainment of more adequate answers, but rather in the evolution of a set of perennial problems.[100] Similarly, Bernard Lonergan conceives the evolution of the theological context as the West's "ongoing discovery of mind."[101] The very fact of being aware of having a history and of being faced with a choice between a number of points of view is itself a kind of "progress," at least quantitatively, in the potential for asking questions and conceiving various solutions.[102]

Moreover, Lonergan holds that the progressive discovery of the subject, leading finally to the exploration of interiority, "identifies in personal experience one's conscious and intentional acts and the dynamic relations that link them to one another. It offers an invariant basis for ongoing systems and a standpoint from which all the differentiations of human consciousness can be explored."[103] That is, historical consciousness, with its awareness of incommensurable paradigms or points of view, need not, in theology any more than in science, lead to relativism or "fideism." According to Lonergan, there are basic positions on human knowledge and on being that, while not universal in formulation, express the common dynamism of the human mind. Lonergan's positions refer not to particular concepts but to the ever-revisable formulations of the subject's performance of the acts of knowing and loving. As such, they can serve as a reference point and principle of interpretation for different systems of thought. Thus it is possible to recognize the legitimacy of different paradigms or points of view while at the same time preserving the possibility of dialogue and (to some degree) of judgment among them.

This point is particularly important because Christian theology more than any of the other arts and disciplines is radically tied to its history. One can function perfectly well as an empirical scientist without having any knowledge of premodern scientific theory. Christian theology, on the other hand, is based upon a notion of historical revelation and its transmission through time;[104] thus, it can never simply leave the past behind but must always be involved in a retrieval of its origins and traditions.[105] Hence, a form of paradigm theory or horizon analysis that in some way deals with the continuity of the message in different contexts is vitally important to the hermeneutical enterprise that is central to theology.

D. THE CONTEMPORARY PARADIGM OF ROMAN CATHOLIC THEOLOGY AND ITS TRAJECTORY TOWARD THE FUTURE

As we have seen, for Kuhn there are two elements that bring about paradigm change in science: (1) a crisis occurs because the "normal science" of the older paradigm can no longer adequately account for the data; and (2) a new paradigm is ready to take its place (not necessarily as a total world-view, but as a new set of questions or way of approaching the data). In theology, as we have already indicated, the situation is more complex. In Roman Catholic theology, the paradigm shift occasioned by the European Enlightenment was to a great degree resisted, and the facing of the issues that caused it was largely put off until this century. As a result, Catholic theology began to face the problems of the modern paradigm at the same time that the postmodern shift was already under way. In the following, I shall attempt briefly to summarize both the modern and the postmodern crises (which are, in my opinion, to a large extent continuous) and attempt to delineate some of the characteristics of the paradigm being formed in response to them. In doing so, I will expand on Bernard Lonergan's analysis but will restrict my consideration to Roman Catholic theology.

Lonergan uses 1680, the year in which Herbert Butterfield places the origins of modern science and Paul Hazard the beginnings of the Enlightenment, as the symbolic date when Catholic theology began to fall behind the changes affecting other areas of culture.[106] (Velázquez painted the Conde-Duque de Olivares in 1634; in art, therefore, the shift of point of view to the subject was already well under way.) Before this time, many discoveries had been made that eventually became part of modern science, but the intellectual framework into which they were accepted was still Aristotelian. The tension between the new ideas and old doctrines grew until, toward the end of the seventeenth century, a new context emerged that could replace the older Aristotelian system.[107]

Roman Catholic thought did not adopt that new context; instead, it invented dogmatic theology. The word *dogmatic* is not used here to distinguish one branch of study, opposed to moral or historical theology, but to designate a method distinct from the older Scholastic method. The Scholastic *quaestio* was replaced with the thesis, and the quest for understanding became secondary: What was important was the certitude of faith, reached through proofs based on authority.[108] This kind of dogmatic theology lasted into the twentieth century and was only finally superseded through the legitimation of a new mode of theological thinking by the Second Vatican Council. During the long period of its dominance, however, factors were accumulating that made the collapse of this classical theological paradigm sudden and violent. As Küng points out, it is possible within a particular science to shelve the issues that call out for new perspectives.[109] But when this happens, the issues do not simply disappear; they may remain as an external challenge to the unaltered paradigm because, as we have seen, the credibility of a paradigm rests not only on its internal consistency, but also on its coherence with the rest of human experience.[110] Theology could be isolated from the general intellectual current of the modern era; but it became increasingly difficult to cut off the lives and minds of believers from the currents of surrounding society. Hence, by the twentieth century a situation had resulted in which Roman Catholic theology to a large degree no longer spoke to everyday life or resonated with contemporary experience.

Without attempting exhaustive analysis, we may briefly summarize some of the major and frequently interrelated cultural movements that shaped modern consciousness, and to which theology (as well as church structure) eventually had to respond:

1. The discovery of history. The Renaissance had reinforced classicism but also showed the relativity of Christian culture. The humanistic values of paganism were appealing and challenging and provided an alternative to prevailing Christian views. The discovery of America and access to the Orient further widened the world, confronting European Christianity on the one hand with the myth of the "noble savage" living in communion with nature, and on the other with the ancient Oriental civilizations and religions. The opening of the European mind to the plurality of the world was accompanied by the discovery of its own past. New his-

torical method led to new exegetical tools, comparative literature, and the higher criticism of classical texts; first the scriptures and then dogmas and church history were subjected to critical scrutiny and their accepted meanings questioned.

2. The rise of empirical science. The discoveries of positive science need not have been seen as a challenge to faith. Copernicus, Galileo, Newton, Einstein, Heisenberg—to mention only some of the major innovators in physical science—were all "believers" in God. But the method of empirical science was opposed to the deductive system based on authority that prevailed in medieval science and theology: Hence, a new paradigm for thinking about the sources of knowledge and the relation of faith and revelation to human reason was needed.

3. Movements of liberation. From the insurrections of the Fraticelli and other marginal groups in the late Middle Ages through the peasant uprisings of the Reformation, the American and French revolutions of the eighteenth century, the socialist and democratic revolts of the nineteenth, and the Marxist and anti-Marxist revolutions of the twentieth century, democratic and egalitarian ideas challenged the feudal and hierarchical structure to which the church was wedded.The ideal of the bourgeois individual, self-determining and independent, reached its climax in the Enlightenment. The notion of authority was questioned on both the social and private levels. At the same time, church authority was undermined intellectually in the critique of ideologies, which portrayed Christian religion as self-alienated consciousness (Feuerbach), a mental superstructure of unjust economic conditions (Marx), a self-degrading rejection of healthy human impulses (Nietzsche), and an infantile regression or neurosis (Freud). The church faced a personal, organizational, and intellectual loss of credibility.

4. The turn to the subject in philosophy. In line with the new Western ideal of personality developing since the Renaissance, thinkers increasingly rejected the authority of the past and took individual consciousness as the starting point for reflection. Philosophy became increasingly estranged from the realm of the transcendent. Descartes already proclaimed the autonomy of reason from faith in confronting the problem of God; yet for him God remains necessary as the final explanatory principle of his rational system—as also of the systems of Leibniz, Malebranche, and Spinoza. But with the rejection of those systems went the rejection of their "God of explanations." The world is explained on its own grounds, without the need to turn to a supernatural hypothesis. The Kantian critique threw into doubt the very possibility of knowing transcendent being. Nietzsche proclaimed the philosophical death of God (and ultimately the death of human meaning as well), while the critiques of Feuerbach, Marx, and Freud questioned the motives of faith.

What kind of theological paradigm change was necessary to meet the crisis posed by the emergence of the modern world? In general terms, it may be characterized as an anthropological shift, modeled on the philosophical turn to the subject. Like art and science, modern theology became increasingly occupied with its own methods, materials, and conditions of possibility.

Lonergan's analysis of this first stage of the transformation of Catholic theology (i.e., its confrontation with modernity) is once again helpful. A major element was the move from classical to historical consciousness.[111] It was recognized that theology is not only the product of the religion it investigates, but also of a culture that sets its problems and directs its solutions.[112] Meaning could no longer be seen as a matter of eternal, objective truths definitively formulated; it is rather a complex reality, in large measure constituted by subjects and their personal and societal interactions.

This insight led to the need for theology to employ something analogous to an empirical method, rather than its former deductive dogmatic procedures. Whereas for neo-Scholastic theology, theses were conclusions to be proven from premises given in the scriptures and tradition, now these sources are not regarded as premises but as data which must be approached in historical perspective. The classicist model had misconceived theology in terms of universality and permanence, reflecting Vincent of Lérins's description of doctrine: *"quod semper, quod ubique, quod ab omnibus"* ("what was always [taught], everywhere, by all"). This ideal is now seen to be impossible. Fixity gives way to development, and the results of theological investigation are not intended to be certain and unchanging, but probable, difficult, and progressive.[113] Theology also adapts itself to a new cultural and linguistic context. This context is ecumenical and pluralistic and presumes a model of conversation rather than authoritarian imposition.

As already noted, even as Roman Catholic theology was moving into the modern context, a new postmodern consciousness was beginning to emerge. In large part continuous with the concerns and context of the Enlightenment, it both carries these farther and reacts against their limitations. The threat of nuclear destruction, the ecological crisis, and the failure of technological progress to produce individual happiness or a just social order point to the inadequacy of the positivist notion of progress. Modernity is itself seen not as the inevitable summit of a progressive evolution in a single direction but as one paradigm among others that have partially incommensurable goals and values. There is a corresponding rediscovery of the past and of tradition. At the same time that the electronic information explosion makes possible a more universal consciousness, there is also an increasing awareness of the irreducible pluralism of human communities and of the value of the small, the local, the different.

An important element in the emerging contemporary paradigm is the radicalizing of the turn to the subject in a realization of the symbolic constitution of the human being and hence its socioeconomic and cultural conditioning. There has previously been an awareness of language and symbol, but these were largely treated in an "expressive" mode.[114] There is now a shift from attention to subjects using language to language itself—just as in painting there has been a shift to art as medium and as "event" rather than as expression of subjectivity.[115] One thinks not of a subject using symbols to express a preexistent, substantial self, but of our very selfhood as the product of language, which makes thought and self-consciousness possible. One important corollary is the recognition that reason and evaluation themselves are not independent, universal, foundational realities but are cultural products exercised in different ways. A second, related corollary stems from Nietzsche: namely, that thought itself either inevitably is (for radical postmoderns) or can be (for the more moderate) an ideological superstructure that represents a certain group's interests and serves its quest for power. Hence, it is important always to ask whose interests are being served by any form of discourse and to attend to those "others" who are left out of the conversation.

Naturally, it would be rash to attempt to predict the course that theological thought will take, even in the immediate future. Some elements of the emerging paradigm are not predictable because they will be reactions to external factors that have not yet fully come into play: What will be the effect on theology of reemergent Islam? of the fall of communism? of the precarious world economy? of the cybernetic revolution in communications? We may expect that the context of human thought may be profoundly influenced by happenings in economics, politics, technology, and the like that are as yet unforeseen; other elements are perhaps hard to recognize because we are still to some extent limited by our present concerns and point of view.

Furthermore, one may wonder whether current tendencies point to a full and revolutionary paradigm shift in theology, or rather to a shift on the level of "mesoparadigms," that is, concepts and theories within the current paradigm. The answer to this will depend largely on the degree of continuity one perceives between the "modern" and contemporary paradigms and their successor(s). If we take the model of art, however, we may perhaps ask a different and more limited question: What elements not now in focus are becoming focal points for theology? What is the "way of seeing" that is emerging?

Some general directions of thought seem quite clear. Humanity is beginning, of necessity, to adopt an ecological point of view. This represents a shift from the anthropocentric emphasis of the recent past. A theology of creation may once again come to the fore in which we rethink the basis for humanity's relation to nature in a nondomineering context—in contrast to an ideology based on the notion of "subduing" the earth.[116] Similarly, the paradigm of unlimited growth and use—a remnant of the positivist belief in inevitable progress?—is being reevaluated; perhaps we must think more in terms of balance. A theology that presents the human good in terms of aesthetic and mystical contemplation rather than consumption may have something to contribute to such changes. In these regards, Western theology may be further enriched by dialogue with the Oriental religions: Such diverse ideas as the Taoist notion of "economy" (so richly influential in Chinese and Japanese art) or the Buddhist doctrine of the interconnected arising of all things may provide fruitful expansions of Christian world consciousness.

Theological thought already manifests another concern that it seems must remain central in the postcontemporary world: attention to the voices of neglected "others" who have been and are on the margins of society. One aspect of this awareness is seen in a theological concern for liberation, on its many levels. The term *theology of liberation* has primarily been associated with currents of contemporary thought in the Third World, and particularly in Latin America,[117] where it arose from the concern for freeing people from the impersonal and depersonalizing forces of economic and social servitude, poverty, and injustice. In recent years, the theme of liberation has become important in other theological contexts. In particular, the liberation of women has contributed a new dimension to thinking in general, and specifically to theology, which has frequently been dominated by analogies and concerns that reflect a male bias. Moreover, Christian theology has much to say about liberation on a psychological level from compulsion and obsession, from the blind spots that keep us from facing reality, and from anxiety about our finite condition; on the intellectual level from prejudice and bias, uncritical thinking, and a merely material horizon of life; on the moral level from egotism of the individual or the group; and on the spiritual level from our finite and disconnected selves to attain the communion and freedom of children of God.

Hans Küng characterizes the emerging theological paradigm as ecumenical. Certainly one of the tasks of theology

will be to deal with the question of the plurality of paradigms in the worldwide context. This means not only con-
versing with and learning from the many "others" who have
become our neighbors in the global village, but also facing
the intellectual problem of relativism that seems to be
raised inevitably by the linguistic and methodological turn
of thought mentioned above. The turn to the subject has
been shown to be inadequate, for the subject itself is the
product of a world and a culture or language. But can the
different worlds and languages speak to each other? Is
there a dimension of human existence that—in some way
and to some extent—can transcend social-linguistic
conditioning? In terms of Ortega's analogy, the question
becomes: Where can the point of view go after the subject?
In thought, as in art, the answers are varied.

One reaction to the insight into the conditioned and
partial character of all human knowing is the total deconstruction of the subject into a Nietzchean nihilism: Art and
philosophy can ultimately only discourse about and within
the flow of evanescent conscious events. But the
abandonment of the centrality of the individual subject
can also lead in positive directions. On one hand,
one may return to the objectivity of a past system.
Philosophical relativism permits the fideistic option for
some particular linguistic world or paradigm. Or, on the
other hand, one may go beyond the subject in an effort to
reach a "deep structure" of human subjectivity and inter-
subjectivity that provides a basis for interparadigmatic
dialogue.

In both the latter cases, there is a recognition of an
essential pluralism and perspectivism (but not necessarily
total relativism) in human thought. But there are two
divergent reactions to this pluralism. One tendency, at its
extreme, opts fideistically for a single point of view or "language game" (frequently a traditional one) as divinely

revealed and normative. Hence postmodernity is for some a cipher for traditionalism: The critique of modernity, combined with the idea of incommensurable paradigms, is used to defend the legitimacy of opting for a premodern theological system. In this movement Christian theology, at the limit, may become purely intratextual: The scriptures and/or tradition are used as a divinely given "lens" (in Calvin's metaphor) through which the world is viewed. The other tendency, while also attempting to reintegrate legitimate insights from the past, rejects the fideist option for a single paradigm or language. Instead, it proposes the possibility of holding several paradigms at once in complementarity and/or of formulating a methodological principle that can function as a metaparadigm leading to retrieval in a new context.

In each tendency, however, there is a common element that unites them despite their differences. The move beyond the independent subject opens up not only an awareness of the conditioning community but also the awareness of the transcendent as the ultimate condition. The existential experience of the event of the nonself—that which has in itself no independent substantial foundation—can lead to the mystical apprehension of the noncategorical source of every "suchness" (much as in the Buddhist experience of *tathatā*).

The integration of the arts and of aesthetic theory into theology is a contemporary tendency that also promises to provide valuable insights in the attempt to formulate a genuinely ecumenical theology that will face the problems of pluralism and relativism. The model of art allows further insight into the pluralism and perspectivism we have noted above. It is important, as Frank Burch Brown points out, for theology to recognize "the role of aesthetic proclivities and sensitivities in the formation of religious communities"[118]— so that, for example, diverging Christian intellectual and faith traditions may be seen not necessarily as opposed positions, but at least in part as different "performances" of a single Christian "classic."[119] Such insight not only allows greater mutual understanding and tolerance, but also provides the basis for separating out genuine commonalities and oppositions on the conceptual level and for seeking a "higher viewpoint" beyond these.[120]

As Lonergan points out, since the Middle Ages theology has tended to look on itself as a science and to model itself on the successful science of its age: In the medieval period, this meant philosophy; in the modern world, empirical science. In our present crises, science and technology are not seen as universally successful; indeed, for many they have become part of the problem. The considerations outlined here may indicate that the successful science of the future must reintegrate areas of our full humanity—including the humanity of the scientist—that have been neglected in positivism.

Clearly, then, theological method and indeed even the self-concept of theology are challenged by contemporary postmodern consciousness. In the light of our increased awareness of the symbolic nature of all discourse, and especially of religious discourse, it is perhaps not unreasonable to project that the theology of the future—along with other forms of intellectual endeavor, including empirical science itself—will at least in part be modeled more on art and on the humanities than on an ideal of objective evidence and material progress.

It also seems increasingly clear that the emerging contemporary paradigm means a shift not only in the method, but also in the content of theological study. The concrete locus of God's symbolic self-revelation, on which theology reflects, is conceived in a wider fashion. In this sense, we can foresee that the "focal subject matter of theology must itself be modified and extended in several ways....Most obviously it must be expanded to include more thorough study of the arts themselves...."[121] In the following chapters I will attempt to exemplify some ways in which this may take place, first by examining how art may serve as a theological locus or "text," and then by considering the convergence of theology and art in the practical life of the church, in the specific case of preaching.

Web sites for viewing illustrations———

a. Several views of Michelangelo's *David* are available online. Two good examples may be found at:
   www.sbas.firenze.it/musei/acca01.htm
   ocaiw.com/galenug6.htm
b. An excellent view is provided at:
   gallery.euroweb.hu/art/b/bernini/sculptur/1620/david.jpg
   • See also the side view at:
   www.mcad.edu/AICT/html/renbrq/RMS/RMS004.html
   •From the latter, a more detailed view is also accessible.
c. The symbol of the fish:
   www.catacombe.roma.it/symb_gb.html
   •Scroll down to locate the image.
   Cf. the fish combined with loaves as symbol of the eucharist:
   www.catacombe.roma.it/regio_gb.html
   •Scroll down to locate the image.
d. The Last Supper from the Rossano gospel:
   www.lib.haifa.ac.il/www/art/med/8_5d_last_supper.GIF
e. Mosaic of the Last Supper in St. Apollinare Nuovo, Ravenna:
   www.bowdoin.edu/dept/religion/rel233/jchang2/page6.htm
   •Scroll down to locate the image.
   also viewable at:
   www.lib.haifa.ac.il/www/art/med/7_1_details.html
f. Duccio di Buoninsegna: "La *Maesta*:
   sunserv.kfki.hu/_arthp/tours/siena/index_b.html

•Click on the image for a full-screen view, or go directly to:
sunserv.kfki.hu/_arthp/art/d/duccio/buoninse/ maesta/verso_3/verso18a.jpg

g. Giotto, *The Last Supper*, Assisi, Lower Basilica:
www2.iinet.com/art/14th/italian/giotto/giott92.jpg

h. Workshop of Fra Angelico: *Communion of the Apostles*, from *Six Scenes from the life of Christ*. Museo di San Marco, Florence.
metalab.unc.edu/cjackson/angelico/p–angeli18.htm

i. Cosimo Rosselli: *The Last Supper*, Sistine chapel:
Several views can be selected at the Christus Rex site:
www.christusrex.org/www1/sistine/L-Christ.html
•Click on the desired image to enlarge.

j. Several excellent views of both versions are available at:
www.ocaiw.com/carava1.htm
•Choose from the list of illustrations.

k. Velázquez, *The Supper at Emmaus*:
sunsite.unc.edu/wm/paint/auth/velazquez
•Choose the image and click on it to enlarge.

l. Velázquez: *Los borrachos*:
metalab.unc.edu/wm/paint/auth/velazquez/ velazquez.feast-bacchus.jpg
•Or choose the image from the above "Velazquez" site and click to enlarge.

m. Georges Seurat, *A Sunday Afternoon in summer on the Island of La Grande Jatte*:
www.artchive.com/artchive/ftptoc/seurat_ext.html
•Choose from the list and click to enlarge.

n. See for example *The Bay from L'Estaque* or *Château Noir*, both viewable by clicking on "Cézanne" at:
artchive.com/ftp_site.htm

o. Wasily Kandinsky, *Composition VIII*:
metalab.unc.edu/wm/paint/auth/kandinsky/ kandinsky.comp-8.jpg

p. Salvador Dali, *The Sacrament of the Last Supper*:
   www.ionet.net/_jellenc/dali.html
   •Click on the image to enlarge.
q. Jackson Pollock, *Number 1A*, 1948:
   www.artchive.com/artchive/ftptoc/pollock_ext.html
   •Choose title from the list.
r. Mark Rothko: see for example the following, with links to other paintings:
   www.nga.gov/feature/rothko/classic2.html
s. Pablo Picasso, *Baigneuses dans une forêt*:
   www.tamu.edu/mocl/picasso/bathers.html
   Sir Lawrence Alma-Tadema, A *favorite custom*:
   www.sappho.com/lart/tadema1.htm
   •Click on the image for more detail.

Chapter 3
Art as a Theological Text

In the previous chapters, we first looked at beauty as a revelation of God, concentrating especially on beauty in sacred art as a human mediation of the transcendental divine word to humanity. Second, we considered Western art as a historical phenomenon whose concerns and viewpoints present certain parallels with those of theology. We suggested also that the new paradigm of theology emerging toward the beginning of the twenty-first century will include, among other forms, a theology that attends to and is integrated with aesthetic concerns.[1] The present chapter considers one aspect of such an integration: the use of art as a theological "text."

A. THE DIMENSIONS OF ART AS TEXT

It is obvious that some forms of art—one thinks particularly of manuscript illustration, vocal church music, and the rhetorical art of preaching—are intimately connected with literary texts of a religious or theological character and may be considered an extension of these. Some aspects of this relationship have been explored in the first chapter. Our present concern is with forms of art, especially the pictorial, that in a certain analogous sense may serve as theological texts in themselves—that is, without the necessity of accompanying words. We shall look at two overlapping aspects of the functioning of art works as theological texts. First, and foremost, works of art are a locus of the faith tradition and an embodiment of religious practice and, hence, can serve as texts *of* Christian theology. Secondly, insofar as it expresses the human situation of various ages, art can also serve as a text *for* Christian theology, especially in its correlational function.

As a text *of* theology, art can serve two distinct but complementary functions. First, the study of Christian art can serve as an important aid to the history of theology. In this regard, the study of artistic texts functions primarily as an auxiliary to verbal, conceptual theology. Second, art itself, precisely as art, can be seen as a mode of reflection on and embodiment of Christian ideas and values and, hence, as constituting a form of theology. In this sense, artistic texts form an integral part of systematic theology. Finally, as a text *for* theology, art is especially related to both fundamental and practical theologies. Art reveals significant aspects of the particular human situations to which God's word is addressed, and on which theology must therefore reflect if it is to be relevant and intellectually responsible. Art is also one of the means by which the message is presented in a way that is persuasive and attractive, giving a vision that can lead to moral conversion and action.

B. ART AS LOCUS OF THE FAITH TRADITION

Nineteenth-century critic John Ruskin wrote:

> Great nations write their autobiographies in three manuscripts;—the book of their deeds, the book of their words, and the book of their art. Not one of these books can be understood unless we read the two others; but of the three the only quite trustworthy one is the last.[2]

What Ruskin says of great nations is also true of the great religions. They constitute and communicate themselves not only through their scriptures and theological writings, through their institutions, movements, and ethical practices, but also through their rites, poetry, architecture, music, painting, and sculpture. Although the third "book," consisting of religious art, cannot be understood without the previous two, it gives us perhaps the most vivid and accurate sense of the religion as lived, thought, imagined, and felt by its adherents. For this reason the books of religious deeds and of religious words are also incomplete without the accompaniment of the book of religious art.

Of course, an important aspect of the art of Christianity is that which is directly contained in its literature, including its scriptures. Contemporary scripture studies explicitly advert to the different literary forms contained in the Bible and are increasingly involved in dialogue with the aesthetic as well as the historical/critical study of literature. Our concern here, however, will be sacred images and pictures as mediators of the Christian tradition. These have long been the subject of exploration by historians of art and culture. In the last few decades, they have assumed increasing importance in religious studies as well.[3]

This importance is comparatively new, even more recent than the application of methods of literary theory to the scriptures. Reasons for the previous neglect of art in Western theology are not difficult to think of. In the past a certain "logocentrism"—preoccupation with the verbal, and especially the written word—has in general dominated the study of Christianity, both because of its own insistence on the normativity of the "word" contained in the scriptures, and also because of the literary emphasis that is generally characteristic of Western intellectual culture and scholarship (which in turn derives, at least in part, from the Judeo-Christian tradition of scriptural study).[4] In the contemporary period, however, a major shift has occurred, largely due to the emergence of the study of religion as a cultural phenomenon. Here the influence of anthropology, especially in the study of nonliterate religious traditions, has led to the study of material culture as an auxiliary means of examining scriptural religions, in particular Christianity.[5]

Hence, it is already well established in the discipline of religious studies that art and other artifacts of material culture are an irreplaceable source of information about the phenomenon of Christian religion and civilization, revealing not only their content, but also the attitudes, ideals, and emotional reactions associated with them. (Naturally, such visual texts do not stand alone but are illuminated by Christian literature.) As we remarked above, in their origins religion and art formed a unity,[6] and even when they became conceptually differentiated in Western culture, the two remained closely united—so much so that until the modern era the greater part of Western "fine" art was explicitly tied to religious themes and patronage.

The reasons that make the use of art as a kind of text about religion a significant aspect of the disciplines involved in the phenomenological study of religions are also applicable within the field of historical theology. The latter has moved beyond simple institutional church history to engagement with the critical history of ideas; and it is increasingly clear today that the history of theological ideas must attend to more than dogmatic statements and theological systems. Even study that concentrates specifically on intellectual history must take account of the cultural contexts in which thinking inevitably takes place. One of the most revealing aspects of such contexts is the history of religious art.

This marks a change in the method and style of theological inquiry. As Frank Burch Brown writes,

religious truth that is expressed beautifully, figura-
tively, and artistically has long had the reputation of
being (at the very most) a vivid but less precise expression of what can be said more properly in systematic,
conceptual discourse....Similarly, for the Church's
ongoing interpretation of the truth as truth, the
inquirer has looked not to its poetry and art or even to
its liturgy (though these are acknowledged to have
their own unique value) but rather to doctrinal statements and theological texts.[7]

However, this situation is rapidly changing. Present-day
historical theologians are becoming aware that what Tillich
wrote about art and the contemporary situation applies also
to the past. As we have seen in the preceding chapter, there
are significant parallels between the historical paradigms of
art, philosophy, and theology that are enlightening for the
study of each of these fields. The art of any particular period
is significant for determining the context of its theology: the
life-situations and existential questions in response to
which it was formulated. If one essential part of historical
hermeneutics is entering into the "common sense" of an
era[8]—what people believed, felt, took for granted in their
lives—then the historical theologian must look not only to
explicitly theological texts, but also to works of art, both secular and religious, that embody and partially express the
context of the times.

The study of religious art thus provides a supplement and
a corrective to the purely conceptual approach to the history
of Christian thought. It is also relevant to the question of the
history of the reception of doctrine. The currents of religious
art not only show us concretely what was intended to be
handed on, but also give us some idea of what was actually
received; that is, how the concrete religious imagination
was formed (or failed to be formed) by the intellectual

content of faith and/or theology, and what the themes that actually occupied the minds of the faithful were.

In the same vein, art is relevant to the recovery of the tradition of Christian spirituality and popular "piety." As long as religion exists on the level of undifferentiated consciousness, there is no distinction between "piety" and "doctrine," just as there is none between religion and art. But once a certain level of reflection and differentiation is reached, it becomes necessary to distinguish between the institutional and official dimension of the church (*Amtskirche*) and the worshiping or cultic church (*Kultkirche*). The former expresses itself above all in its doctrines, which are closely allied to scientific or academic theology; the latter comprises the attitudes, practices, images, and styles of life and worship of particular communities.[9]

The differentiation—and sometimes tension—between these two aspects of ecclesial life stems from an element that is intrinsic to Christianity. Because of its claim to be grounded in the unique and universal salvific event of Christ, it is of the nature of the church to be universal or "catholic" (καθ' ὅλου, "according to the whole"). This universality is understood both extensively and intensively. Extensively, the church is oriented to the salvation of all people; intensively, it is oriented to the salvation of the whole of each person. Catholicity in the first sense ("for all people") is the source of the church's inclusiveness and its missionary impulse. Christianity could not be the religion of a single people (like ancient Judaism or Hinduism, which were defined by belonging to a racial or geographical community),[10] nor of a spiritual elite (like Hinayana Buddhism, whose full practice demands entry into the order of monks and nuns). To conform to and continue the salvific act of Christ, the church must be "for all."

On the other hand, catholicity in the second sense ("for the whole person") is the source of the church's cultural and intellectual impetus. If the wholeness of the human being is to be respected, then faith must address also the rational nature of the human person: As the church fathers insisted, faith must be a *rationale obsequium* (reasonable submission of the person to God). This meant that the church had to encounter philosophical thinking and develop a theology that could use its categories. Hence, Christian theology emerged as a mode of understanding, explaining, and communicating that goes beyond the simplicity of the originating gospel message and its imaginative forms of discourse. But the pursuit of the intellectual aspect of human wholeness can come into tension with universality of extension, because believers live on different intellectual and cultural levels and in different stages of meaning,[11] and not all are capable of or interested in theology in its theoretical-conceptual form. Therefore Christianity always exists simultaneously in different realms of meaning: in the realm of transcendence in its spirituality, in the realm of common sense and imagination in its preaching and worship, and in the realms of theory and intellectual interiority in its conceptual theology.[12]

Ideally, these levels and realms of meaning are complementary, but in fact, the history of Christianity shows that only too frequently they have been the source of divisions: between office and spirituality, theology and piety, clerical and lay forms of religion, and so on. Although a careful and detailed examination of the history of such divisions is beyond the scope of this work, it will perhaps be worthwhile to mention briefly some noteworthy moments that contributed to the separation of the aesthetic realm from the theoretical in Christian life.

Already in the second century B.C. the Stoic Panaetius had differentiated between the common level of worship of the gods and a deeper understanding according to *logos* (word or reason). He posited a progression from a mythic to a political and finally to a philosophical form of religion.[13] This schema, which St. Augustine learned from Varro, could be adapted by Christianity to explain the presence of different levels of intellectual participation in the same faith: The *rudes* (the uneducated; in Christian discourse, simple believers) truly have faith; at the same time, faith is also called to participate more deeply in the intrinsic rationality (*Logos*) of God's economy of salvation by seeking understanding. But in the earliest ages of the church, the coexistence of different levels of understanding of the faith does not seem to have produced an unbridgeable gap between the popular and theological levels of religion.[14] Certainly, we find various of the fathers correcting the content of popular piety, especially practices and understandings that were carried over into Christianity from paganism. Still, there was in general a strong interdependence between theology, spirituality, and liturgy.

According to the well-known thesis of historian Arthur Mirgeler, the problem of different levels of religion became acute only with the mass entry into Christianity of the Germanic peoples, frequently with little catechesis. These tribes had no direct experience of the Hellenistic culture to which the early church's intellectual life had been adapted, nor did they speak the Latin and Greek languages that were its media of thought and transmission. The result was that the Christian liturgy and theology, as well as the mystical side of Christian spirituality, became the exclusive preserve of the clergy and hierarchy. Movements in these directions on the part of the laity were generally absorbed into the religious orders. This resulted in a Christianity that existed on two levels: the religion of the people, which mixed Christian doctrine with pagan ideas and practices, against the literate and theological religion of the priests and monks, to whom the scriptures were effectively reserved and who preserved the cultural forms of antiquity. The great Gregorian reform of the eleventh century widened an already existing gap between clergy and laity and strengthened the notion of a class structure in Christianity, with the laity representing an imperfect and inferior state of life.[15]

Aspects of such a division have continued to haunt the church, although to greater or lesser degrees, into modern times. At the time of the introduction of Aristotelianism to theology in the high Middle Ages, some church leaders already saw the danger of theology's being separated from the life and practice of faith. In a celebrated passage, St. Bonaventure warns against thinking "that it suffices to read without unction, speculate without devotion, investigate without wonder, examine without exultation, work without piety, know without love, understand without humility, be zealous without divine grace, see without wisdom divinely inspired."[16] But the shift in the center of intellectual life from monasteries to universities virtually assured the emergence of a theology that was increasingly academic and conceptual, in which the Augustinian model of wisdom was largely replaced by the Aristotelian ideal of science.

The crises subsequently brought about by philosophical nominalism and by the emergence of the empirical sciences increased the need for a strongly intellectual and academic theology. The Protestant Reformation added new factors: The Reformers attacked the exaltation of the clerical state above the laity; the Roman Catholic response, although adopting the Reformation program of educating the laity by catechesis and preaching, insisted on reaffirming the principle of hierarchy.[17] With regard to the relation of theology to piety, the heritage of the Protestant and Catholic reformations of the church was ambiguous. On the one hand, there was an impetus to a reintegration of Christian life. Personal and communal piety and spirituality underwent significant developments during this period and frequently reflected different theological orientations. On the other hand, in the long run, the controversies stemming from the Reformation tended not only to concentrate theological attention on particular and highly nuanced academic questions, but also fostered a polemical context for their pursuit.

Perhaps most significant for the separation of theology from popular religion is the knowledge explosion and consequent specialization of studies that has typified the Western world since the European Enlightenment. From the seventeenth century onward, a number of factors have promoted increased specialization in theology. Among these factors are the ever-increasing intellectual challenges posed by unbelief, the expansion of intellectual horizons beyond the Western context, and, perhaps above all, the emergence of historical consciousness. This specialization in turn has tended to reinforce the separation between the realm of theology and that of spirituality or piety, especially in its popular forms. Although theology has often been castigated by believers for being excessively abstract, conceptual, and lacking in existential relevance, popular Christian piety is frequently attacked from outside the church (and sometimes from within) for its superstition, intolerance, superficiality, and lack of intellectual honesty.[18]

Given this recurrent situation in the church, explicit attention to the history of Christian piety is an important addition to the history of theoretical theology in the retrieval of the tradition in its wholeness. In this study, Christian art has a significant role. As we shall see more concretely in the next section, art was frequently and purposely used as a "mediator" between conceptual theology and the religion of the uneducated masses. On the one hand, much religious art, especially in the Middle Ages, had an explicitly didactic function. On the other hand, the use of art works as votive offerings (given in gratitude for a favor or the answer to a prayer) assured the connection of art with the religious motives of its patrons. Art therefore provides a partial entry into the world of the popular piety that was (and is) for most people the primary expression of religion. Of course, literary documents are also crucial. But art—for those who are able to "read" it—gives us a particularly direct look into the heart of piety.

Naturally, the history of piety as expressed in art also reveals negative elements. It is important that these be acknowledged, lest we fall prey to nostalgia for a romanticized past. Dom David Knowles writes that

> Church historians in general say too little about the changes of cultures and of mental climates, and still less about the extravagances, ignorances, and misconceptions of sentiment and devotion that have coloured or deformed the purity of the spirit in past centuries and that may well be obscuring for us now in this respect or that the full vision of revealed truth.[19]

The study of Christian art, then, should allow theology to engage more deeply and concretely in the function that Lonergan calls dialectics: the sorting out of conflicts within the Christian tradition and the horizons or "viewpoints" that cause them, with the purpose of evaluating such conflicts in the light of the dynamism of intellectual, moral, and religious conversion.[20] It is to be expected that in theology, this dialectic will take place primarily on the conceptual level. But the study of art makes us realize to what extent even our concepts are linked to emotionally laden images. Frequently our thought is tied, unconsciously, to certain imaginative concretizations and the feelings that accompany them, which in turn provoke and embody a personal religious stance. The encounter with the plurality of images in the tradition can therefore be liberating insofar as it allows us to imagine differently, to make new associations of ideas with concrete visions, to expand the affective range of the message, and therefore to think of it in new contexts, with new possibilities of association.

Of course, there are also limits to art's usefulness as a historical-theological source. Margaret Miles reminds us that Christian literature throughout most of the history of the church was produced by a small minority that was almost exclusively male and was predominantly clerical.[21] A similar qualification must be made regarding a great deal of Christian art. Sacred art's involvement in popular piety and its direction to a largely uneducated audience, even in its didactic doctrinal function, make much of Christianity's art intrinsically less elitist than its written texts. To a certain extent, art allows the emergence of minority points of view neglected by the official tradition; to a much greater extent, it reveals the cultural context and spiritual implications of that tradition. Nevertheless, because the artifacts of the "fine" arts were most frequently produced under clerical and/or aristocratic patronage and were sometimes dedicated more or less exclusively to the edification of educated patrons, art does not totally escape from the limitations Miles notes in our literary tradition. It is important, therefore, that the social context of art works be taken into account in any discussion of its theological relevance, and that folk art, to the extent that it survives, be included in any historical treatment.

C. Art as the bearer
of a theological message

In the above sections we have considered art as a text insofar as the aesthetic realm provides artifacts that aid us in understanding the literary and historical texts of the Christian tradition. But works of pictorial art may also serve as genuinely theological texts in another sense. They are symbols that convey to religiously committed persons not merely information *about* the tradition (looked at from "outside," so to speak), but that actually *are* tradition—that is, the act of mediating the content and attitude of faith (*traditio* in the active sense of "handing on").[22] Sacred art does not merely give us information about the concrete "addressee" of the message in a particular era, but also conveys dimensions of meaning (both cognitive and affective) that directly accomplish the communication of God's word. Moreover, in calling this mediation by art theological, I am implying that art's transmission of faith-meaning can take place not only on the level of receiving or celebrating of some aspect of the Christian message, but also as part of the process of interpretation, understanding, formulation, affirmation, and appropriation of the viewer's faith. That is to say, art can also operate on the level of faith's intellectual self-appropriation, or "theology." I will be contending, therefore, that the "logos" of "theology." may be taken in a wider sense than that usually at work in the verbally dominated Christian tradition.

In what follows I will first consider some general principles. Because the first chapter has already given some consideration to sacred vocal music, the pictorial realm will be the explicit focus of attention here. But these considerations may also be applied in analogous way to other forms of non-literary art, particularly those historically connected with the Christian tradition: nonvocal music, architecture, and dance (especially when taken in its widest sense to include the choreographed ritual movements of liturgy).

1. PICTORIAL ART AS SCRIPTURE

One dimension of the idea that pictorial art may serve as a kind of religious text has been classical in Western Christianity at least since the time of Gregory the Great. While repeating the biblical and patristic admonition against the worship of images, Gregory nevertheless rejects the iconoclastic conclusion that images should be banished from the church. On the contrary, he asserts that they play an important role in the communication of the Christian message to the unlettered—that is, to those who were at his time (and remained, until the modern era) the greater part of the faithful: "for what writings present to those who read, pictures present to uneducated viewers; for in them the ignorant see what they should imitate, and in them the illiterate are able to read; hence, especially for the [common] people, pictures take the place of reading...".[23]

In subsequent centuries Gregory's defense of images was frequently repeated. The West never adopted a view of images as quasi-sacramental mediators of a divine presence or "energy," as the Orthodox Eastern church did (although not without prolonged and bitter controversy—including the "iconoclast controversies" that occupied the Eastern church during the greater part of the eighth and ninth centuries). But until the Protestant Reformation, the legitimacy of the use of pictures as the "scriptures of the illiterate" was scarcely challenged, even in the recurrent ascetical protests against decorative luxury in the church.[24] The thirteenth-century canon lawyer, liturgist, and bishop William Durand (Durandus—called Speculator, from his work *Speculum Judiciale*) even gives a certain preference to images over the written word:

> for paintings appear to move the mind more than descriptions: for deeds are placed before the eyes in paintings, and so appear to be actually carrying on. But in description, the deed is done as it were by hearsay; which affecteth the mind less when recalled to memory. Hence, also, is it that in churches we pay less reverence to books than to images and pictures.[25]

It is notable that although Durand appeals to St. Gregory's justification of pictures on the basis of the illiteracy of the laity, here he seems to go beyond that rationale by referring to a general efficacy of pictures as compared to words. This point is central to the consideration of pictorial art as a theological text in its own right.

The notion of the pictorial representation of the scriptures might lead us to think of ecclesial art as having a primarily narrative function. This function is obviously of major importance and is present from the very beginnings of Christian art in the catacomb frescoes and through every succeeding period. Nevertheless, pictorial narrative by no means exhausts the functions of ecclesial art. The scriptures themselves, of course, are more than narrative. In them there are many story- or historylike accounts of events, for example, the narratives found in much of the Old Testament and in the gospels. But there are also genres that center not on historical-type events but on imaginative presentations of the supernatural (such as the visions of the prophets and of the Book of Revelation, both favorite sources for Christian art) or on more or less abstract theological ideas (such as the Lordship of Christ or the concepts of *faith* and *love* in the Pauline and Johannine epistles) or on practical moral precepts. Moreover, the reading of the scriptures for the Christian is not merely the imparting of information but is meant to be an event of encounter: through God's indwelling Spirit, the Word in person acts in the believer's mind and heart.

Hence, from very early on, alongside the narrative, Christian art produced pictures and sculptures with symbolic and "iconic" functions. (The word *icon* [ἐικών] in Greek means "image." In the Byzantine churches, the term *icon* includes narrative paintings as well as sacred portraits. I am using the term *iconic* here to designate the type of painting that is intended not merely to narrate, but more especially to mediate the presence of its subject. This is in accord with the common theological understanding of the purpose of icons in the Byzantine tradition, from which the Western use of the term—as distinguished from the more general term *image*—principally derives.)

Already in the narrative paintings themselves there is symbolism and allegory at work. Thus in the Roman catacomb frescoes, the frequently presented story of Jonah swallowed by the fish for three days and then released[a] is a symbol of death and resurrection (the uncharacteristic and unscriptural nudity of the figure of Jonah in the last scene of the story makes sense only when we realize that Jonah lying under the gourd—sometimes in a posture reminiscent of pagan representations of Endymion—symbolizes the resurrected spirit in paradise); Noah emerging from the ark[b] evokes baptism, the journey through the waters of death to new life; in the story of Daniel in the lions' den[c] or of the three young men surviving the fiery furnace, the young church saw an encouraging image of itself, triumphing amid the persecutions of the powers of the world.

Moreover, in the catacombs we also already find paintings that cannot be construed as pictorial "translations" of particular scriptural narratives. They are rather imaginative symbolic representations of the content of Christian faith, or of the spiritual world, or of the present world in process of transformation (for example, the frequently encountered figure of the orant,[d] representing at once the church and the faithful soul). We find as well the beginnings of what might be called the theological or spiritual portrait, especially in representations of Christ in glory, often surrounded by the apostles. These portrayals are sometimes explicitly linked with the vision of the Lamb enthroned from the Book of Revelation (as in the famous fresco in the catacombs of Marcellinus and Petrus, where the figure of the enthroned Christ is doubled by the Lamb standing above the rivers of paradise). But in others, no concrete visual reference to a scriptural scene (historical or visionary) is immediately apparent except the evocation of the theological idea of the Lordship of Christ. Some such portrayals represent the adaptation of pre-Christian symbolism to the expression of theological ideas (see, for example, the third-century portrayal in the necropolis under St. Peter's Basilica[e] of a young and beardless Christ—the Apollonic *Cristo bello*, the "beautiful Christ"—represented as the "sun"); others are clearly related to and perhaps derived from the apocalyptic scenes referred to above (for example, see the frescoes in the ex-Giordani catacombs and the catacombs of Domitilla, where Christ is seated in the midst of the apostles, all dressed in the togas of the Roman upper classes), but any visually recognizable scriptural context is lacking.

In the course of time, this kind of "dogmatic" portrayal of persons rather than events became a major and independent genre of Christian art. The emphasis in such paintings is not on the narration of sacred history (although this is presupposed as the basis for Christian doctrine) but on two complimentary functions of the religious portrait: on the one hand, the presentation of theological ideas that identify the subject and his or her relevance to the viewer (e.g., Christ as Savior or as Judge); and on the other hand the evocation of the personal presence of the subject to the viewer. That is to say, the image becomes a reminder of the saving power of Christ or the saints, and it aids worship by giving a concrete image of prayer's intended recipient. One may think, for example, of the many representations of the Madonna and Child in both Eastern and Western art. Sometimes, indeed, the figures are represented in the context of the Nativity story, but very frequently, no such reference is present. The figures may be shown in a nonhistorical earthly setting (a local landscape, for example, as is frequently the case in Renaissance art[f]), or enthroned,[g] or without any representational background at all[h] (as in many Eastern icons and in Western free-standing statuary). Such figures do not simply relate the scriptural affirmation of Jesus' historical birth, but proclaim Mary's motherhood and Jesus' humanity as permanent realities of religious and theological significance. Hence, the image may mediate an existential consciousness of relation to the picture's subject (realizing an aspect of the doctrine of communion of saints) and may evoke in the viewer religious sentiments of gratitude, awe, devotion, and so on.

In the light of such examples, religious painting can be seen to have a function beyond that of "illustrating" the written scriptures. It can be, in fact, a form of "writing," a "scripture," in its own right: a text whose spiritual message goes beyond any specific biblical content, even when the latter is the subject of the picture. This idea is particularly developed in Orthodox thinking. Thus Leonid Ouspensky writes in his *Theology of the Icon*:

> ...the visible image is equivalent to the verbal image. Just as the word of Scripture is an image, so is the painted image a word....In other words, the icon contains and proclaims the same truth as the Gospel. Like the Gospel and the Cross, it is one of the aspects of divine revelation and of our communion with God, a form in which the union of divine and human activity, synergy, is accomplished....
>
> In the eyes of the Church, therefore, the icon is not art illustrating Holy Scripture; it is a language that corresponds to it and is equivalent to it, corresponding not to the letter of Scripture or to the book itself as an object, but to the evangelical kerygma, that is, to the content of the Scripture itself, to its meaning, as is also true for liturgical texts. This is why the icon plays the same role as Scripture does in the Church; it has the same liturgical, dogmatic, and educational meaning.[26]

Although Ouspensky's claim for "equivalence" of the (canonical) icon to the scriptures would no doubt be disputed by many Western theologians, particularly in the Protestant tradition, the Orthodox view of the icon gives theological significance to a point that emerges clearly from an examination of the history of sacred art, namely, that the meaning of a sacred image cannot be reduced to its illustrative function. Abstracting for the moment from Ouspensky's claim that icons are on an equal level with the scriptures, we may note that the visual image transcends scriptural content in at least two ways: First, the visual specificity of painting means that it will always be an interpretation and localization of what it portrays; second, the image always adds a further dimension—by the way in which something is portrayed, the artist implies an affective reaction to its content, a comment on its meaning, and an attempt to relate it to the personal experience of the transcendent.

Already in St. Augustine we find a recognition of the first point: the concretizing nature of Christian imagination. We have a tendency to "give a face to" people we hear about in the scriptures:

> ...when we believe some material or physical facts we read or hear about but have not seen, we cannot help our imaginations fabricating something with the shape and outline of bodies as may occur to our thoughts.... Anyone, surely, who has read or heard what the apostle Paul wrote or what was written about him, will fabricate a face for the apostle in his imagination, and for everyone else whose name is mentioned in these texts. And every one of the vast number of people to whom these writings are known will think of their physical features and lineaments in a different way, and it will be quite impossible to tell whose thoughts are nearest the mark in this respect.... Even the physical face of the Lord is pictured with infinite variety by countless imaginations, though whatever it was like he certainly only had one.[27]

Augustine recognizes that our imaginative pictures of historical events or persons will rarely, if ever, correspond to reality:

> when our eyes are confronted with the features of a man or a place or any physical object which turns out to be exactly the same as we pictured it to ourselves when we were thinking about it before we had ever seen it, we treat it as no little miracle, so rarely, almost never in fact, does it happen.[28]

Nevertheless, Augustine does not see this variety of physical images as problematic:

> Our faith is directed to something else of use and importance which is represented by this picture in our imagination…. Nor is our faith bothered with what physical features [Paul and his companions] had, but only with the fact that they lived like that by the grace of God and did the things which those scriptures bear witness to.[29]

However, as we have seen, the artistic portrayal frequently intends not merely to give a realistic form, but to convey a message about its object that is relevant to our faith relation to it. Frequently a painting's localization includes an explicit attempt to convey a theological truth and/or to show the relevance of the subject matter to the viewer's circumstances (by showing scriptural events against a local background, for example, or by portraying secondary characters in the story in contemporary dress rather than in the conventional representations of biblical costume, or even placing later figures at the scene,[i] thus reinforcing the feeling of transtemporal "presence"). Durand notes that "the diverse histories of the Old and

New Testaments may be represented after the fancy of the painter. For

Pictoribus atque poetis
Quod libet addendi semper fuit aequa potestas.

(Painters and poets have always had equal license to add things.)"[30] Hence even narrative paintings are more than simple renderings of the scriptural text(s). Through the painter's "fancy" (which is in fact generally exercised within the confines of a definite natural and/or conventionalized symbolic language), pictures become an auxiliary text, an interpretive "gloss" that consciously or unconsciously bears a further dimension of message. The same holds true, analogously, of more iconic paintings: The theological message and the evocation of the person are concretized, interpreted, and given emotional resonance by the artist's vision.

(The recognition of this fact raises a question that takes us beyond Augustine's unproblematic acceptance of a variety of imaginative "pictures" of Christ; that is, the possibility of conflict between the artist's explicit or implicit message and the scriptural witness and/or conflict with other artistic/theological visions. This problem becomes particularly acute with regard to the portrayal of Christ according to the ideals of different ages: How is the unavoidable process of projection reconciled with Jesus' particular historical humanity? How do the values implied or presupposed—for example, in portrayals of Jesus as Roman emperor or feudal lord—relate to those of the gospel? As Augustine notes, "the spirit which believes what it does not see must be on its guard against fabricating something that does not exist, and thus hoping in and loving something false."[31] The resolution of such questions is beyond the scope of the present treatment of the positive functions of the visual image. It should be noted, however, that the problems raised by a "hermeneutic of suspicion" do not apply only to the arts, or to the later tradition, but they also apply to the originating images of the gospels themselves. A consideration of the criteria for sorting out such issues would involve something like the theological specialities that Lonergan calls dialectics and foundations.[32])

Even when it is intended as a communication of scriptural events and ideas, then, sacred art transcends its scriptural content by adding an interpretive element. This consideration leads us to yet another dimension of art's function as a religious and theological text: Sacred art aims not merely at the practical catechetical goal of communication of a message, but also at the more specifically artistic goal of visible representation of experience, in this case the experience of the divine.

2. ART AS VISIBLE REFLECTION OF THE DIVINE BEAUTY AND MYSTERY

In addition to illustrating and substituting for the scriptural word, the religious painting, whether narrative or iconic, can also be in a more direct way a word of God, independently of its content. This occurs in a way we have discussed earlier: by the mediation of beauty. I will not repeat here all that was said in the first chapter on this subject in the context of music but will merely recall the central thrust of the argument: that the beautiful is not only an attribute of God's "official" word of categorical revelation; it is also in itself a word about God and of God, even when it is not explicitly tied to the sacred. Explicitly religious art combines, in varying degrees and proportions, both the word as idea and the nonconceptual word of beauty, to produce in the properly receptive viewer an event of meeting with the sacred.

We noted above that the reading of the scriptures for the Christian is not merely the imparting of information but is meant to be an event of encounter. The church teaches that when the word of God in the scriptures is heard in faith, God's Word in person acts in the believer's mind and heart to evoke the presence of God as savior, through the power of God's indwelling Spirit. In the successful work of religious art, something analogous takes place. This analogy is most obvious when art operates in the way we considered in the last section—as a presentation or recollection of the content of the scriptural message, that is, as the appropriation of and response to the narrative of salvation, the person of the savior, or the communion of saints. But the evocation of presence and invitation to encounter takes place on another level as well: Insofar as it is beautiful, the art work evokes God as the object of desire, as what we are implicitly drawn toward by the Spirit through the dynamism of our innermost "heart." In sacred art, then, we encounter not only the beauty of the narrative, of the salvific message, but also the beauty of form in general. Like music, even when it is connected with the remembered or represented word, beautiful art is also a sacred word in its own right, a direct mediation of encounter with God.

In this sense also, in addition to its functions as a repository of history and as a nonverbal form of communication, sacred art can be regarded as a theological text. Indeed, I would suggest that it should be seen as a theological text in the strongest sense, that is, as a "locus" of revelation.[33] Patrick Sherry, in the context of a discussion of Simone Weil, remarks that "if indeed she is right in thinking that beauty is the attribute of God under which we see Him, then what she says is of inestimable importance for theology, for it would seem that both natural and artistic beauty might be what was traditionally referred to as a theological 'source' (a term usually restricted to Scripture, Church doctrine, and so on)."[34]

Sherry notes that the traditional enumeration of the *"loci theo-logici,"* or sources of theology, derived from Melchior Cano, does not mention art or beauty—nor, for that matter, prayer, liturgy, or personal experience.[35] However, Roman Catholic theology consistently affirms that there is a genuine knowledge of God through creation and human history—a self-manifestation of God that is attainable independently of explicit connection to biblical revelation (although not for that reason independently of grace).[36] The beautiful may be seen as an element of such natural divine revelation, functioning in a way parallel to intelligibility and goodness.[37]

Moreover, as Karl Barth and Hans Urs von Balthasar have both emphasized, God's categorical self-revelation in history, culminating in what Christians consider the "fullness" of revelation, the Christ event, is intrinsically beautiful: it is a manifestation of God's glory.[38] This glory is experienced as beauty because of the correspondence of God's being, as ultimate Goodness, to the deepest human desire for happiness. Hence, the beauty of the message and of its media is not merely incidental to what is communicated in revelation, namely, God's being for us and self-communication to us. Beauty is intrinsic to its meaning and must be an element of the forms that revelation takes historically.[39] (I shall return to this idea in the next section, in the consideration of the Christian "classic.")

Hence we may legitimately speak of beauty as an intrinsic element of both revelation and its tradition, and of sacred art as one of its primary texts or theological sources. Having said this, however, we must also introduce certain cautions and qualifications.

With regard to beauty, we must note that the term is analogous, that is, there are different kinds and levels of beauty. The divine beauty, the source and final cause of all that is beautiful, at the same time transcends all of its visible manifestations. In a famous passage from the revelations of the anchoress Julian of Norwich, God says, "I am the one that makes you to long: I am the endless fulfilling of all true desires."[40] Dame Julian is expressing the idea that the beauty of God corresponds to our *deepest* creaturely desires. But our present life, even in God's grace, is "concupiscent"; that is, our desires are not completely orderly—they go in different directions and not always straight toward their ultimate goal. They can be focused on incomplete and lesser goods, rather than on the ultimate good. Therefore, we need to be taught how to desire rightly and what true beauty is. The Christian spiritual tradition frequently expresses this insight. In a prayer of the Roman liturgy, for example, the church confesses to God: "the love you offer always exceeds the furthest expectations of our human longing, for you are greater than the human heart..." and prays that "the limits of our faults and weaknesses may not obscure the vision of your glory."[41] We need God's grace to open our eyes to see God's work at hand in creation and the beauty of human life,[42] despite its sorrows and tragedies.

It is for such reasons that Karl Barth, although he acknowledges the need for the category of beauty in theology, also expresses severe reservations about its use. He fears that the transcendent divine glory may be reduced to a function of finite and sinful human desire.[43] Balthasar, while "correcting" Barth by placing God's glory within an ontology of beauty, also cautions that the meaning of this beauty transcends our natural desires and capacities and can only be known from revelation. For the Christian, the idea of God's revealed beauty must include God's forgiveness of sin and Jesus' acceptance of death on the cross. Hence, spiritual beauty for the Christian is not simply unalloyed sensible pleasure, but includes what is ugly and alienating—insofar as it is transformed or transformable by God's triumphant love. In this way, art may attain spiritual beauty by the evocation of what Edward Schillebeeckx calls "contrast experiences": experiences of human suffering and need, placed in the context of a more fundamental hope.

> As a *contrast* experience, the experience of suffering presumes, after all, an implicit impulse toward happiness. And as an experience of injustice, it presumes at least a dim consciousness of the positive prospects of human integrity. As a contrast experience, it implies indirectly a consciousness of an appeal of and to the *humanum*. In this sense, activity which overcomes suffering is only possible on the basis of at least an implicit or inchoate anticipation of a possible *coming* universal meaning.[44]

It is in this perspective of eschatological hope that Jesus can proclaim the poor and persecuted "blessed" or "happy" (Mt 5:1–11). Human suffering and need are not beautiful in themselves, any more than they are blessed or happy in themselves; but for the Christian, the portrayal of suffering and need can be "beautiful" insofar as it makes us realize the truth of the human situation in need of salvation, evokes the beautiful vision of hope, and stirs up the beautiful moral response of compassion. Such art is sacred in a prophetic-ethical sense.

The apprehension of this level of beauty, like that of truth and moral goodness, demands conversion. Deep religious beauty, therefore, challenges worldly aesthetics, even while affirming that its basis is godly.[45] The pleasure that sacred beauty gives is mixed with awe, and it draws us beyond ourselves, rather than simply allowing us to rest. Or, better, it gives a certain repose and comfort even within the paradoxical dynamism of losing one's self to save it. The experience of sacred beauty is the anticipation of fullness, rather than its total presence, and as such can have various admixtures of satisfaction and longing. To call God beautiful and to say that this is revealed in history, in Christ, is a statement of faith; like all such statements, it stands under the "eschatological proviso"—we will be able to "see" and enjoy God's beauty fully only at the end, only when we have been totally transformed, and only in communion with all, including those whose lives at present are far from beautiful.

Qualifications must also be made when we speak of sacred art's serving as revelation of God precisely through its beauty. Two points call for clarification: (1) that the characteristic of artistic beauty applies to some sacred art, but not equally to all; and (2) that the revelatory word of beauty can stand in different relations of complementarity or tension with the word, or the specific intellectual content of Christian revelation.

First of all, not all art succeeds equally in attaining beauty; more fundamentally, not all art even seeks beauty as its primary goal. Many pieces of sacred art are simple and crude, sometimes purposefully so. As we have seen, religious art can mediate the sacred by means other than beauty, for example, by the illustration of texts or tradition, or by evoking experiences that have associations with the sacred, or by creating a sense of strangeness that mediates the "otherness" of the divine. Art may achieve "an evocation of the sense of the absolutely unknowable"[46] not so much by creating a beautiful object as by reproducing and drawing attention to the very act of experiencing: drawing the viewer into contemplation and a sense of wonder at existence and experience itself and, hence, evoking its source in an ultimate mystery. Such art may not be beautiful in the ordinary sense of the word.

Moreover, when sacred art does seek beauty, it can achieve its goal to a greater or lesser degree, and the kind of beauty achieved can be more or less well suited to the specific religious content to which it is attached. That is to say, the *implicit* religious content of the aesthetic medium (beauty, the evocation of sacred desire, or a sense of grateful awe at the fact of existence) may have different degrees of relationship to the *explicit* religious content of the message. Here there is a possible tension between the different ends of art: as an embodiment of beauty existing for its own sake, and as an instrument of communication whose purpose is the mediation of a message outside itself.[47] Hence, the "word" of beauty in sacred art can have different and sometimes ambiguous relations to the "word" of scripture, theology, and Christian life.

In Western art there are many pieces that are thematically Christian and that are skillful and aesthetically deep (in the sense of engaging the viewer not merely by pleasant sensation, but on the level of mind and affect)—but in which the specifically Christian content of the work is secondary or even incidental. It has frequently been remarked, for example, that the popularity of the theme of the martyrdom of St. Sebastian in Renaissance painting is explained by the fact that it gave an excuse for painting the male nude.[i] Certainly the first reaction evoked in most viewers by such paintings may have more to do with a humanistic appreciation of the body than with earnest meditation on suffering and death in witness to Christ. However, this does not mean that we are here confronted with mere paganism or with Platonism in Christian clothing (or, in this case, lack of clothing). The humanistic affirmation of the body connects also with Christian theology: with the doctrine of creation in God's image, and again with eschatology, resurrection and glory. (Indeed, insofar as Renaissance sacred paintings retain elements of the medieval iconographic style, such themes may be implicit in them.) Nevertheless, despite this more ultimate coherence, there is at the immediate level some degree of tension between the word mediated by beauty and the word evoked by the conceptual themes of martyrdom and sharing in the sufferings of Christ.

On the other hand, in some sacred art the earnestness of the message can be subverted by various forms of aesthetic inadequacy: lack of skill, inappropriateness of style, triviality of presentation. Religious kitsch is all too common. Moreover, there is also sacred art that is primarily decorative; it may please visually without engaging the mind, so it fails to challenge the viewer with the existential quality of the message. Of course, both good and bad art can be wedded to poor theology: time-conditioned misunderstandings or cultural accretions that have little to do with the originating "word."

3. SACRED ART AS EMBODIMENT OF THE CHRISTIAN "CLASSIC"

However, when Christian content is combined successfully with aesthetic form, art may be a living event of the Christian tradition that is complementary to the scriptures, liturgy, and doctrinal formulations. The combination of the Christian message (or some aspect of it) with aesthetic power and/or beauty constitutes a new way of communicating—through the evocation of ideas and feelings that reach beyond the merely conceptual level and touch the core of the person. In great Christian art, the content is presented in a way that is replete with spiritual meanings and associations that both connect with the verbal message (directly, as in narrative pictures, or indirectly, as in sacred portraits) and at the same time go beyond it so that the viewer is drawn into the presence to what is represented, and invited to take a personal stance toward it. In the terms made famous by the philosopher Martin Buber, the viewer is brought out of an objectifying frame of mind, into an "I-Thou" relationship with God.

When works of art so mediate the Christian message that they disclose an "excess of meaning" not only to a particular historical situation, but to people through different ages, we may speak of such works as Christian "classics." David Tracy uses the term *classic* to designate "those texts, events, images, persons, rituals and symbols which are assumed to disclose permanent possibilities of meaning and truth..."; "expressions of the human spirit [that] so disclose a compelling truth about our lives that we cannot deny them some kind of normative status."[48] The religious classic is "an event of disclosure, expressive of the 'limit-of,' 'horizon-to,' 'ground-to' side of 'religion.'" "Explicitly religious classic expressions will involve a claim to truth as the event of a disclosure-concealment of the whole of reality *by the power of the whole*—as, in some sense, a radical and finally gracious mystery."[49] The specifically Christian classic par excellence subsists in the event and person of Jesus Christ,[50] experienced in the present through manifestation and proclamation as an event from God and disclosing God.[51] Because of the intrinsically historical nature of the Christ event in Jesus of Nazareth, this supreme classic must be mediated by a tradition which transmits the original apostolic witness.[52] This tradition includes subsidiary classics, above all the texts of the New Testament scriptures,[53] but also minor classics, including some that are both aesthetic and religious.[54]

Clearly, there are degrees of intersection between religious and aesthetic classics. A work of art with a Christian subject may be a cultural classic without being a religious classic; and religious classics (for example, credal or dogmatic formulations) may have little aesthetic value. Nevertheless we may suspect, as was intimated above, that for many Christians art is a (if not the) major mediator of both ideas and presence of the sacred. As Frank Burch Brown remarks, "Christian theologians by and large seriously underestimate the extent to which classic artworks, within and without the church, have historically and legitimately functioned for many people as classics of the faith."[55] Moreover, in the light of our earlier discussions of the mediation of God's presence through beauty (including, especially in religious art, the evocation of longing for a final beauty beyond what is present), we can agree with Brown that works of art can be Christian religious classics precisely *because of* their aesthetic nature.[56] Such works will be specifically *Christian* classics provided that a classical Christian content is present, even though what is primarily mediated by the work may be a personal stance toward the transcendental,eschatological goal of hope rather than knowledge of its categorical and provisional formulations.

Such artistic-religious classics may be specific works of sacred art. But the notion of *classic* is analogous; therefore, as Brown points out, we may expand Tracy's notion and see the Christian classic as embodied also in *styles*.[57] (Just as a similarly expanded use of the term classic could apply to the theological paradigms spoken of in the last chapter.) The romanesque, the Gothic, the Counter-Reformation baroque, and other general forms of art were invented in a Christian context and for the sake of expressing spiritual ideas and feelings. "Thus in a sense the Gothic style itself is as much a classic as is Rheims or Chartres or York Minster; for these Gothic churches are far more similar than they are different in artistic and religious meaning and effect. Again, the Masses of Palestrina and Victoria and even Byrd…are valuable to the Christian tradition more for what they share stylistically than for their individuality."[58] Besides individual works and epochal styles, we may also speak of classic Christian artistic "genres": the crucifix; the *pietà*; the basilica; the oratorio; and so on. One might debate whether a particular *pietà* is a genuinely Christian or aesthetic classic, but the genre itself is both.

D. ART AS TEXT FOR THEOLOGY:
EXPRESSION OF THE HUMAN SITUATION

We have thus far considered art as a text *of* theology, that is, as an expression or embodiment of the Christian tradition and, hence, as an extension of the revelatory word of God in Christ. But art can also be a text for theology, not insofar as it is religious, but insofar as it embodies and expresses the "spiritual situation" of a particular culture to which a religious message is addressed.

Paul Tillich has provided a classic description of theology's function as correlational, that is, as forging a link between the "questions" implicit in the human situation of a particular era, and the "answers" given by God's revelation;[59] or, in another of Tillich's formulations, between the conditioned forms of human culture and the unconditioned term of our "ultimate concern."[60] If the task of theology is conceived to be, at least in part, correlational,[61] it becomes clear that art has a special role to play with regard to theological thought, namely, as a primary factor in the discernment of the "human situation" to which the Christian message must be addressed. This situation is perhaps most explicitly formulated in conceptual terms by the philosophies of a particular age. But by their very abstractness, philosophical forms of thought must necessarily lose much of the concrete human dimension. Hence Tillich writes:

> Art indicates what the character of a spiritual situation is; it does this more immediately and directly than do science and philosophy for it is less burdened by objective considerations. Its symbols have something of a revelatory character while scientific conceptualization must suppress the symbolical in favor of objective adequacy.[62]

In particular, art unconsciously expresses the ultimate concern of its society: The artist "cannot help but betray by his style his own ultimate concern, as well as that of his group, and his period...in every style the ultimate concern of a human group is manifest."[63] As Nicholas Wolterstorff points out, this is not the same as saying that art necessarily expresses the artist's religion, for some have no religion to express. However, there is always a "world" behind the work, and frequently the artist's religious attitudes or lack of them will play a central part in that world.[64] Moreover, the artist's own world standing behind the work will seldom fully account for it; almost always, elements will enter in that come from beyond the artist's consciousness. These elements often stem from a way of seeing of which the artist is hardly aware[65] and which will frequently, if not always, contain clues as to the ultimate concerns of the artist and/or of his age.

Hence, the theologian intent on presenting the Christian message in a way that is relevant to the thought forms of a particular age can find in its art a significant text, a concise embodiment of the spirit (or spirits) of the age, including, in Tillich's terminology, the implicit "questions" to which God's revelation is the proposed "answer." From another point of view, we may say that such art, insofar as it embodies an implicit and unthematic stance toward the transcendental horizon of God's grace, is itself a formulation of revelation in its most general form, and hence may also be called a word of God—although one that remains ambiguous and possibly unrecognizable as such until it is explicitly brought into contact with the special revelation formulated in religious consciousness.[66]

This "correlational" function of art is first of all relevant to theology as "apologetic." This kind of theology attempts to show the reasonability of the personal act of faith by demonstrating that the content of faith is coherent with other dimensions of our human experience. Insofar as this function is conceived in terms of presenting arguments that can in principle be recognized as reasonable even by those outside the Christian community, this form of theology (Tracy's "fundamental theology") is primarily directed to the academy.[67] However (as I shall argue more concretely in the next chapter), the themes of fundamental theology have a direct pastoral relevance, especially in an increasingly well-educated world where questions to the faith arise precisely from the difficulty of integrating it with the perspectives learned from secular experience. Moreover, apologetics, or the effort of theology to give reason for the faith, is not directed solely to those outside; on the contrary, it is addressed above all to those within the faith community. Apologetics addresses the necessity of integrating faith with our total humanity. It therefore takes seriously the questions and doubts that arise for faith from the contemporary situation. It sees these questions not as expressions of a hostile world that should be rejected out of hand, but as legitimate challenges that are intrinsic to establishing the full humanity of Christian belief. (As Pannenberg points out, the "debatability" of assertions about God is intrinsic to their nature and corresponds to the eschatological nature of faith.[68]) The art of an era is generally an important embodiment and interpretation of its secular perspectives, and it is therefore a crucial element in a theology of correlation.

Art as revelatory of the contemporary situation also relates to the practical and liberational aspects of theology. If Christian faith is to move people to action, it must be able to present a concrete and attractive vision of the good: it must move the heart and stir the imagination. In this sense, theology itself must become aesthetic. (This theme also will be treated more concretely in the next chapter, in the context of preaching.) Although the church can and should call upon the vast store of religious beauty from the past, at least part of its theological/aesthetic task will be to discern those sensibilities of the contemporary imagination that are manifest in art.

E. LIMITATIONS OF ART
AS TEXT AND AS REVELATORY WORD

In the previous sections, we have spoken of art as a religious text, embodying God's historically expressed word. We have distinguished three basic and frequently overlapping realities that can be mediated by art: the Christian tradition, known through its material artifacts; the contemporary human situation, epitomized and interpreted in its artworks; and the transcendent itself, apprehended in beauty or aesthetic power. But there are limitations to art's ability to mediate these realities to us.

We have already adverted to some of the sociological limitations of art as a historical text. Aside from these objective limitations, there are also limitations to be overcome on the part of the viewer; that is, there is a hermeneutical task to be accomplished if we are to "read" works as expressions of a human situation, either past or present. Symbols and representations do not necessarily yield their original meanings easily, even when they have a positive aesthetic or spiritual effect on the viewer. As with any text, there is a need to understand not only the content of the work, but also its historical and aesthetic context and the symbolic language it employs. Hence, the emphasis on the hermeneutics of texts in recent theology must be extended to the realm of art as well.

There are also objective and subjective limits to the ability of art (as of any symbolic reality) to mediate the religious transcendent. On the subjective side, the ability of a work of sacred art to be revelatory and inspiring depends largely on the degree of aesthetic and religious "conversion" operative in the viewer.[69] Objectively, there are intrinsic limitations to art's ability to be a medium of divine presence and grace or revelation—that is, its capacity to serve as (to repeat Tracy's description) "the event of a disclosure-concealment of the whole of reality *by the power of the whole*—as, in some sense, a radical and finally gracious mystery."[70] Indeed, as Tracy says, it is the mark of the subject matter of the religious classic always to be beyond adequate expression by any form.[71]

F. THE SACRAMENTAL POWER OF ART

To the extent that it attempts to give (always provisional and inadequate) form to the transcendental mystery, religious art may be described as being sacramental—in a general sense, referring to those acts by which the church expresses and realizes itself, in which it gives concrete form to its essence as the historical presence of God's self-gift in Christ.[72] The church does not consider sacred art itself a sacrament in the narrower sense of the term—this sense of the word is normally reserved for the specific symbolic liturgical acts, linked with performative words, through which the church incorporates people into its life and mission. But the Roman Catholic Church has long recognized that the concept of *sacrament* itself is analogous, applying differently to the major sacraments of Eucharist and baptism than to any of the other acts that are officially included under the term. Moreover, Catholic theology adds the notion of *sacramentals* to apply to things or acts that are used as aids to its principal acts of worship and fellowship. For this reason, we may say that sacred art, like the preaching of the word, is sacramental. The iconoclast controversy brought the church to the decision that the production and use of pictorial symbols is in fact a legitimate actuation of its nature, and, in this sense, art shares in the sacramental character of the church itself.

However, the iconoclast controversy also brought to light the need to distinguish sacred art's sacramental ability to mediate presence of and communion with God from the widespread notion of the religious image as a material abode of the deity or repository of divine power; that is, the idea of *sacramentality* must be distinguished from the notion of religious idolatry. The idea of religious images as living repositories of supernatural power is found in "high" religions such as Hinduism and Buddhism as well as in animist "folk" religions. Apologists for these religions sometimes claim that the function of idols in them is purely symbolic and educational, but Buddhologist Robert H. Sharf notes that it is "misleading to view Buddhist icons as primarily didactic—intended merely to symbolize the virtues of buddhahood or to nurture a sense of reverence toward the Buddha and his teachings.... [R]itual consecrations are intended to transform an inanimate image into a living deity, and both textual and ethnographic sources indicate that icons thus empowered were treated as spiritual beings possessed of apotropaic powers, to be worshipped with regular offerings of incense, flowers, food, money, and other assorted valuables. Chinese Buddhist biographies and temple records are replete with tales of miraculous occurrences associated with such images...."[73]

Christianity also has a tradition of "wonder-working" images,[74] and although it forbids the explicit kind of idolatry that is approved in Hinduism and Buddhism, pastors and observers of popular religion will recognize vague but sometimes disquieting similarities to it in the way images function in the piety of some of the theologically unsophisticated faithful. To combat such tendencies, church teaching distinguishes between the legitimate use and veneration of images and an idolatrous misinterpretation.[75] The doctrine of the Western church in particular insists that there is no divinity or supernatural power "inherent" in sacred images that makes them worthy of veneration.[76]

Yet, at the same time, it seems appropriate to speak of the "power" of great religious works of art. If such works can embody the Christian religious classic, and if, as Tracy says, it is characteristic of the encounter with such classics that it conveys the conviction of being confronted with a disclosure brought about by the gracious power of God, then it seems we must think of sacred art as a medium of that power. The analogy of the sacraments suggests an explanation of how we can hold this can be true without falling into any form of idolatry.

According to a maxim of Scholastic sacramental theology, *sacramenta significando efficiunt gratiam*—the sacraments cause grace by signifying. Without going into the precise meaning of this maxim with regard to each of the official sacraments, we may apply it analogously to the symbolic mediation of grace in general and, more specifically, to the case of sacred art. Religious art mediates grace by signifying. What is peculiar to its mode of signifying is that it not only communicates a Christian message, but also, insofar as it is aesthetic, implicitly represents (to varying degrees) the ultimate goal of human desire, in one or more of several forms: in the form of beauty; in the form of human creativity, which reflects the Creator; and in the form of wonder at the act of experiencing (and hence of conscious being) itself.

It would be misleading, then, to think of the work of sacred art as a special repository of divine power or grace, as though the latter were somehow "materially" present; rather, the work is a symbol that refers us (if we are capable of receiving it) to the unique source of grace.[77] Its only power is aesthetic and symbolic, and this power depends upon the spiritual engagement of the viewer with both the subject matter and the enhanced consciousness of the act of experiencing (and hence of being) that is associated with artistic representation. Grace is not "inherent" in the image in an objective way, but the image can be a medium of grace insofar as its beauty and/or aesthetic intensification of experience points beyond itself and engages the viewer in dialogue with its subject matter. In this case, the subject matter is (1) the Christian message and (2) God's self, as the creative source of beauty and of the consciousness of which art provides a concrete and heightened experience. The power of religious images is that of images in general: the ability to unite ideas with an affective state evoked by associations (some explicit, some unconscious) that are connected with a heightened visual experience of a concrete reality. This power is "subsumed" into the workings of God's grace ("grace presupposes nature")[78] and becomes sacramental by its explicit connection with religious and Christian conversion.[79]

Obviously, the actual operation of such signifying has conditions and limitations, on the part of both the work of art and its viewer. Naturally, the work's communicative and aesthetic power are in part determined by the degree of the artist's vision, skill, and materials. But the primary limitation is more fundamental and unavoidable, namely, the provisional nature and the ambiguity of every sign as compared with both the transcendent as such and its hoped-for eschatological realization in us. Even within this general condition of finite symbols, there is the further factor of the intrinsic limits of every language, whether spoken or non-verbal. The concreteness and specificity of the work of art are an integral part of its evocative power; but at the same time they can also overdetermine the message. On the other hand, signs are by their nature polyvalent, capable of expressing many meanings, and are open to different interpretations. Either of these factors can vitiate a work's ability to "speak" to some viewers because of differences of linguistic or historical context.

There is also a yet more serious aspect of the polyvalence of signs. Every human sign of the transcendent—including the church and its essential self-realizations—also has the potential to be an anti-sign, to the extent that it fails to reach or to communicate transcendence on the moral, intellectual, aesthetic, or religious level. That is to say, even in the context of the representation and communication of God's definitive victory over sin and death in Christ, no human sign completely shares the absoluteness of the Christ event (which by definition includes the resurrection, which places its final meaning beyond death, in the transcendence of God).[80] Every categorical realization of grace is also marked, to some greater or lesser extent, by the human context of sinfulness and frailty ("original sin"), by concupiscence, and by personal sin. Hence, signs can point in more than one direction at once, or they may draw attention to themselves as signs, rather than to what they represent.

To call a work a religious classic is to say that these limitations have largely been overcome—that a particular sign succeeds to a great degree in transcending its historical and linguistic limitations and points beyond itself in such a way that many people in different contexts find in it a challenging excess of meaning. However, even the classic is to some extent ambivalent, and if it is true that the classic can be called normative[81] so that in a certain sense it is the classic that judges us and makes a claim on us, it is nonetheless also true, as Frank Burch Brown insists, that critical judgment must be applied to the classic.[82] We may apply to art as well as to literary texts the questions of deconstructive hermeneutics concerning the work's unexplicit presuppositions and conditions of production. These conditions may include sociopolitical inequities and implicit assumptions of power, and as indicated above, artistic-religious classics should enter into the dialectical function of fundamental theology. There will be multiple forms of this dialectic: (1) between different images—in Brown's terms, between aesthetic-religious classics and counterclassics;[83] (2) between the different ends of art (communication of ideas, mediation of beauty, heightening of experience, etc.); (3) between image and word; (4) between formulation and experience; and (5) between different kinds of experience, both aesthetic and religious.

We have already alluded to some of the subjective limitations on art's functioning as a revelatory event. In addition to education in the language of the art, attentiveness, and the aesthetic sensitivity that comes with the habit of seeing, the viewer must have some degree of religious conversion—in classical language, must have the interior testimony of God's Spirit—to be grasped existentially by the revelatory possibilities of the word in any of its external forms. It is the experience of the Spirit, as participation in God's life and anticipation of ultimate union, that gives us a taste for what is spiritual in sacred art and allows us to be moved by it and so enter into its movement. The degree of conversion, combined with the subject's particular circumstances, introduces a further relativity into art's revelatory possibilities. Poor art can sometimes inspire; on the other hand, the beauty of religious art can leave one unmoved, can incite a banal reaction, or can distract from the message. It can even, at the limit, arouse misdirected desire (as is symbolized in the penultimate scene of Goethe's *Faust, Part* II, when Mephistopheles, seeing the beauty of the angels, is incited not to worship but to lust).

For these many reasons, art will not always occupy the same place in the spirituality of either the individual or the church community. Nevertheless, it is my hope that this chapter has uncovered some of the ways in which it can serve as a sacred text that can exercise a sacramental function similar to that of the sacred word. For its specifically Christian content, sacred art is materially dependent on the scriptures (at least if one rejects as legendary the idea that certain images were painted during Christ's life and as mythological the idea of icons "not made by hands"[84]); at the same time, as art it has a revelatory dimension that is formally independent of its material content, although (ideally, at least) in service of the same ultimate goal.

In the exercise of this quasi-sacramental function, Christian visual art has similarities to the art of preaching—to which, as we have seen, it is intimately related historically and of which it may be considered a special form. In the final chapter, I will attempt to explore these affinities further, turning now to Christian preaching in its normally accepted sense. I will attempt to construct the outline of an understanding of preaching as an exercise of aesthetic or artistic theology: the activity in which theology, art, and spirituality combine in the service of communicating God's word and presence.

Web sites for viewing illustrations———

a. Jonah, from the catacombs of Callixtus and the catacombs of Via Latina:
**www-lib.haifa.ac.il/www/art/med/
late_antiq_cata.html**
•Choose from images and click to enlarge.
b. Noah emerging from the ark, from the catacombs of
Peter and Marcellinus:
**www-lib.haifa.ac.il/www/art/med/
late_antiq_cata.html**
•Choose from the images and click to enlarge.
c. Daniel in the lions' den, from the catacombs of Giordani:
**www/lib.haifa.ac.il/www/art/med/
late_antiq_cata.html**
•Choose from the images and click to enlarge.
d. The orants from the catacombs of Priscilla (two views):
**www-lib.haifa.ac.il/www/art/med/
late_antiq_cata.html**
•Choose from the images and click to enlarge.
e. Christ as the sun (*sol Christus*) from the necropolis under
St. Peter's Basilica:
**www-lib.haifa.ac.il/www.art/med/
late_antiq_cata.html**
•Choose from the images and click to enlarge.
f. See for example Giovanni Bellini, *Madonna con il Bambino
benedicente* (1510):
www.grisnet.it/arte/bellini.htm
•Click on the image to enlarge.
g. Giovanni Bellini, *Madonna con il Bambino, Santi, e angeli*
(1487):
www.grisnet.it/arte/bellini.htm
•Click on the image to enlarge.

h. Among many examples, see Raphael, *Madonna del Granduca* (1505):
   metalab.unc.edu/wm/paint/auth/raphael/ granduca/granduca.jpg
i. See for example Giotto's portrayal of the crucifixion in the lower basilica in Assisi, where St. Francis and his companions are placed at the foot of the cross of Jesus along with the figures whose presence is indicated by the gospels:
   www.christusrex.org/www1/francis/lower.html
   •Choose from the images and click to enlarge.
j. See for example the portrayal of St. Sebastian by Antonello da Messina at:
   www.grisnet.it/arte/antonello.htm
   •Click on the image to enlarge.
   Or see Perugino's version, at:
   metalab.unc.edu/cjackson/perugino
   •Click on the image to enlarge.

Chapter 4
Theology, Aesthetics, and the Art of Preaching

Urgently preach the word in and out of season; convince, rebuke, and exhort; be unfailing in patience and teaching. (2 Tm 4:2)
The word is near you, on your lips and in your heart (that is, the word of faith which we preach); because, if you confess with your lips that Jesus is Lord and believe in your heart that God raised him from the dead, you will be saved....For "everyone who calls on the name of the Lord will be saved." But how are they to call upon him in whom they have not believed? And how are they to believe in him of whom they have never heard? And how are they to hear without a preacher? And how can people preach unless they are sent? As it is written, "How beautiful are the feet of those who preach good news!" (Rom 10:8–15) (NRSV)

A. THEOLOGICAL AESTHETICS AND AESTHETIC THEOLOGY

This book began with a practical theological concern: the place of beauty in the human apprehension of and response to God. The first chapter closed with an example of the concrete religious questions raised by aesthetics, reflecting on the place of music in liturgy. In the following chapters, we turned to theological concerns of a more theoretical nature. We have seen that the often implicit dialogue between theology and aesthetics leads in contemporary thought to the recognition that aesthetic categories must be admitted as genuine theological concepts that refer to and transmit a basic type of human experience, one that is incommunicable in any other way.[1] (Even scientists and mathematicians, after all, use such ideas as *beauty* and *elegance* as criteria of judgment for theories.) I have therefore argued for art as a special kind of theological text on several levels. In the last chapter, we noted a special affinity between art and the church's sacramental self-realization and intimated that it has a special relationship to preaching. Our primary concern up to this point can be designated as "theological aesthetics": the examination of aesthetic experience and its descriptive categories in their relation to the language and categories of philosophical and theological discourse.

However, the conjunction of aesthetics and theology can also be eminently practical, and in this chapter we turn again to the first chapter's concern for art as a way to God, specifically in liturgy. We shall also expand on the third chapter's recognition of sacred art's kinship with the preaching of the word and its sharing with the latter a kind of sacramental status and power.

The methodologically conscious and purposeful introduction of aesthetic concepts into the formal study of theology is a fairly recent phenomenon, but (as we have seen in our historical overviews) the possibility of attaining and expressing theological insight in the language of art and of everyday experience has long been recognized. Indeed, for most people this frequently has been and probably always will be the more normal way of encountering theology. As the heroine Lara remarks in Pasternak's novel *Doctor Zhivago*, "I don't like purely philosophical works. I think a little philosophy should be added to life and art by way of seasoning, but to make it one's specialty seems to me as strange as eating nothing but horseradish."[2]

These sentiments may be distressing to those who find academic philosophy a sufficiently nourishing diet for themselves, but such people are no doubt a small minority. The same may be said of those within the church whose faith is nourished directly by the formal study of theology. At the same time, there is an ever-increasing level of intellectual sophistication among believers, raising the dual problem of (1) relating religious belief to the ordinary life-forms and experiences of secular society, and (2) discerning the rational justification of commitment to particular religious beliefs, in the midst of the pluralistic "marketplace" of ideas. This problem is exacerbated by the contemporary lack of a single philosophical system or religious worldview. The common grounds shared by most Westerners are media culture, the sphere of politics, and the worlds of business and commerce, all of which are secular and often lacking in reflective depth. Nevertheless, there is a human thirst for substance, value, and beauty, although they are often sought confusedly and erratically. Hence, there is a need for faith to address the genuinely philosophical and theological concerns of believers in a language that is both more locally attuned and more accessible to them than the normal discourse of those disciplines. In distinction to the theological aesthetics spoken of above, we might call this practical approach aesthetic theology.

By this term I mean to denote the operation of theology on the aesthetic level—not a watered-down version of abstract theology nor a simple "translation" of the latter into a different language, but the performance of critical reasoning on the symbolic and metaphorical level that speaks to the human "heart" and "feeling" and that is the primary religious sphere of discourse[3]—in short, theology practiced as an art and in conjunction with the arts.

Liturgy and sacramental practice are obviously major fields for the practice of such aesthetic theology. A treatment of these areas, however, would demand another book, longer than this one. I shall instead take as an example of the project of aesthetic theology a more restricted field, namely, the theology of preaching. This topic again will be restricted to preaching in the context of the eucharistic liturgy. We shall examine such preaching's foundations in the nature of Christian revelation and the church, its status as an art, its relation to conceptual theology, and its connections with spirituality and aesthetics.

In preaching, Christians encounter God's word in the form of paradigmatic images as well as concepts. In previous chapters we have seen how music and pictures can serve as a means of mediating the sacred. We now turn to the mediation of the Christian message by the word. My contention will be that here also there is a need for art as well as theology so that God's self-revelation may be communicated in such a way that its intrinsic beauty—its attractiveness and its promise of joy—may be apprehended by contemporary minds and hearts.

Our first concern will be to examine the nature of preaching and to explain why Christian preaching has both intellectual and aesthetic dimensions. After looking at the context of the contemporary renewal of preaching, we shall examine the New Testament basis for the connection between faith and the proclaimed message. It is this connection that establishes the intellectual dimension of faith and prevents its reduction to a matter of feeling alone. We shall then try to establish that three essential elements in successful proclamation are theology, spirituality, and art. After considering in detail the rationale for each of these elements in the nature of preaching, we turn in the second section to specific problems posed by the contemporary situation. We shall see that the exercise of liturgical preaching is conditioned by an aesthetic context that is problematic for many people in contemporary Western society. Finally, we will take a closer and more practical look at the relation of theology to the art of preaching and suggest one way of attempting to construct an aesthetic theology that overcomes the aesthetic distance between the tradition and the contemporary congregation.

B. Preaching as Aesthetic Theology

1. THE RENEWAL OF EUCHARISTIC PREACHING IN THE CONTEMPORARY CHURCH

A recently retired Roman Catholic priest, reflecting on the status of preaching in the early days of his ministry, recalled that he was assigned to his first parish at the beginning of July. He celebrated mass in that parish every day and several times each Sunday. Nevertheless, he never preached a homily at a eucharistic liturgy until the last Sunday in October, the feast of Christ the King. He explained that this was not exceptional but was the rule in the church of his youth. Sunday sermons were simply eliminated during the warm weather; they were not considered crucial to the celebration of mass. Preaching at the Eucharist during the week was unheard of.

By contrast, it would be very unusual today to find a Catholic Sunday eucharistic celebration without a homily, and in most parishes, preaching is the norm even on weekdays. The contemporary status of preaching is the result of the directives of the Second Vatican Council and is in line with its teaching that the homily is not an optional addendum but an intrinsic part of the liturgy itself.[4] This perspective has a strong basis in the early liturgical practice of the church, which served as an inspiration and source for contemporary renewal.

The restoration of the practice calls for an equally vigorous return to the theology of preaching as well as for an appreciation of its nature as an art. To grasp the meaning and goal of preaching and to understand its relation to theology and to aesthetics implies seeing its connection not only with liturgy, but with Christian faith itself. The church's renewed practice is in danger of becoming mere routine unless it is accompanied by a truly personal appreciation of the reason for the centrality of this act in the church's life. In what follows I shall first explore briefly the connection of preaching and faith as it is seen in the New Testament perspective. In the light of this, with no pretension at completeness or systematic rigor, I will then offer a few suggestions concerning the nature of preaching, especially in its connection with theology, spirituality, and art. Finally, I will look at some of the difficulties that face the preacher in the contemporary Western world and suggest some general principles for approaching them in practice.

The context I will primarily have in mind in this chapter is that of liturgical preaching. In most Christian churches that have an ordained ministry, preaching in this context is normally restricted to such ministers—although this rule applies in greater or lesser degrees and with varying breadth of exceptions. In the Roman Catholic Church, liturgical preaching is at present officially restricted, in most circumstances, to ordained ministers. Nevertheless, even there the ministerial restriction is not necessarily intrinsic to liturgical preaching,[5] nor is the liturgy the only place where "preaching," in its wide sense, takes place.[6] Hence it is my hope that these reflections will have some relevance to the communication of the gospel by religious educators, teachers, and members of the Christian community in general in their relations within and outside the church.

2. FAITH AND PREACHING:
THE NEW TESTAMENT BASIS

The New Testament conveys a sense of urgency about the communication of the message: Jesus himself sees preaching as central to his mission (Mk 1:38, for example); the disciples after the resurrection declare that they are under compulsion to bear witness to Christ (Acts 4:20); Paul sees preaching as necessary for salvation (Rom 10:8ff.) and as a personal necessity for himself (1 Cor 9:16—"Woe to me if I do not preach the gospel!"), for which he is willing to suffer hardship (2 Cor 11:23–28).

This emphasis on preaching corresponds to the New Testament's theology of faith as the all-inclusive salvific act and its stress on belief in Jesus as faith's central aspect.

In general contemporary parlance, *faith* and *belief* are nearly synonymous. When Christians make their profession of faith, they enunciate a series of statements prefaced by the words, "I believe...." Yet it is by no means obvious either that our relation to God should be summarized by the attitude of faith or that the principal expression of faith should be a creed—a series of beliefs or assertions. Indeed, these ideas, far from being a universal characteristic of religion, reveal precisely what is specific to Christianity and its claim.

There is little direct or systematic reflection on faith in the Old Testament; in fact, as Gerhard Von Rad tells us, the Old Testament has no single word to signify the human person's turning to God with his or her whole being.[7] Nevertheless, the story of Israel's relation to God clearly expresses such an attitude of conversion in various terms: trusting in God, fearing God, obedience, hope, faithfulness, covenant love, belief in God's word, being secure in God.[8] The crux of this relation is the acknowledgment of God's sovereignty and trust in God's self-revelation to Israel through word and act in its history.

For the New Testament, *faith* becomes the word that summarizes the whole process of conversion. In continuity with the spirit of the Old Testament, faith indicates a total personal relation to God and response to God's word. Thus it includes obedience, trust, hope, fidelity, and love. But the crucial and specifically Christian aspect of faith for the New Testament writings is the mediation of our relationship with God by Christ as God's final and definitive word. Hence the knowledge and acknowledgement of God's saving work in Christ becomes central to the living relation to God. This means that there is a particular emphasis on the intellectual aspect of faith: faith as belief, as the affirmation of the content of the divine revelation in Christ as being real.[9] Thus the primary New Testament meaning of *faith* is the acceptance of the kerygma, the preaching about Jesus, as true. Faith now has a specific content that must be heard and accepted as real and determinative for one's relation to God, namely, that Jesus was raised up by God from death and is the Messiah, Lord, and Savior who was foretold by the scriptures.[10]

The acceptance of the kerygma is of course not merely a detached intellectual judgment; the message is received as a message about salvation and, hence, implies the acceptance of a saving significance for one's life and the corresponding conversion to a new way of living. One accepts the message of life to give oneself to God who is revealed in it. Concretely, to accept the kerygma means to acknowledge Jesus as Lord. But while Old Testament faith implied obedient response to a Lord already known, the acceptance of Jesus as Lord can only come about by hearing and believing the message proclaimed about him. Although the Old Testament relation to God is a trust in future action of the Lord who has acted in the people's history, the New Testament sees the Christ event as the definitive and eschatological act of God, so our future is here already revealed. God meets us definitively only in Christ (Col 1:19, 2:9).

Moreover, the validity of our self-giving to God through Christ is seen to depend upon the truth and reality of what is preached. If Jesus was not raised from the dead, Paul writes, faith is in vain and we are still in our sins (1 Cor 15:17). In short, the quality of faith as intellectual assent (belief or "knowledge" in the Johannine sense[11]) corresponds to the reality of God's saving action in Christ in history. We can participate in that action, present above all in Christ's resurrection, only by accepting it in its saving power for us, and we can only accept it through hearing and assent, hence, Paul's insistence that "faith comes through hearing" (Rom 10:14–16); and, hence, the centrality of preaching the word to bring about the encounter with the Lord.

The truth of the message that is preached about Jesus, however, is not obvious. What is apparent in history is the cross, the apparent failure of Jesus' mission, not its eschatological success. Therefore preaching includes an aspect of personal "witness" to the community's and the preacher's own encounter with the risen Lord. In itself, however, this external testimony, even if accompanied by "signs" of its divine origin and inspiration, is insufficient for the response of faith without a corresponding internal movement from God: the interior "witness" of God's grace moving the mind and heart to assent to the word that is heard (Jn 6:4). Preaching the gospel, then, is not merely human discourse or reflection but is the announcing of what God has done in history. Moreover, its acceptance presupposes a present act of God in the heart of the hearer. In this way, both preaching and its reception in faith are divinely empowered acts so that the message is received not as the word of humans but as the word of God (1 Thes 2:13).

The New Testament has no single word that exhausts this concept of *preaching*.[12] It uses a number of terms to describe various forms of communication of God's message. By far the most common verbs used to describe the activity are *kerussein*, meaning "to herald or proclaim," and *euangelizesthai*, meaning "to announce good news." Correspondingly, the content of preaching is "proclamation" (*kerygma*) or "the good news, the gospel" (*euangelion*). It is natural that the New Testament should emphasize the missionary aspect of preaching, the public proclamation of the "news" of Christ to a non-Christian world. But closely allied is the idea of *teaching* (see for example Mk 4:23, 6:30, 11:1; Mt 2:23, 28:20; Acts 8:31), which is addressed also to those who accept the message and form the believing community. Although the proclamation announces the good news of what God has accomplished in Jesus, teaching expounds upon this message, explores its implications for life, and demands an "existentielle" decision.[13]

In what follows we shall see that the dual aspects of proclamation and teaching remain central to Christian preaching, albeit in varying proportions. We shall also suggest that their proper functioning today involves not only theology and spirituality—dimensions that are already implicit in the New Testament conception of preaching—but also an explicit attention to their nature as art.

3. ELEMENTS OF PREACHING: THEOLOGY, SPIRITUALITY, ART

"But as for sermons! They are bad, aren't they!" So exclaimed J. R. R. Tolkien in a letter to his son Christopher, dated April 24, 1944. If we take as our starting point the New Testament conviction that Christian faith centers on the vital personal affirmation of and reaction to the message of what God has accomplished for us in Jesus, it is clear that the preaching of that message remains always an essential element of the task of the Christian community. But the fact that Tolkien living in England and his son living in South Africa both had the same experience forty-five years ago that many in the church complain of today testifies to the fact that this central element faces long-standing and widespread problems. A major reason has been the failure to recognize that the church's teaching and proclaiming must also constitute a form of art.

Tolkien's letter continues:

> The answer to the mystery is probably not simple; but part of it is that "rhetoric" (of which preaching is a department) is an art, which requires (a) some native talent and (b) learning and practice. The instrument used is very much more complex than a piano, yet most performers are in the position of a man who sits down to a piano and expects to move his audience without any knowledge of the notes at all. The art can be learned (granted some modicum of aptitude) and can then be effective, in a way, when wholly unconnected with sincerity, sanctity, etc. But preaching is complicated by the fact that we expect in it not only a performance, but truth and sincerity, and also at least no word, tone, or note that suggests the possession of vices (such as hypocrisy, vanity) or defects (such as folly, ignorance) in the preacher.
>
> Good sermons require some art, some virtue, some knowledge. Real sermons require some special grace which does not transcend art but arrives at it by instinct or "inspiration"; indeed the Holy Spirit seems sometimes to speak through a human mouth providing art, virtue and insight he does not himself possess: but the occasions are rare.[14]

Once the rhetorical dimension of preaching has been noticed, it seems obvious that preaching is, as Tolkien says, an art (in the wide sense of the word), one which in its practice touches upon the mystery of grace. It requires skill (or *art* in the narrower sense), insight, and virtue. But given the fact that grace presupposes nature and that arts can be learned, there is no reason why these requirements should be left either to the chance of native talent or to an unpredictable miracle of the Spirit. As the French preacher Olivier de La Brosse remarks, amateurism should not be regarded as a special privilege of the clergy; the art of preaching can and should be developed in its practitioners to a professional level.[15] It is true that St. Paul speaks of preaching to the Corinthians without either eloquence or wisdom—so that the power of God alone would be manifest in the persuasiveness of the message (1 Cor 2:1, 4–5), but it would be rash to interpret this to mean that Paul's preaching was without either theology or art. Even if Paul was sometimes "artless" in proclaiming the Christian kerygma among the Gentiles for the first time, it hardly follows that this can be a model for addressing contemporary Christian congregations. In our post-Christian age, a better example might be found in Paul's letters and in the gospels, where both theology and art are used in setting forth the message and teaching its implications to their respective audiences. This is in no way to minimize either the intrinsic power of the message or the efficacy of God's spirit, but it is to affirm that God's work and human agency are directly, and not inversely, related—that is, that we are most apt to be a medium for God's grace when we are most humanly sensitive, intelligent, and responsible.

In the contemporary exercise of preaching, then, I will suggest that both art and theology have an important role to play. On one level—that of content—the connection of theology with the art of preaching is obvious. The concrete procedures of the two, however, would seem to be radically different. In particular, it would seem that the method of theology should have little in common with preaching. Although theology has traditionally been thought of as a science, I have been arguing that preaching should be seen as a pastoral art. Of course, if one defines *method* in a wide enough way—as for example in Bernard Lonergan's notion of "a normative pattern of recurrent and related operations yielding cumulative and progressive results"[16]—it is clear that the arts have their own methods and are not merely the result of spontaneous creativity. But such methods are generally learned through example and practice, and their mastery has more to do with intuition and imitation than with the analytical and objectifying concerns of scientific methodology.

It will be my suggestion, however, that the contemporary situation reveals a particular overlapping of theological and pastoral concerns and that—the peculiar nature of every art notwithstanding—contemporary reflections on the method of theology are relevant to the development of a methodical approach to the art of preaching in the modern world. Before broaching the topic of the relation of theology to preaching today, however, it will be helpful to consider briefly the essential components of the art of preaching itself.

In his classic treatise on Christian rhetoric, *De Doctrina Christiana*, St. Augustine draws upon the tradition of Cicero and Aristotle to define the three essential goals of preaching: to teach, to please (or "charm"), and to persuade (or "touch") the listener (*De Doctrina Christiana*, IV, 17). In contemporary theology, Bernard Lonergan writes that preaching consists in "leading another to share in one's cognitive, constitutive, effective meaning."[17] An examination of these three dimensions of meaning will show a close agreement with Augustine's three aims of preaching. Indeed, a phenomenology of speech reveals that the sharing of these three aspects of meaning (in varying proportions) is intrinsic to all human discourse.

Speech between persons is first of all (at least implicitly) an act of interpellation. One is addressed by another; there is a personal "call," an imperative to attend to the other as a person, rather than as a thing: an invitation to dialogue. To the extent that we respond to this call positively, the other becomes for us not merely a function of our own existence or an object within the horizon of our minds, but another mysterious "self" over against our own. Through this call and response, the new reality of a "we" comes into being. Speaking and hearing are aimed at a communion of life at some level (although admittedly the degree of shared life may at times be very superficial). Dialogue is thus an event of purposely and freely uniting separate persons and is therefore (implicitly, and to different extents) a potential act of love.

But human speech is rarely pure invitation to intersubjective attention. It generally also has a cognitive dimension: It intends to communicate some content. This content may be primarily objective ("there's a gas station just past the next light") or may be intersubjective, inviting a further and more explicit extension of the sharing of life ("I love you"). But although the levels of significance and involvement may vary widely, every true assertion is meant to contribute in some way to the other's being. When we share something of our mind, we are giving of ourselves to another, contributing to that person's life project. Because the reality of what is communicated is crucial, speech also involves an invitation to trust: Saying something implies a claim to communicate the truth and asks the hearer to put faith in the one who speaks.

In what follows we shall see that these intrinsic dimensions of human communication ("speech," in the widest sense) correspond to what Lonergan means by the sharing of cognitive, constitutive, and effective meaning. This communication becomes rhetoric when it is raised to the level of art, and it is Christian preaching when that art is concerned explicitly with communicating the relationships, values, insights, and projects, the sharing of which constitutes the

Christian community. It will also become apparent that Tolkien's three requirements of the preacher—insight, virtue, and art—can be correlated to Lonergan's three aspects of meaning and that they designate precisely the qualities that permit the attainment of Augustine's three goals of Christian rhetoric.[18]

a. The Need for Insight: The Sharing of Cognitive Meaning: The Rhetorical Goal of Teaching

Human discourse, we have noted, normally involves the communication of information. When such information goes beyond the level of immediate sensible experience and involves understandings of the world, judgments, values, personal relations, it belongs to the sphere of what Lonergan calls "cognitive meaning"; and when the sharing of such cognitive meaning takes places as an art, one has the realization of the rhetorical goal of teaching or informing. In the Christian context, as we have seen in our examination of the New Testament, preaching involves primarily the cognitive meaning which is the "good news"—the message of salvation centered in the remembrance of Jesus—and, secondarily, all the implications that message has for human life, that is, Christian theology. In this perspective it is obvious why insight is, as Tolkien points out, a necessary requirement of the preacher: insight into the message to be preached and into its implications; into the audience to receive the message, and into the preacher's own self in the light of the message; in short, theological insight. These brief and undeveloped observations will suffice to introduce what will be the major concern of the final section of this essay: the relation of theological insight to art in the practice of preaching.

*b. The Need for Virtue: The Sharing of Effective Meaning:
The Rhetorical Goal of Persuading*

Human meaning is also effective or efficient; that is, it involves not only the contemplative knowing but also the active making of the world and of human life itself in accord with our ideas and values, hopes, and plans. To share one's effective meaning with others is to invite them to act in accord with one's insights and values, that is, rhetorically to "touch" their minds and hearts and persuade them to a certain course of behavior. In the case of Christian preaching, this means the calling of people to conversion and to the life of self-giving charity in response to God's initiative of love. It is clear, then, why virtue is a requirement for the preacher. Intellectual insight and moral goodness are not the same; yet neither can they be completely separated, particularly when the object of insight is the moral life itself. Without the habits of virtue, the preacher would be lacking the experience that spiritual insights and value judgments must be based on. Moreover, persuasion is the effort to bring others to share the value of one's judgments and decisions, and, hence, it is also an invitation to put faith in the speaker. But such an invitation can hardly be convincing or moving if one does not practice what one preaches, and, as the adage says, "actions speak louder than words" in conveying one's own conviction of the message.

In the contemporary world, the need for "virtue" in the preacher takes on a broader meaning. As the world has grown smaller and the interdependence of all people with each other and with the natural world has become more apparent, we are more than ever conscious of the social and ecological dimensions of morality. The human good and the good of the world depends ever increasingly on human collaboration.[19] In this circumstance, the virtue of the preacher must consist not merely in personal goodness on the level of immediate relations; he or she must be one who is further able to realize and to communicate the moral connections between individuals, communities, and the wider world.

The habitual exercise of such moral insightfulness corresponds with what the Thomist tradition calls the virtue of prudence, not in its common degenerated sense of caution, but in the sense of right practical reasoning in situations, through which we know what is concretely good. Today especially the practice of this virtue will imply the ability to take the long-term moral view, overcoming the biases or blind spots that narrow our horizon to egotistical or group interests and prevent us from seeing that our short-term benefit may be at the long-term expense of other persons and communities (including those yet to come).[20] Although examples of this dimension of virtue could be taken from many areas (ecology, world peace, political responsibility, etc.) a single illustration must suffice for our purposes here.

In the last months of his life, the great author Leo Tolstoy came to a personal crisis which had been building for many years. Shortly before he ran away from his home and family and died in a provincial railroad station, Tolstoy had written in a letter to a peasant:

> You ask whether I like the life I am now leading. No, I do not. I do not like it because I am living with my family in luxury, while around me there is poverty and need, and I can neither extricate myself from the luxury nor remedy the poverty and need. This I do not like. But what I do like about my life is that I do what is within my power, and to the extent of my power, to follow Christ's precept and love God and my neighbor. To love God means to love the perfection of good and to draw as close as you can to it. To love your neighbor means to love all men equally as your brothers and sisters. It is to this, and this alone, that I aspire.

And since I am approaching it little by little, though imperfectly, I do not despair but rejoice.

You ask too whether I rejoice, and if so over what—what joy I expect. I rejoice that I can fulfill to the extent of my powers the lesson given me by the Master: to work for the establishment of that Kingdom of God toward which we all strive.[21]

The anguish that Tolstoy experienced in his personal situation—being chained by family and circumstance to a life of comparative comfort, while seeing around himself abject poverty—might easily find an echo in the conscience of Christians in the contemporary First World. As a society, we enjoy a disproportionate amount of the world's products and use the major portion of its energy and resources; we live in comparative comfort and security, and we take for granted a standard of living and enjoyment unprecedented in history. At the same time, we are surrounded by the almost unbelievable condition of misery of a vast portion of the human race—the Third World—and, like Tolstoy, we find ourselves unable either to eliminate the poverty and misery or to escape from our own sometimes complacent comfort, or perhaps even from the desire for ever more riches in the form of goods, services, experiences.

It is notable, moreover, that Tolstoy saw not only the poverty, but also the luxury as a problem; if poverty dehumanizes, so does excessive comfort. As Tolstoy saw, the life of luxury is spiritually deadening for two interconnected reasons. First, the well-being of the few seems to be—at least in part, and perhaps involuntarily—dependent upon the exploitation of the poverty of the many, a situation that remains problematic even when that "exploitation" is at the same time the means of the economic development of Third World countries. Second, material satisfactions and attractions can close our hearts to the true values of life and its ultimate meaning: the kingdom of God, the value of persons and of love, with the attendant need for self-discipline and self-criticism, for conversion and sometimes self-sacrifice.

Thus the contemporary Christian, like Tolstoy, must feel somewhat uncomfortable with our situation; if we have an awakened mind and conscience, we cannot totally like our lives. But, again like Tolstoy, we find there is something that we can like: the fact that we can do something about our condition, that we can strive to free ourselves to follow Christ's commandment to love God and our neighbor.

It follows that Christian virtue in our society (and the preaching that flows from it) must have an essential concern with liberation. Although the term *theology of liberation* has primarily been associated with currents of contemporary thought in the Third World, and particularly in Latin America,[22] a reflection on our situation shows that it is by no means out of place in the prosperous First World as well.

Indeed, liberation is one way of stating the essential meaning of the Christian message, the good news itself. In Luke's Gospel in particular, the work of Christ is seen as the power of God's Spirit bringing the freedom of the Kingdom to the alienated world. In the "program discourse" (Lk 4:18–21), Jesus announces that the prophecy of Isaiah has been fulfilled in his person:

> The spirit of the Lord is upon me;
>> therefore he has anointed me.
> He has sent me to bring glad tidings to the poor,
>> to proclaim liberty to captives,
> Recovery of sight to the blind,
>> and release to prisoners,
> To announce a year of favor from the Lord. (NAB)

There are many levels to liberation. Its goal is the attainment of freedom: the ability to be or to act; more deeply, the capacity to determine one's existence toward the good. Human freedom, however, is always to be attained by the overcoming of the existential obstacles to such self-determination; and these obstacles are of different kinds.

On a physical level, there is a lack of freedom which consists in subservience to alien forces: the impersonal forces of uncontrolled nature, manifested in accident and sickness (conceived in the ancient world as the reign of personal demonic powers); or the impersonal and depersonalizing forces of economic and social servitude, poverty, and injustice. Obviously, this form of lack of freedom is most significant in those areas of the world which are materially underdeveloped and are dominated by internal and external forms of exploitation.

There are, however, other levels of freedom to be attained even when physical, material, and political liberty are taken for granted. On a psychological level, freedom is the ability to act without compulsion or obsession: freedom from anxiety, from psychic "blind spots" that prevent us from facing reality,[23] from the fear of self-knowledge. Although mental health is to a large extent conditioned by physiological and chemical factors, a dimension of meaning is also present: To be free psychologically means also to have the liberty to hope, to find life meaningful, to face the truth about one's self and the world, to be able to apprehend and be attracted by the beautiful, to be capable of giving and receiving love.

On an intellectual level, freedom means the overthrow of prejudice and bias, the courageous opening of the mind, the surmounting of mythology, the ability to attend to the data, to imagine new possibilities, to reach insight, to achieve and to criticize formulations and concepts, to weigh evidence dispassionately, to make sound judgments. It means liberation from inattentiveness, stupidity, and rashness; overcoming the power of obscurantism, the myth of materialism, the narrowness of ideology and unexamined presuppositions.

On a moral level, freedom is the ability to orient one's existence on the basis of values: the beautiful and the good. It implies liberation from slavery to the unintegrated drives of the lower levels of our animal being, to societal conditioning, and, above all, to the spontaneous egotism that marks our being as "fallen."

Finally, there is the "freedom of the children of God," the liberation that comes from the acceptance of God's gift of self: liberation from death and sin, from the constraints of the Law, from the intrinsic limitations of our finitude, and freedom for life in the Spirit and for absolute love. This is what St. Augustine referred to as the freeing of freedom itself: The love of God grounds every other dimension of freedom and integrates the whole of human transcendence into a final meaning and goal.

The attainment of any level of freedom implies a "conversion," a transformation of the subject and his or her world.[24] Each level of conversion implies and calls for every other. Furthermore, the attainment of internal or spiritual freedom is intrinsically connected with the achievement of political and social freedom because it is only by an act of self-transcendence that we can overcome the prevailing group bias that prevents us from seeing that the interests of our particular class, group, or society may be achieved at the expense of the good of others.[25]

Hence—to return to Tolstoy's insight—the spiritual freeing of the "haves" in our society is inextricably connected with the political, social, and economic liberation of the "have nots," both among us and in the materially underdeveloped nations of the world. Moreover, without a basis in personal conversion the preaching of the "social" dimension of the gospel will almost invariably be seen as an unwarranted interference of religion—conceived as a purely internal and "otherworldly" phenomenon—with the unspiritual realm of the world, and will meet with resistance and resentment. The preaching of social justice must be able to make a connection between the spiritual—the realm of transcendence—and the concrete circumstances of our daily existence, including our sociopolitical and global situation. Hence, virtue today means that the preacher must have attained a certain degree of freedom on its various levels, from the psychological to the spiritual.

c. The Need for Art: The Sharing of Constitutive Meaning: The Rhetorical Goal of Pleasing

Meaning is "constitutive" when human insights, judgments, and values in themselves create a new reality, that is, create the human world, the world constituted by meaning. Our interpretation of life shapes our conscious being and, hence, makes us what we are as human subjects. Our personal meanings make us individuals; our shared meanings make us communities. To share one's constitutive meaning, then, is to build community, for community is nothing other than the achievement of common meaning: Common experiences, understandings, judgments, and decisions constitute families, nations, religions.[26]

If we understand Augustine's rhetorical aim of "pleasing" or "charming" the audience in its deepest sense, we will see that it has an intrinsic connection with sharing the constitutive dimension of meaning. Human dialogue in general aims at some kind of communion of life and sharing of the good. The attainment of that goal brings satisfaction to a basic human need and desire. Thus every positive act of communication in some way and to some degree affirms the other's being and contributes to the other's life. On its most profound level, then, the pleasure (or perhaps better, fulfillment) aimed at in rhetoric is not merely that provided by well-turned phrases and elegant discourse (to which the contemporary ear, at least, is in any case not very well attuned), but that of finding common meaning or communion of life. The hearer is charmed or engaged by a discourse that reveals meaningfulness and therefore gives a vision of beauty. In Christian preaching, the goal is the communication of the joy and peace that characterize God's kingdom.

The sharing of constitutive meaning is necessarily a work of art (in the wider sense of *creativity*): not the creation of beautiful objects, but of ourselves and our communities as embodiments of moral and spiritual beauty. It should result in the joy of hope, the inner assurance of fulfillment of our total being. Art (in the narrower sense) is required of the preacher to bring forth that joy; the style of speaking (as well as the spirit of the speaker) must evoke and sacramentalize the beauty that it proclaims. The rhetorical skill of speaking well, of pleasing the ear by well-constructed and well-spoken discourse, is therefore important. But even more significant is that what is communicated be beautiful in itself, through its correspondence to the deepest human desire. The manifestation of this correspondence requires in the preacher a certain poetic skill: the ability to engage the minds, hearts, and affects of hearers with a vision of goodness based on faith.

The achievement of this task implies a further dimension of the liberation of which we spoke in the last section. Crucial to the preacher is the poetic liberation of the imagination. Every person lives and thinks within a context, a mental "horizon," which at the same time gives meaning to our thoughts and actions and limits their possibilities. The meaning of conversion is the opening of our horizons (at the various levels of our being) to what is "other" or "beyond": to the transcendent and mysterious, that which is not within our control but challenges us and draws us

190 • Theology and the Arts

out of ourselves.[27] The "other" is to be encountered in every human person, as well as in the absolute Otherness of God. But the encounter is possible only on the condition that we allow the other to be itself, rather than reducing it to a function of our consciousness and world.

The imagination is critical in enabling this encounter to take place. Through it, what initially is simply "other" can be seen to be in some manner analogous to what one has already experienced. Hence, the encounter is revealed as genuinely possible: The unknown, the other, is not merely alien, but corresponds to an openness in one's own being. Our true identity is not locked within our present selfhood or horizon but is to be found precisely in the dialogue with the other.

It is the function of the preacher to enable the imagination to function on this level of analogy and empathy. This will mean liberating the imagination from its usual and familiar courses, breaking it free of its common sense, attracting it to a different vision. (As the contemporary movement of virtue ethics reminds us, we learn moral behavior more effectively by the examples of concrete models and paradigms of goodness than by codes of prohibitions or by deduction of norms from abstract principles.) Moreover, this vision must be seen *as* attractive, as beautiful in the deepest sense. The preacher's problem is not merely to inculcate moral principles, but to show convincingly the *goodness*, the attractiveness, of what is right, thus making it a psychologically possible option: to manifest the ultimately "fulfilling" nature of Christian love, even thought it demands self-sacrifice.

This means that preaching aims at the creation and nurturing of the "converted" and specifically Christian sense of beauty of which we have spoken earlier, so that this beauty and our pleasure in it, far from being escapist, have an intrinsic element of commitment to others, especially in their suffering. Eucharistic preaching takes place in the immediate context of the *anamnesis*, or ritual recollection, of the death and rising of Christ. In this sense, it is true to say that the goal of the homily will always include bringing this remembrance to existential awareness, making it a "dangerous" memory, one that has the power to (further) change our lives and (re)orient our values. This means also the relating of the Christ event to the ongoing history of suffering of humanity. The message of the cross and the resurrection allows us to see that history in terms of "contrast experiences"; that is, the experience of evil itself reveals our essential rejection of it, our hope for its overcoming, which is in turn based on our intrinsic orientation to goodness and beauty, our hope for the final peace symbolized by the biblical notions of peace, forgiveness, resurrection, the life of God's kingdom.[28]

In other words, the preacher must continually illustrate the gospel truth of the cross and resurrection, of finding one's self only by losing it. As we have seen above, this dimension of conversion is multileveled. Christian virtue must be conceived not only in terms of each individual, but also on the interpersonal, community, social, political, and ecological levels. This implies the need for aesthetic theology, that is, a theology that does not merely teach, but provides attractive and convincing images of "the good life" and the means of achieving it: a communal vision corresponding to the notion of God's kingdom and the kind of compassionate social relationships symbolized by the Eucharist.

Here there is need for profound art as well as profound insight because evil can easily seem more varied and interesting than good (is not Dante's *Inferno* much more fascinating than the *Paradiso*, and is not Milton's Satan the most appealing dramatic figure in *Paradise Lost*?). Novelist Brian Moore, when asked by an interviewer why he so frequently chose to write about people who have failed in life, replied simply that failures are more interesting than successful people. Similarly, Leo Tolstoy remarks in *Anna Karenina* that all happy families resemble one another, but each unhappy family is unhappy in its own way. *Bonum ex integra causa—malum ex quocumque defectu*, says the old adage—the good is integral; evil stems from any defect at all. Does this mean that evil will have more variety, more individuality, more intrinsic aesthetic interest than the good? C. S. Lewis writes to the contrary that "life is not like a river but like a tree...creatures grow further apart as they increase in perfection. Good, as it ripens, becomes continually more different not only from evil but from other good."[29] The better people become, the more like God, the more distinctive and unique they become; the goodness of God is simple, but its finite reflections must be infinitely varied. Why then are so many modern religious portrayals of goodness stereotypical, lacking in intellectual interest or appeal? Why are they all too frequently artistic kitsch? Unimaginative, shallow presentations can make virtue and community seem a dull and unappealing conformity rather than high adventure and the deepest, most intelligent and unique self-realization. Here lies the great challenge for preaching as aesthetic theology.

The concrete means of approaching this poetic task of preaching are multiple. Jesus uses parables to allow the breakthrough of an analogy to our situation. The contemporary preacher may through a careful exegesis and explanation of the scriptures attempt to draw the hearer's imagination into an unfamiliar view of the world that challenges our presuppositions and, hence, into an insight into the moral challenge of our contemporary world: If the ancient world can be seen as revealing genuine possibilities of the human for us, then the "others" of the contemporary situation may be seen likewise as inviting us to a reevaluation of our lives. (Such a method is particularly inviting in the light of the themes of Luke's Gospel, in which Jesus' compassion for the poor and oppressed plays so large and clear a part.) Or, as I shall suggest below, the preacher may adopt a more explicitly "correlational" strategy, appealing to the hearers' experience and attempting to raise from it the question about human existence to which the gospel message of love presents the answer. In this process, references to poetry, literature, film, and art are frequently effective means of evoking experience in a concentrated and vivid way that invites both insight and affective openness.

C. PREACHING AND FAITH
IN THE CONTEMPORARY WORLD

We have seen that preaching had a primary place both in the mission of Jesus and in the New Testament period. We have noted that because for Christian faith the good news concerning God's historical acts in Jesus has the central place, the act of preaching has a nearly self-evident importance. It is also clear that our context has radically changed from that of the early church, and this change forces us to ask exactly what the preaching of the message means for us today, in the light of the nearly two thousand years of history since the first proclamation of the Christ event.

Obviously the existence of that history itself is a major challenge to a contemporary understanding of the Christian preacher's task. For many people, the good news is no longer new. Of course, there remains a task of evangelization in the missionary sense of bringing Christianity to new areas of the world. But most preaching today takes place within the church, that is, within a context in which the message has been heard and incorporated into a long tradition of reflection, structures, and modes of behavior. In this context, the New Testament emphasis on proclamation of something hitherto unknown is largely supplanted by the function of teaching—not merely repeating, but interpreting and showing the relevance of the message of Jesus and the message about Jesus for the contemporary situation.[30]

This is not to say that the function of the preacher as herald is lost, for the presentation of the message in a way that is understandable and applicable to contemporary life in general or to the particular here and now situation of a congregation makes it good news to the hearer, even if its content has long been known in an extrinsic way. Indeed, insofar as the purpose of the message is not merely to impart information, but to foster a present encounter with God through Jesus as the living Lord, what is preached is always new and unrepeatable: My encounter with God in the present moment itself constitutes a new reality for my being and a new imperative for my life. Faith as belief is oriented toward faith as living relation and dialogue, and the latter depends on hearing not merely facts to be accepted but a message that corresponds with and brings to explicit consciousness the interior dynamism of God's presence, whether experienced as questioning, as desire, as need, or as fulfillment and beauty.

Of course, for committed Christians such experiences are already largely formed and shaped by their faith language and culture—the tradition as appropriated by a particular group. At the same time, they contain an element that seeks to go beyond what is already known: They point to the inadequacy of any word or concept or language to contain God or our relationship to God. Hence, the preaching of the message has the task not only of evoking the associations of a faith already present, but also of provoking new faith experience by challenging us to growth.

As was noted above, to conceive faith as belief in the kerygma about Jesus or, in other words, as acceptance of Jesus as Lord, is to acknowledge that God is really and definitively manifested historically in the Christ event. But that event, culminating in Jesus' resurrection, is not simply a past fact: It includes the communication of the principle of Jesus' life—the Spirit of God—to his followers. Hence, as we have seen, virtue, in the Christian sense of our own living of the resurrected life according to and because of the model of Jesus and in his Spirit, is both a crucial element of what we profess and a condition for our making a credible profession.

The communication of the message about Jesus, therefore, remains central to Christian faith. The Christian preacher must not only evoke an interior sense of the divine life within us, but must also relate that life to the historical community gathered in Christ's memory. God's revelation is not merely "in" us, seeking outward symbolic expression but is always also what encounters us as "other" and through others, as an external word that constitutes our experience and forms our possibilities in certain concrete directions. This word is first of all the kergymatic message we have been speaking of.

The knowledge and celebration of the Christ event constitute a new dimension of the saving presence of God and of the human possibility of faith as relation to God. They propose a vision of the value of history and community and a model of love that are perhaps more than ever relevant to the world. They point to the indispensability of Jesus as the witness and sign or sacrament of God's love actually triumphant in history. Nevertheless, the affirmation of Christian faith does not exclude more universal access and relation to God, by God's self-revealing gift. Hence, there is also another dimension of the external word of God: that which is implicit in our human experience in

196 • Theology and the Arts

general, including both its non-Christian religious aspects and its secular manifestations. To this word—which is frequently ambiguous and mixed with the distortions stemming from human sinfulness—the preacher must also attend.

The complexity of the contemporary world makes it difficult to integrate these two dimensions of revelatory experience, which is exactly what Christian preaching attempts to do. In a general way, preaching may be described as speaking the Christian message—the word—to a particular situation. The word mediated by preaching is first of all the scriptural witness to God's action in Jesus. But it is this word insofar as it is interpreted and reflected on by the church's tradition and especially as it is connected with the liturgical, symbolic celebration of the sacraments, in particular the Eucharist. Hence, the scriptures "on" which we preach are not taken simply in their historical sense, but in the light of the whole scriptural and ecclesiastical tradition. They are juxtaposed with other texts and read and expounded in liturgical contexts both immediate (this community in this eucharistic celebration) and more general (the church's feasts, times, and seasons). Similarly, the situation to which the preacher addresses the word is complex: It includes the general culture, the changing world-historical context, and the particular circumstances of a congregation. For this reason, preaching today particularly needs to be integrated with the reflection on faith that is theology. I will suggest that, although there are different theological methods that are compatible with the contemporary preacher's task, there is a particular relevance of the methods of a correlational type of theology, especially of that kind that the Roman Catholic tradition names fundamental or foundational theology.

D. THEOLOGY IN THE ART OF PREACHING

A significant part of the art of preaching, as of any art, is the mastery of technique. A major part of this concerns physical delivery: proper breathing and good projection, clear enunciation, pace, variation of pitch, and so on. Beyond these are more properly rhetorical concerns like the effective use of pauses, periodic sentences, grammatical construction, modulation of voice, choice of language, and the various "styles" of speech. As anyone who has ever prepared a homily knows, however, the method of delivery is only the last part of the process of communication. As in any profound art, as distinguished from the merely decorative, it is not technique but content that is the decisive factor: Good communication is fruitless unless there is something significant to communicate. In the art of preaching, it is theological depth that marks the significance of content.

1. TYPES OF THEOLOGY AND OF PREACHING

As we have already remarked, the content of Christian preaching will naturally have some connection with the systematic reflection on faith which is theology. Nevertheless, the degree and kind of connection can vary widely, depending upon the context and purpose of the preaching. In some circumstances preaching is principally oriented to eliciting an emotional or ethical response: to comforting, encouraging, exhorting. In such cases, the preacher will draw primarily on the poetry of religion. At other times, preaching more explicitly envisages teaching or instruction. Even here, however, different modes are possible, ranging from pure exegesis and exposition of biblical texts to reflective analysis of current events.

Moreover, theology itself has different forms and methods that may be auxiliary to preaching. Paul Tillich spoke of two fundamental kinds of theology: kerygmatic theology, which emphasizes the unchanging truth of the original Christian message (*kerygma*), and apologetic theology, which attempts to respond to the current human situation by correlating its implicit questions with the answers implicit in the Christian message.[31]

David Tracy goes a step farther than Tillich, dividing theology into three complementary types or "specialties," distinguished by points of view corresponding to the principal audience of each.

Foundational theologies are directed primarily to the academy. The specialty of foundations attempts to provide arguments that all persons, religious or not, can recognize as reasonable. Of the traditional transcendental qualities of being, it emphasizes truth. Like philosophical metaphysics, to which it is related, it stresses honest and critical inquiry and uses argument and dialectic in its conversations.[32]

Systematic theologies are directed to the church: They re-present and reinterpret "what is assumed to be the ever-present disclosive and transformative power" of the theologian's tradition. Their primary value is loyalty or creative and critical fidelity to that tradition.[33] Such theologies emphasize the transcendental "the beautiful" insofar as it is true and is related to the religious or holy. Systematics is cognate to the disciplines of poetics and rhetoric; its major mode of operation is interpretation as "conversation" with the religious classics.[34]

Practical theologies are directed to society. Their primary criterion is praxis—practice informed by and informing theory. They value especially responsible commitment to and/or involvement in the situation envisaged by praxis.[35] Practical theologies embody the transcendental "the good" as true and related to the religious or holy. Because it is oriented to socially transforming faith-praxis, practical theology relates particularly to the disciplines of ethics and politics. Its major mode of conversation is the Christian critique of ideology, sometimes combined with positive proposals for the future ideal situation.[36]

Without insisting on an exact correspondence, we may discern suggestive affinities between Tracy's three theological specialties (foundational, systematic, practical) and Augustine's three goals of religious rhetoric (teaching, pleasing, persuading); Tolkien's trinity of qualities required of the preacher (insight, art, virtue); and Lonergan's three dimensions of shared meaning (cognitive, constitutive, effective). Just as the latter triads refer not to three different types of preaching but to the characteristics of all preaching (although one or the other aspect may be stressed in a particular situation), so Tracy's three specialties represent not so much three different theological sources for preaching or three different methods it may pursue, but rather three theological elements that may be present to varying degrees in any homily or sermon, depending on its context, audience, and purpose.

Nevertheless, it might appear that because of its normal liturgical context, there is a natural congruence between preaching (at least of the kind we are concerned with here) and the systematic branch of theology that is addressed *ad intra* to believers within the church and that stresses the coherence and beauty of the message.

This connection seems to be illustrated with particular aptness by the seasons of the liturgical year. The readings for each Sunday of Advent and Lent, for example, are not only carefully arranged in thematic relation to one another; in addition, there is a thematic sequence from one Sunday to the next. These seasons therefore provide the opportunity for an eminently intratextual approach to preaching, one that sees the scriptural passages in relation to each other and expounds from them a coherent view or picture or paradigm of the world and of human life in relation to God. The scriptures, read in the light of the church's tradition, become a lens (to use Calvin's metaphor) through which the believer is invited to see the world and his or her experience. It is the unveiling of the coherence of the message in its spiritual beauty, its convincing attractiveness as a God-given way of viewing reality that is (or should be) the preacher's main concern. From this alluring beauty flows the imperative—indeed, the desire—to imitate the moral examples that show what it is to live by this vision.

Christian preaching within the church—that is, leaving aside the special case of missionary situations—seems classically to have taken primarily this approach (although—as Tolkien's remarks remind us—this is not by any means to say that preachers have always followed the classical pattern or, when they have attempted it, that they have done so successfully—i.e., insightfully, persuasively, and artfully). Nevertheless, without denying the legitimacy and fruitfulness of this kind of preaching, in what follows I shall argue that there is a particular suitability in contemporary preaching, even within the church, for attention to the perspectives and methods of the foundational type of theology, especially as embodying a method of correlation between faith and secular existence.

2. FOUNDATIONAL THEOLOGY AND CONTEMPORARY PREACHING

There is a great attractiveness to the idea of a poetic, rhetorical approach to preaching, centered on the intrinsic beauty of the message itself. At the same time, it must be acknowledged that preaching must take account of the difficulties inherent in presenting the Christian message in the contemporary context in which most Western believers live. That context is marked by pluralism, secularity, and the absence of a Christian or even religious context for daily existence. As we have remarked several times above, the kind of beauty present in the Christian message not only calls for spiritual conversion (which may be presumed to be present, to a greater or lesser degree, in the normal congregation), but also requires familiarity with an intellectual and aesthetic language that is increasingly foreign to those brought up in the contemporary world, including believers. We may ask, then, whether there is not a particular need for another kind of preaching alongside the intratextual and systematic: a kind of preaching that might be called foundational in that it explicitly addresses the problem of faith's relevance (or lack thereof) to the contemporary situation. Such preaching must also be artful and must ultimately unveil the intrinsic beauty, the attractiveness and joy, of the Christian message, but it does so in a way more conscious of the difficulties many contemporary people have in relating to the beauty of the message, precisely because of its aesthetic and intellectual distance from their lives.

A seminary classmate once preached a homily that he began by speaking about the importance of the Word of God in our lives. He had not spoken more than a few sentences when the sound of a radio became audible, apparently coming from immediately outside the windows. At first it was a minor distraction, but the volume gradually grew to a point where the speaker could no longer be heard. He stopped and stood in obviously perplexed silence as the harsh noise of rock music filled the chapel. After a few moments, the radio stopped, and the preacher made his point. It turned out that the whole incident had been prearranged to serve as a parable illustrating the situation that the church faces in general today: The Word of God is drowned out by the noise of secular society.

The same point has been made on numerous occasions by the Nobel laureate author Aleksandr Solzhenitsyn.[37] Western society has the blessing of free speech. But freedom does not guarantee responsibility; freedom of speech applies to falsity as well as truth, hatred as well as love, shallowness as well as profundity. The result in practice is that every message of truth must compete with error, ignorance and shallowness in an uncontrolled intellectual "free market." In some ways, Solzhenitsyn says, this is a great deal more dangerous than the suppression of truth by totalitarian societies, because when truth is persecuted, it is all the more sought; when spoken by courageous spirits, it stands out all the more clearly against the background of official lies. But what can the speaker of truth do when the message is perfectly permitted but is drowned in a sea of trivia?

In this context, the essential challenge to preaching is to find a point of contact for the Christian message in the lives and consciousness of its hearers. It can no longer be assumed that the intrinsic beauty of the message (whether biblical, dogmatic, or ethical) immediately resonates either with contemporary people's experience or with an unquestioned acceptance of traditional views; on the contrary, the preacher's exhortations will frequently be met with a (perhaps only half-conscious) suspicion of romanticism or mythology. As Karl Rahner has written,

> ...until now preachers have usually taken it too much for granted that they are operating within the framework of the Church as something indisputable and self-evident, so that they need only set forth whatever the Church says. But nowadays, even in mystagogical preaching within the bosom of the Church preachers are addressing people whose relation to the teaching office and even to the faith-consciousness of the Church as a whole is not as ingenuous and naive as it used to be.[38]

Preaching today and in our society must be explicitly cognizant of the unbelief that is a part of the context of each believer so that "proclamation 'inside' should not differ now from proclamation 'to the outside.'"[39]

It may be argued—as it is by Karl Barth and Hans Urs von Balthasar—that the most effective kind of apologetic theology is systematic (dogmatic) theology—the presentation of God's revelation in its coherent beauty and persuasiveness—and that the same applies to preaching. Balthasar's method in particular envisions a form of apologetics intimately united with dogmatics. He enunciates his "fundamental conviction" that

> you do good apologetics if you do good, central theology; if you expound theology effectively, you have done the best kind of apologetics. The Word of God (which is also and always the activity of God) is self-authenticating proof of its own truth and fecundity—and it is precisely in this way that the church and the believer are inserted into one another. The man who wants this Word to be heard in what he has to say... does not need to resort to another discipline (called Fundamental Theology) to gain a hearing for it.[40]

As commentator John Riches puts it, for Balthasar "Divine authority in its revelation as *doxa* [glory] requires no other justification than itself; its rightness, like that of a work of art, has its own evidential force for those who see it."[41] This may be true; but only for those who "see" it. The problem is that many—even among believers—do not "see" the Christian message as self-evidently beautiful, or they "see" its beauty but only as one claimant among many to truth. Keats's dictum—"What the imagination seizes as beauty must be truth"—may strike some people as the opposite of self-evident: Beauty can be deceitful, and human beings are prone to self-deception. Hence, there is

204 • Theology and the Arts

a need for the explicit examination of the question of the truth of this beautiful vision and a dialectical comparison with the alternative options for our commitment.

Few people are so integrated in their faith or its tradition that these form the sole context for hearing the message. For most of us, there is a constant mixture of belief and unbelief, conversion and unconversion; there are areas of our experience that have not yet been confronted by or integrated with the vision of faith; there are areas of faith that have not yet been examined in the light of our life decisions and worldviews.

Furthermore, more and more people today are located, at least in part, in the sphere that for Tracy is the primary "public" of foundational theology, that is, the "academy"—not that most congregations will be composed of professional academics, but increasing numbers in every congregation will have a higher education, and almost all will have more secular education than religious education, so that their primary mental language is that of secular society (science, technology, commerce, the market) rather that than of religious faith or tradition. Questions to faith that once might have been considered academic have attained currency within educated society, while the conditions for the practice of intratextual Christian discourse are weakening. Even George Lindbeck, a strong proponent of intratextual systematic theology as opposed to a fundamental-theological approach, admits this problem: "Those who share in the intellectual high culture of our day are rarely intensively socialized into coherent religious languages and communal forms of life."[42]

Even the practicing Christian in our society is to some extent living in a world of unbelief and to some extent unconsciously shares its presuppositions.[43] Hence, the preacher must be concerned with the horizon within which the message is to be received. It cannot necessarily be presumed that there already exists in the hearer an *explicit* spiritual and intellectual context that allows the message to make sense. The preacher's task will include the need to elicit in the hearers the kind of concerns that can bring about or make explicit the realization that the Christian message is of interest and worth listening to on an intellectual level at all, that it is beautiful not merely as an aesthetic object, but because it truly corresponds to our deepest human desires and needs. A post-Christian secularized society like those of the United States and Western Europe may indeed be more in need of "preevangelization" than the pre-Christian societies of the great missionary era, because in the latter there could usually be assumed a general sense of the "supernatural" and a concern for some transcendent meaning to existence; the preacher in a secular society, however, must frequently deal with deadened sensibilities and a widespread if unexamined cynicism about the reality of anything beyond the material values of the surrounding culture. Even if such attitudes are combined with an attachment to religious habits, symbols, and rituals, these may be valued for their cultural or sentimental associations, while their intellectual faith content is more or less consciously disregarded by the "cultural" Christian and is given a dogmatic assent by the pious that frequently remains on a notional level that offers little intellectual nourishment or moral guidance in facing the complex realities of everyday life.

Another challenge to contemporary preaching arises from the modern knowledge of competing religious interpretations and our democratic as well as religious presumption in favor of a universal divine revelation. The assertion of God's universal salvific will and of the value of non-Christian religions as means of salvation, as taught by the Second Vatican Council,[44] can lead to an emphasis on faith as a transcendental relationship, realized in various forms and languages. What then becomes of the specifically Christian good news, so essential to the very meaning of faith in the New Testament? In an age of cultural pluralism, why should the Christian tradition be normative, even for a Westerner, rather than a syncretism of ideas and beliefs? Why and in what sense is the proclamation specifically of the kerygma necessary to faith in its fullest dimension? Or, to put the question Christologically: What exactly does the Lordship of Jesus mean in relation to universal history and the plurality of approaches to God or the Ultimate?

Such questions touch on the essence not only of Christian preaching, but also of its principal setting, the liturgical celebration of the memory of Jesus' death and resurrection. The message *of* Jesus, the good news of the kingdom, is proclaimed in the context of the message *about* Jesus: that through the resurrection God's kingdom has been accomplished and made present for us in an anticipatory way, giving vision and power to our lives and relations with others. The contemporary preacher will have the task of showing how faith in Jesus is not a matter of affirming lifeless facts about the past, but is a dangerous memory with liberating implications and demands for our societal and individual lives; that the necessity and credibility of faith as belief in Jesus are not merely intellectual matters but are shown in this belief's actual world-transforming power, embodied and exemplified in the community of faith, living in love.

In short, although there is a constant and shifting relationship of preaching to theology in general, there is today a particular need for contemporary preaching to integrate within itself the theological specialty of foundations: the attempt of faith to "give answer" for itself (cf. 1 Pt 3:15) by an appeal to human reason and experience; that is, to find in the human subject the "connecting point" for faith. If this is so, then not only the content but also the method of fundamental or foundational theology will have a special relevance in the development of a contemporary exercise of the art of preaching.

3. METHOD IN FOUNDATIONAL THEOLOGY

Contemporary foundational theology explicitly aims at making possible the communication of the truth of faith or revelation to the concrete subjects of our society. To this end it generally follows some form of what Tillich called a method of correlation,[45] an attempt to find the correspondence between the concrete human situation and the message of Christianity. Human life is seen to imply ultimate questions whose answer is to be found in God's self-revelation. The answers given by God and preached by the church can only be meaningful insofar as they correspond to existential questions; hence, a crucial aspect of the method of correlation is the analysis of the human situation out of which such questions arise. It must then be shown that the symbols used in Christian faith are the answers to these questions.[46] David Tracy modifies Tillich's project by including the insights of the "hermeneutical turn" of contemporary theology. In Tracy's formulation of a "revised method of correlation," Christian theology is seen as the attempt to establish mutually critical correlations between an interpretation of the Christian tradition and an interpretation of contemporary experience.[47]

A specific form of the analysis of the human situation in its dimension of ultimacy is the transcendental method. Taking as its starting point the acting human subject, this method attempts to uncover the necessary "conditions of possibility" of our actual experience, in particular of every act of knowledge and love, and to show that these can provide philosophical warrant for considering the truth claims made by Christianity for its revelation.[48]

On a first level, transcendental method (particularly as explained by Lonergan) consists simply of the recurrent operations of the mind or spirit by which it functions on a human level. In this sense, it is the basic method that underlies all methods whatsoever and comprises the pattern of being sensitive, attending to data, inquiring, coming to insights, formulating them, weighing evidence, judging, evaluating, and making decisions. Its norms are not formulated rules but are the spontaneously operative "transcendental precepts": "Be attentive, Be intelligent, Be reasonable, Be responsible."[49]

On a second level, transcendental method means the explicit knowledge, objectification, and formulation of these norms. The procedures of knowing are applied to the process of knowing itself. In this sense, transcendental method is a philosophical pursuit that consists of heightening one's consciousness by objectifying it.[50] The results are the answers to the questions, "What am I doing when I am knowing? Why is doing that knowing? What do I know when I do it?"—or cognitional theory, epistemology, and metaphysics.[51] In other words, transcendental method on this level unveils the basic condition of all human knowledge and responsible action by objectifying the permanent and invariant structures of the subject who does the knowing and acting.

The relevance of this method to theology now becomes apparent. It is transcendental not only in the Scholastic sense of going beyond any particular ("categorical") field, but also in the Kantian sense of revealing the a priori conditions of possibility of our knowledge in general.[52] It therefore also provides an analysis of the anthropological conditions of possibility for revelation and faith; that is, the very structures of the act of knowing disclose the human subject as transcendent, or as "open" to an infinite horizon beyond the self.[53]

Critical to transcendental method is the performance of the subject. Because this method is essentially the thematic appropriation of one's consciousness, it necessarily depends upon one's having and adverting to the relevant conscious experiences. Only in the *act* of knowing or loving can their conditions of possibility be discerned. Hence the affirmations arrived at by transcendental method are in principle verifiable by each person through the examination of experience and its implications.

The turn to the subject as the starting point for basic method also implies the possibility of an "anthropological turn" for theology. Transcendental method shows that every statement discloses not only the object about which it is affirmed, but also the subject who makes the affirmation; that is, we can discern the conditions of possibility of reasonably and responsibly making such a statement and the limitations of its validity. Applied to theology, this insight implies the possibility of an "anthropological reduction" of theological statements: that is, every affirmation about God can be restated in terms of its conditions of possibility in the human subject. This in turn implies that every theological statement should be capable of being articulated in terms not only of its verifiability, but also of its existential meaning for human being and, therefore, also its beauty and its capacity to draw our assent and commitment.

Finally, transcendental method as I conceive it necessarily includes a dialectical moment.[54] This dialectic has two principal aspects: the contrasting of every theological affirmation with opposing positions, and the contrasting of both with the experience and performance of the subject in which it is grounded. Hence transcendental method is at the same time self-critical and intersubjective or dialogical.

It will be clear that this method offers a fruitful approach to correlating the affirmations of faith with the human subject as such and, hence, is of great significance for apologetic or foundational theology. It is my suggestion that the concerns of this branch of theology ought also to be those of contemporary preaching. I will further suggest that the theological method outlined here may be applicable—in an analogous way—to the art of homiletics and that its characteristics correspond to the major goals of preaching.

E. INSIGHT, VIRTUE, AND ART
IN FOUNDATIONAL THEOLOGY

The Christian dimensions of cognitive, effective, and con-stitutive meaning are clearly central to the concern of theol-ogy as a whole. The possibility of the sharing of these dimensions is of particular concern to the special field of foundational theology. Although this theological specialty is not per se dedicated to the rhetoric of faith, given the situ-ation of the contemporary world it is logical that the area of theology involved with believability should be especially relevant to the pastoral concern for communication of the message. That is to say, foundational theology is concerned with uncovering the "connecting point" of the message with its audience: the conditions in the hearer that make it possi-ble for this message to instruct, persuade, and please—to be apprehended as true, good, and beautiful.

By the same token, the attributes of the effective preacher —insight, virtue, and art—come to play a particularly important role in this branch of theology, especially in the exercise of the transcendental method. As has been noted, this method consists in a heightening of the subject's own consciousness and an appropriation of its performance. Although all theology should in theory involve personal engagement rather than mere concepts, this kind of method is more explicitly personal in that it depends upon and for-mulates the theologian's actual *practice* of responsible faith: attaining insight, living the converted life, and constituting a symbolic community with others through shared Christian meanings.

The practitioner of transcendental method must advert to this practice and ask about its conditions of possibility. If Christian faith (or any particular part of the message) is the answer, what is the *question* in ourselves that it corresponds to? What is it in human experience—in *my* experience—that permits and calls for conversion and self-giving love as a responsible option? What makes the Christian message—whose central focus includes the cross—a source of joy and peace, a reason for hope, a revelation and fulfillment of our deepest desires? In short, what is it in us that allows us to perceive this message as beautiful? If the conditions of possibility of receiving a revelation from God do exist in us, then why is our performance so frequently at variance with its acceptance? What are the obstacles to conversion, and why do they exist? Such will be the kind of questions the transcendental theologian will ask in discerning the possibility of faith. It is my suggestion that the same questions could profitably be adopted by the preacher in discerning the relevance of the message to the contemporary congregation.

F. THEOLOGICAL METHOD AND ART
IN HOMILY PREPARATION

In conclusion it will perhaps not be amiss to offer some suggestions on how the project of transcendental theological method might figure in the concrete preparation for preaching.

If one begins with Tillich's idea of correlation of the Christian message with a human situation, the first step for the preacher will be to determine the content of the message to be communicated. In the case of the Sunday homily, this content is generally mediated by particular texts and by their liturgical context. This means that careful *exegesis* will ordinarily be a necessary factor in homily preparation. (There may be occasions, of course, when simple exegesis will suffice for preaching, but these will probably be exceptional. On the other hand, even when exegesis of the text will occupy a minimal place in the actual preaching, it remains the indispensable starting point for the preacher's preparation.)

The interpretation of the liturgical readings will have several dimensions. One must begin with an understanding of each text's words and the author's intent and context, but one must also go beyond these in one's understanding of the matter being treated in the text and of one's own context.[55] Furthermore, the liturgical texts are not read by themselves or in their original scriptural context but in a specific aesthetic/theological framework; that is, in relation to other selected texts, with which they stand in greater or lesser thematic unity and (within that unity) in complementary or dialectical relation. This juxtaposition of texts—in the context of the eucharistic celebration—constitutes in effect a new redaction and brings to light further dimensions of meaning that go beyond those of the single passages. From this multiplicity of meanings the preacher must determine a theme, which may be based on one of the readings, on their conjunction, on their relation to the liturgical season, or on their relation to some extrinsic factor: current events, the particular congregation, and so on.

The determination of a theme brings the preacher into the second major aspect of correlation: the human situation to which the message is addressed. A second major step in preparation, then, will be *meditative prayer*. One must not merely read the texts intelligently in their context(s); it is crucial that one reads them "before God" and in the context of one's own life. Before preaching can become a genuine and personal encounter with the Christian community, it must first be the preacher's face-to-face encounter with God. Here the preacher's virtue comes into play as the readiness to be converted more deeply by the word to be preached. The preacher must ask: What is the word of God being presented *to me*? One will find in prayer what Bultmann called the existential imperative of the message: the dimension of conversion or relation to God here and now that is implied by its acceptance. (This process may also imply the demythologization of certain texts, that is, getting beyond its objectification of the supernatural in finite terms to the transcendent meaning symbolized.)

From the act of encounter and conversion in prayer arises the theological moment of methodical *transcendental reflection*. Having discerned an existential meaning in the message, one may ask about its conditions of possibility. Here, existential intellectual insight is crucial. What is the "point of insertion" of this message in a human being? What horizon must be present in order to receive it, specifically as beautiful, as attractive, desirable, lovable? What does it say about the receiver? What is it in our common humanity that makes this message relevant for the author, for myself, for the church? On the other hand, one may inquire dialectically: What are the obstacles to receiving this message or fulfilling this imperative? Why do I not see its beauty or, seeing it, shrink from its beauty, rather than welcoming it? What implicit presuppositions of my thought or behavior does it challenge? In asking about the conditions in the subject for receiving God's word, one states its theological content in anthropological terms; one uncovers the question to which this word is the response. One arrives then at a statement of the message, which is immediately relevant to our human being, which reveals our selfhood in its most profound dimension of possibility: its openness to God.

Finally, there is a need for *concretization*. One must find examples of the anthropological dimension that has been revealed in the life experiences shared by the congregation. Such examples may be positive or negative, showing the implicit presence of the transcendent horizon or its absence. It is here that imagination and art are crucial. It might seem that a form of preaching that emphasizes cognitive meaning and truth might place less emphasis on art than those that are oriented primarily to the coherent beauty of the message itself. In practice, however, the reverse may be true. Preaching as teaching, if it aims at genuine insight, does not require less virtue or art than preaching as persuading and pleasing do; it must on the contrary be particularly attentive to these aspects of preaching, without which it would be arid and divorced from life. (This of course remains the perpetual danger of any "intellectual" discourse.)[56] The method of correlation will not merely show an intellectual correspondence, but will also expose the practical existential imperative of God's word to us, and its inherent desirability or beauty as the ultimate fulfillment of our being. Moreover, the intellectual aspect of preaching (insight) should of course be complemented by a mode of celebration that bespeaks sincerity and prayerful encounter (virtue) rather than mere ritualism, and by a liturgical context that is beautiful (art).

Art should not only be a part of the liturgical context, but should enter into this form of preaching itself in two ways. First of all, the presentation must be rhetorically pleasing, skillful, and interesting. Second, the content will frequently depend on artistic examples to evoke insight. One cannot normally take a congregation through one's own lengthy process of reflection and prayer; one must find a dramatic instance that exemplifies the point in a way that captures the mind and draws its attention to the point, an instance in which the hearer's own experience of transcendence (or lack thereof) is evoked in a provocative way. As we have seen above, the arts frequently epitomize the situation that faith must address, the spirit of the age, more fully and certainly more evocatively than its explicit philosophy. Hence, literature and film are particularly good sources for the preacher. But homiletic examples may also be stories from personal experience, items in the news, occurrences in local life. If they are artfully conceived, they will be more than a mere hook to draw the audience into the subject; they will be examples of the unnoticed presence of the transcendent dimension—at least as a question—in every aspect of human life. They should thus provide a basis for recognizing a point of insertion for the Christian message in the hearer's own experience. Finally, the beauty of this message itself, although not necessarily the primary content of preaching, is implicitly present in its correlation with our transcendent desire and need for God.

In preaching itself, of course, the order of the four steps I have outlined will usually be changed and will frequently be reversed. One might generally start with a concrete example and then show how this experience implies, on the one hand, a transcendental dimension in our humanity, a question about God and salvation, or, on the other hand, the refusal of that dimension, which also raises the question in a dialectical way. One would then relate this question to the existential "answer" embodied in God's word in the texts, leading the congregation to a disposition for prayer, reflection, and action, first in the immediate context of the Eucharist and second in their everyday lives.

This foundational approach can be applied also to preaching whose primary orientation is intratextual, as I have suggested might be the case especially in the liturgical seasons. The benefit of the variety of the seasons is that it allows us to relate the *same* central resurrection mystery to the different "limit situations" that are encountered in every life: for example, the experience of incompleteness and longing (Advent); the gratuity of life and love (Christmas); revelation through personal encounter (Epiphany); sin, suffering, and death (Lent); the experience of unexplained courage, hope, and communion (Pentecost), and so on. Taken in their theological context, then, the liturgical seasons provide a structure for a correlational method in preaching, relating these limit situations—the questions inherent in the human condition—to God's salvific answer in Christ.

Such a correlational approach critically examines the scriptures and the traditional Christian worldview from the perspective of historical scholarship and relates it to the contemporary situation, including people's present experiences. The two elements—the scripturally based Christian tradition and our life experience—shed light on each other, interpret each other, and constitute God's present revelation to us. The preacher's role is to assist in this process, especially in interpreting and reflecting on the liturgical readings.

It will be clear that these suggestions necessarily remain very schematic and that they exemplify only *one* way in which the method of foundational theology might be applied to preaching as an aesthetic undertaking. Moreover, this application does not represent a "new" approach to homiletics, but rather intends to make explicit what the good preacher actually does, usually in a more or less implicit and unreflective way. If my suggestion of an overlapping of contemporary theological and pastoral concerns is correct, however, such an explication may not be entirely without use for the development of a methodical approach to preaching in which the insight, virtue, and art of the preacher may more effectively be brought to bear on the meaning of the gospel in the goal of teaching, persuading, and edifying the Christian community.

Chapter 5
Conclusion:
Revelation, Art, and Theology

An old proverb warns against the danger of "not seeing the forest for the trees." The previous chapters were excursions into different parts of a large forest, whose general shape was indicated in the introduction; in this concluding chapter, I will attempt to give a glimpse of the landscape as a whole.

Each of the preceding essays exemplifies a different aspect of the central theme enunciated in the book's title: Christian theology and the arts. It was not the purpose of this book to attempt a systematic exposition of the relationship of beauty and the arts to theology—a project that I have attempted to realize, at least partially, in my earlier work on theological aesthetics.[1] However, the individual examples of the interaction of theology and the arts in the present work are all dependent on a larger theological framework; specifically, they all presuppose several fundamental positions on the nature of God and of revelation. The explication of these presuppositions will contribute to attaining a view of the theological aesthetics that underlies the individual chapters and ties them together.

I will first articulate this vision as a series of three theses that together express an aesthetic theology of revelation based on the classical Roman Catholic tradition. These theses taken together lead to the proposition that the four previous chapters of this book attempt to demonstrate and exemplify. In the sections that follow, I will expand briefly on each of the three statements. I will concentrate especially on the second affirmation, concerning revelation, because it is both the most central to the argument and the least explicitly treated in the preceding chapters. This exposition of the theses will, I hope, serve three purposes: to show the premises at work behind the book as a whole, to make connections between the individual chapters, and to give a brief résumé of the principal points of the book.

The underlying theses are these:

1. God is ultimate beauty, implicitly known as the ultimate desire of the human mind and heart.

2. Revelation is the self-gift of God to humanity. More expansively, God gives a sharing in the divine life to humanity, both within the limited horizon of historical experiences and as the goal that these point toward and anticipate. These events of the self-giving of God and its reception by humanity constitute the history of revelation, which for Christians attains its culminating moment in the person of Christ.

3. Art is one of the primary embodiments of the ongoing history of this revelation and its communication.

The theme that this book elaborates follows as a conclusion from these three premises:

4. Theology, as a reflection on revelation, should be related to art in two ways: academically, theology must reflect on beauty, on art, and on the products of the arts, as part of its object; and pastorally, the arts of ministry must incorporate theology as an intrinsic part of their functioning.

Let us now briefly examine the meaning of each of these statements and the reasons for making them.

1. GOD AS BEAUTY ANTICIPATED
BY THE HUMAN MIND AND HEART

The notion that God is not only ultimate truth and good-ness but also perfect beauty is a classical one. The exact relation of beauty to the other "transcendentals" has been much discussed, but to assert that God is beauty clearly means at least that God is desirable, lovable, glorious, and the ultimate font of the order, beauty, and joy of existence.

The influence of the idea in Western theology stems largely from St. Augustine's appropriation of the Platonic theme of the ascent of the mind from physical beauty, first to its own spiritual beauty and then to the divine beauty. We have examined this idea in the first chapter, using music as an example. The presupposition of the Platonic ascent through beauty to the divine is that creatures participate in God's being at various levels and are thus able to reflect and reveal God's beauty. Above all, the human mind-and-heart itself is a participation in God's being. For this reason, human consciousness implies an innate and nonconcep-tual knowledge of God as its own source, foundation, and goal. It is of this that Augustine speaks when he says that God is to be sought "within"[2] and when he asserts that God is "closer to me than my inmost being."[3] It is the implicit knowledge of God's beauty as our ultimate desire that underlies his famous prayer: "Our hearts are restless until they rest in Thee."[4]

This implicit knowledge of God is what constitutes the mind's dynamism not only toward God, but toward all finite beings as well, precisely because they "participate" in God's being. As the anticipation (or, in Rahner's term, the "pre-apprehension") of infinite Being, this dynamism makes all of our knowledge possible. By establishing in consciousness the horizon of infinite being, it makes us able to question everything that is finite and gives us the ability to make judgments, that is, to make assertions about the being of things. As an anticipation of the ultimate good, it is the basis for the reality of values and underlies every act of freedom. As an anticipation of beauty, it orients our desire and love and grounds the joy of existence.

Beauty, therefore, is understood here in a transcendental sense. It signifies the unity of being, intelligibility, and goodness, insofar as these are the goals of human beings and the source of our spiritual dynamism. The innate sense of beauty is ultimately identical with the natural human dynamism toward being and goodness and constitutes a kind of implicit knowledge of God. To say that God is beauty is to affirm God as the horizon for every experience of the beautiful, in all its aspects: intellectual, moral, interpersonal, and aesthetic. God is what we anticipate and implicitly know and love in all experiences of form, order, loveliness, and desirability, and just as the human openness toward being and goodness is the condition of possibility of a divine supernatural revelation,[5] so the intrinsic openness to what is unconditionally beautiful is what allows us to be grasped by revelation's beauty and rejoice in it.

2. REVELATION AS THE HISTORY OF GOD'S SELF-GIFT TO HUMANITY

In its "Dogmatic Constitution on Divine Revelation," the Second Vatican Council gives a summary of the Catholic theology of revelation. Although the focus of attention is on the history or "economy" of revelation, that is, the "deeds and words [of God], which are intrinsically bound up with each other," the document begins with the assertion, repeated several times, that the object of revelation is the communication of God's self to humanity. The purpose of this self-revelation is to share with us the divine nature and to make us "friends" of God.[6]

When examined closely, these simple statements, which in themselves probably contain nothing particularly striking to the Christian believer, nevertheless have far-reaching theological implications. If we take seriously the idea that revelation is the communication of God's *self* to humanity in such a way that we actually share the divine nature, then a purely propositional view of revelation seems clearly inadequate. That is, revelation cannot be seen simply as a matter of information *about* God; it must instead be understood primarily as an interpersonal event, as the communication of God's own life, in the way that friends share their lives. This means that revelation in its full sense is not merely the bestowal and reception of information, but is an increase in life; it occurs not merely on the level of "mind" but on the personal level of "mind-and-heart." As we have seen above in chapter 4, for Christians an intellectual content is a necessary element of revelation, but it is grounded in a more fundamental communication of being. The essence of what is communicated in revelation is God's self: both in us, as a new principle of our being, and *encountering* us, as the Other who is manifested for the sake of being known and loved in a relation of mutual intimacy ("friendship").

(The specific concept of God's *self-revelation* is frequently identified with German idealism and the liberal Protestant theology that followed it. But the notion of revelation as God's self-gift—i.e., as interpersonal communication and communion—stems from a much more extensive and ancient theological tradition. It has roots already in Philo and Plotinus and is found, with varying degrees of emphasis, in the fathers, in Bonaventure and Aquinas, in the Reformers, and in certain of the neo-Scholastics.[7])

Revelation includes the dimensions of "I-Thou" encounter with God and of sharing in the divine life. In this sense, as

Karl Rahner explains, revelation may be seen as coextensive with grace, the divine self-gift to humanity.[8] There are two inseparable aspects to revelation as received by us. Insofar as it is a genuine communication of God's self, revelation/grace is necessarily Trinitarian.[9] It is first of all a consciousness of an excess of meaning beyond every content, an orientation to absolute mystery. God is always greater than our hearts, even in our sharing in God's life. This transcendental dimension of revelation corresponds to the presence of God as Holy Spirit, the interior dynamism that unites us in the movement of love toward the Father, the unoriginate Mystery.

At the same time, human existence is necessarily bodily, historical, and social. Hence, there is never a "pure" experience of the Spirit: The transcendental for us is always somehow embodied, mediated concretely and historically. It is present in and through events, ideas, and persons that make God's self-gift concretely present by symbolizing it, that is, by pointing beyond themselves to the transcendent. The symbolic, historical dimension of God's self-gift, although it takes various forms, is generally referred to as God's active revealing Word. This Word is genuinely from God, but it takes place in human words. That is, it is realized in and through human minds and hearts, as well as being formulated in human language and symbols. Divine revelation occurs when and to the extent that these human realities are evoked by the Spirit, when they are elevated and transformed by grace. But they remain, nevertheless, limited embodiments of it.

Reflection shows that this limitation is intrinsic to every categorical (historical, spatio-temporal) event of revelation. Obviously, every finite symbol (whether it be in the form of thought or of event) is inadequate to the infinite God who is the gift as well as the giver. But the limitation applies not only to our knowledge of God *in se*, but also to God's revelation insofar as it is about us and our relationship to God. This is because of the irreducible plurality of human situations related to God; because of the intrinsic limits of all symbols, thoughts, and languages, which are always conditioned by their cultural and historical contexts; and above all because of the incompleteness of our transformation by grace. Even when we accept the Spirit's movement in us, there is an admixture of unconverted and even sinful elements in our reception and formulation of God's word. For this reason, revelation has an eschatological orientation: It anticipates a final form in which its present provisional character is overcome.

In this view, revelation is first of all a personal and interpersonal event—it occurs when individuals, who are always located in a social context, are able to enter into a relationship of knowledge and love with God. The knowledge and love of God on the level of personal intimacy means a sharing in the divine life that is beyond the natural horizon of a human being—it brings us beyond the status of mere creatures into a sharing of God's own way of being. Therefore, it is always an event of self-transcendence and, as such, involves a turning away not only from sin, but also from lower integrations of life. In this sense, the acceptance of revelation is always an event of "conversion."[10] It takes place on the religious level by the acceptance of God's Spirit as the orienting principle of our lives. Such conversion is not a once-for-all event, but a lifelong process. Moreover, this orientation calls out for the integration of every dimension of life. Hence, we may also speak of other levels of conversion: intellectual, moral, psychic, aesthetic.

We may therefore say that a basic kind of revelation occurs wherever conversion takes place; that is, when a human life accepts and achieves self-fulfillment through being oriented by God's Spirit toward God (at least implicitly) as the real, the true, the good, the beautiful, the ultimate "Thou."

Intellectual conversion takes place when we attain to authentic intellectual integrity. This means that our personal standard of truth is determined by an inner dynamism toward the real and that the "real" is recognized as what is reached by insightful judgment based on sufficient evidence, not by mere appearances, or wishful thinking, or received opinions, or bright ideas, or the presumptions of "common sense."[11] Moral conversion occurs when we live responsibly, that is, when our standard of behavior is "the good," defined not by pleasure or self-interest or the biases of a group, but by values discerned by prudent decisions based on reasonable, intelligent judgments.[12] Aesthetic conversion is attained when our taste is not simply an accidental by-product of spontaneous appetite, but is formed by disciplined pursuit of the deepest desire of the mind-and-heart, that is, when our standards of beauty are formed by the dynamism of God's love, rather than by pleasure, sensual attractiveness, and the like. In the converted aesthetic sense, the dynamism of human eros is sublated into agape so that we take pleasure in the perception of the good. Sensible beauty is not lost or denied, but is integrated into a higher synthesis that centers on values. Physical form is seen to represent and point to the personal ("spiritual") level of being. This means also that the sense of the beautiful is expanded: It includes not only what gives pleasure, but also what evokes compassion for the needy other. The latter is a beauty not merely experienced passively, but experienced in the compassionate response itself, and calling for a further dimension of action.[13]

Such conversion events, on their different levels, are essentially personal and interpersonal acts, movements of the heart toward God (at least implicitly, insofar as God is the ultimate true, good, and beautiful); but they can only be fully real when they are mentally and physically formulated in some way. This generally happens through the transformed use of the available symbols (actions, words, signs) of a community. The occurrence of conversion is inseparable from some such symbolic formulation.

If we recall that conversion is not simply a human achievement, but is at the same time the realization of God's self-gift,[14] we may say that conversion is the human side of revelation, its acceptance and formulation. In this sense, the history of revelation, in its widest sense, is the history of conversion, embodied in human formulations. (As we have pointed out above, in chapter 3, even though the category of God's word is frequently used to signify every historical mediation of God's revelation, these formulations may consist of thoughts, acts, texts, symbols, institutions, etc.) The clearest and most explicit locus of this general history of revelation is religion, but revelation subsists also in the entire history of human culture, insofar as the latter is implicitly under God's "grace." Intellectual conversion, for example, occurs whenever people genuinely seek truth, and may be formulated theoretically in philosophical theories of knowledge or in scientific methods; moral conversion occurs in good decisions and the practice of virtue, and is theoretically formulated in ethical systems; aesthetic conversion occurs when transcendent beauty is apprehended by the mind in sensible form, and is formulated conceptually in aesthetic theory and nonconceptually in the different kinds of art. In short, every attainment and expression of human transcendence forms a part of this most general revelation history.

But, as we have noted above, this history is ambiguous. Conversion can be incomplete or inauthentic. Even when it is genuine, conversion can nevertheless be inadequately formulated: There can be a disparity between the intention of the heart and the available symbols, between one's willingness and one's ability, and between different aspects of conversion—head and heart, mind and body, self and community. Hence, general revelation is an incomplete and ambiguous realization of God's self-gift, but because and insofar as it is borne by the presence and sense of God, it can recognize its own inadequacy. The Spirit serves as a critical principle, not only toward society, but toward religion itself. General revelation implicitly hopes for a final, eschatological realization.

Christians believe that the interior Spirit testifies to the Christ event as the personal, historical embodiment of a revelation that already makes present that eschatological fullness. That is to say, Christians affirm the life, death, and resurrection of Jesus as God's special and victorious self-revelation: a complete human incarnation or achievement of acceptance of God's self-gift, confirmed by God, a word of God in history that can be final because (in the resurrection and ascension) it anticipates the final union with God and makes its power (the Spirit) present among us. The memory and meaning of this special revelation are continued in the community of the church in an explicit and sacramental way. But if God's love is truly universal, then its salvific-revelatory power is also present, to greater and lesser degrees, in all history: The same Spirit that vivified Jesus and made him the Son of God, makes him also the "first of many" brothers and sisters;[15] that is, the one Spirit is the power that inspires every revelation, every accomplishment of sharing in God's life, "incarnated" in the persons, "sacramentalized" in the ideas, words, symbols, acts, and relations of God's sons and daughters throughout history.

3. ART AS AN EMBODIMENT OF REVELATION

If we combine the above two affirmations (God is beauty; revelation is God's self-gift), we come to themes that we have expounded in chapters 1 and 3: Art embodies revelation, in its transcendental and historical dimensions. It does so in two overlapping ways: first, insofar as it creates and represents beauty, and second, insofar as it symbolizes human conversion.

First, if God is Beauty, then the revelation of God is a revelation of beauty and must itself be beautiful. Beauty, the capacity to produce joy through perception, characterizes God's historical revelation to the extent that the latter is faithfully received. But it is a beauty that demands conversion. Hans Urs von Balthasar has written extensively on the beauty of God's special revelation: the form of Christ and of the Christian message when authentically lived in the church. This includes the beauty of contrast experiences, preeminently the cross, in which eschatological hope is unveiled. The experience of God, as present joy, as the power of transformation, and as anticipated fulfillment of human need, is an experience of beauty. As we have seen in chapter 3, art is one of the forms in which this special revelation is transmitted and appropriated.

But God as the beautiful is also present in a general revelation through all positive experiences of beauty: natural, interpersonal, artistic. If revelation is beautiful, then, conversely, every experience of beauty is a revelation of God, to varying extents, at different levels, and in diverse ways. Art is one expression or formulation of this revelation through beauty. Art is also a medium of general revelation insofar as it serves as a language for intellectual, moral, and religious conversion—that is, as an aspect of human culture, independently of the degree of its beauty.

We may say, then, that art is an element in both general and special categorical revelation—keeping in mind, of course, the qualifications mentioned above concerning the limitations of revelation in its human reception.

4. THEOLOGY AS ACADEMIC AND PASTORAL AESTHETICS

If the previous three theses are accepted, then we may conclude to the primary contention of this book: that the arts have an intrinsic place within theology, and theology within the pastoral arts, at different levels and in various ways.

The mutual relation of art and theology is most obvious in the pastoral and communicative modes of religion. There is clearly an important aesthetic dimension to ritual and sacramental practice, in both their symbolic and verbal aspects. This connection has been explored particularly in chapter 4, where it is exemplified by the relationship between theological reflection and art in preaching.

However, it is my contention that the connection of art and theology in preaching is not simply a concession to the practical necessities of communication, but is more profoundly rooted in the aesthetic dimension of revelation itself. For this reason, art should not be conceived as something to be added on to a theological message to make it palatable or more easily understood, but as an intrinsic part of theology's nature and object.

The preceding chapters have exemplified a number of ways in which this can be true. Art is relevant to theology insofar as it is an expression of the human culture from which theology receives its intellectual challenges, to which theology addresses itself, and in which theology participates. Theology is not a timeless enterprise but is part of a more general intellectual history. An understanding of art and its history is therefore relevant to theology's self-understanding and method. We have explored aspects of this relevance in chapter 2, on the parallels between paradigm changes in art and in theology. We concluded there that the emerging paradigm of theology in the West today should make more explicit the unity between theology and art that has always existed.

As the explanation of my second "thesis" maintains, art is also relevant to theology insofar as it embodies aspects of God's general and special self-revelation in history. This embodiment takes place when art succeeds in awakening a sense of transcendent beauty and its source. This was the theme of chapter 1: art can be a way to God. But it also occurs when art symbolizes other aspects of God's word and the human appropriation or rejection of it. Chapter 3 concentrated on this aspect of the relation, enumerating some of the multiple ways in which art can serve as a text for theology, as a representation of both God's word and of the human situation to which theology attempts to correlate that self-revelation.

This book has concentrated above all on the methodological relationships of Christian theology to the arts. Only a few steps have been taken here toward the actual accomplishment of a theological aesthetics. But it is my hope that my considerations on method and my few examples of content may make some contribution to an emergent paradigm in which the treatment of art is a genuine and fruitful source of theological insight, both on the pastoral and the academic levels.

NOTES

NOTES TO THE INTRODUCTION

Note that all bibliographical and explanatory notes are numbered and appear in this section. Illustrative or discographical notes are indicated in the text by letters and are found at the end of each chapter.

1. Scott Heller, "Wearying of Cultural Studies, Some Scholars Rediscover Beauty." The Chronicle of Higher Eduaction, December 4, 1998. vol. XIV, no. 15, pp. A15–16.
2. Dorothy L. Sayers, "Toward a Christian Esthetic" in The Whimsical Christian (New York: Macmillan Publishing Co., Inc., 1978), pp. 73–91, at p. 74.
3. Frank Burch Brown, Religious Aesthetics. A Theological Study of Making and Meaning (Princeton, N.J.: Princeton University Press, 1989), pp. 178–184. See below, ch. 2, note 126.
4. See St. Thomas Aquinas, Summa Theologica, q. 1, a. 4: Thomas teaches that theology includes both speculative and practical disciplines and that it is more speculative than practical, "because it is more centrally concerned with the divine than with human acts; it considers the latter [only] insofar as they lead humanity to the perfect knowledge of God...."
5. See Summa Theologica, q. 1, a. 9.
6. See Summa Theologica, q. 1, a. 4.
7. Much of the content of this chapter represents a recasting and synthesis of the reflections on homiletics in my series The Word In and Out of Season (New York: Paulist Press, 1990–1996).
8. See my Theological Aesthetics. God in Imagination, Beauty, and Art (New York: Oxford University Press, 1999).

NOTES TO CHAPTER 1

1. Henryk Gorecki, interviewed on National Public Radio, Performance Today, April 5, 1995.

NOTES • 231

2. See Alfred North Whitehead, *Religion in the Making* (New York: New American Library, 1960), pp. 21–23.

3. Iris Murdoch, *The Fire and the Sun. Why Plato Banished the Artists* (Oxford: Clarendon Press, 1977), pp. 76–77.

4. See James McKinnon, ed., *Music in Early Christian Literature* (Cambridge: Cambridge University Press, 1987), p. 3.

5. Murdoch, p. 72.

6. Johannes Quasten: *Music and Worship in Pagan and Christian Antiquity* (Washington, D.C.: National Association of Pastoral Musicians, 1983). The following paragraphs are essentially based on Quasten's study, augmented by James McKinnon, ed., *Music in Early Christian Literature* (Cambridge: Cambridge University Press, 1987), a collection of relevant texts from the patristic period.

7. McKinnon, p. 2.

8. Ibid., p. 1.

9. See *Politics*, book VIII, ch. VI, 5ff.

10. John 4:23.

11. McKinnon, p. 39 and passim.

12. Ibid., p. 2.

13. Ibid., p. 39. Both Patristic ways of dealing with Old Testament music are referred to by St. Thomas in explaining why the church imitates Israel in using song, but not in using instruments: *In veteri autem testamento usus erat talium instrumentorum, tum quia populus erat magis durus et carnalis: unde erat per hiusmodi instrumenta provocandus, sicut et per promissiones terrenas. Tum etiam quia huiusmodi instrumenta corporalia aliquid figurabant.* (In the Old Testament such instruments were used, first because the people were more hard of heart and more sensual; therefore these kinds of instruments were used to incite them [toward God], just as the promises regarding earthly life were. Second, such instruments also presignified something else [viz., a spiritual reality].) (ST II II, q. XCI, a. 2, ad 4.)

14. Ephesians 5:19; cf. Colossians 3:16. The Reformer Zwingli later referred to these same passages in his considerations of church music. Contemporary translators, however, throw doubt on the patristic interpretation of "in your hearts." The RSV, for example, translates the passages respectively: "making melody to the Lord with all your heart" and "sing psalms and spiritual songs with thankfulness in your hearts...."

15. *Confessions*, Ch. X.

16. See Augustine, *Confessions* IX, vii, 15 (PL xxxii, 769–70; CCL xxvii, 141–2); McKinnon, p. 154.

17. *Confessions* X, XXXIII, 49–50 (PL XXXII, 799–800; CCL XXVII, 181–2); McKinnon, pp. 154–5.

18. In the medieval context, the *laus divina* would primarily mean the chanting of the psalms and canticles of the "divine office." See also Aquinas's treatment of the prayer of petition: II II, q. 83, esp. a. 12 (*Utrum oratio debeat esse vocalis*—"Whether prayer ought to be made aloud") and a. 13 (*Utrum de necessitate orationis sit quod sit attenta*—"Whether it belongs to the intrinsic nature of prayer that one be attentive").

19. *Et quandoque intantum abundat haec intentio, qua mens fertur in Deum, ut etiam omnium aliorum mens obliviscatur.*

20. PL XXXVII, 1272; CCL XXXIX, 1394. Quoted in McKinnon, p. 158.

21. PL XXXVI, 283; CCL XXXVIII, 254. Quoted in McKinnon, pp. 156–7.

22. McKinnon, p. 164. The authenticity of this epistle is in doubt, but the sentiment of this sentence is in accord with the passage from the *Confessions* quoted above.

23. Martin Luther, "To Louis Senfl," in *Luther's Works*, vol. 49, ed. and transl. by Gottfried G. Krodel (Philadelphia: Fortress Press, 1972), p. 428.

24. Martin Luther, "Vorrede auf die Gesänge vom Leiden Christi," in Luther, *Sämmtliche Schriften*, vol. XIV, ed. by Johann Georg Walch (St. Louis: Concordia Publishing House, 1898), p. 430.

25. Martin Luther, "The Last Words of David," in *Luther's Works*, vol. 15, ed. and transl. by Gottfried G. Krodel (Philadelphia: Fortress Press, 1972), p. 274.

26. Martin Luther, "Vorrede auf die Gesänge vom Leiden Christi," in Luther, *Sämmtliche Schriften*, vol. XIV, ed. by Johann Georg Walch (St. Louis: Concordia Publishing House, 1898), p. 429f.

27. John Calvin, *Institutes of the Christian Religion*, transl. by Ford Lewis Battles, Book III, ch. XX, n. 31–32, in John T. McNeill, ed., *The Library of Christian Classics* (Philadelphia: Westminster Press, 1960), vol. XXI, p. 894 n. 65.

28. Ibid., pp. 895–6.

29. *Inst.* III, XX, 32. Ibid., p. 896.

30. From *An Essay on Criticism*, 342.

31. Gerardus van der Leeuw uses a similar analysis to establish a general correspondance between different forms of art and

the particular emphases that characterize different religious traditions: "That theology which places the impersonal, the spiritual (in the sense of the immaterial) in the central position will
attempt to follow the movement of the arts from the fixed center to music. Such an immanent, pantheistic, mystical theology
will understand music as the essence of all arts and leave the
image behind....A theology, on the other hand, which thinks
historically and transcendentally, which places the incarnation
of God at the center, will seek the mid-point of the arts in the
image." Gerardus van der Leeuw, *Sacred and Profane Beauty: The
Holy in Art*, transl. David E. Green (New York: Holt, Rinehart and
Winston, 1963), p. 302.

32. Karl Rahner, "Priest and Poet," in *Theological Investigations*,
vol. III, transl. by Karl-H. and Boniface Kruger (New York:
Seabury Press, 1974), pp. 301–2. In what follows, Rahner extolls
the uniqueness of the poetic word, compared with the other
arts, in a fashion that seems to me to be excessively logocentric
and to neglect the wider nonverbal possibilities for symboliza-
tion of the transcendent: "...the other arts can represent in the
first place only what is apprehended and circumscribed. They
can set out the image and the gestures....But among all the
modes of expressing himself that man uses in all the arts, the
word alone possesses something which is not shared by any
other creation of man: it lives in transcendence....The word
alone is the gesture which transcends everything that can be
represented and imagined, to refer us to infinity. It alone can
redeem that which constitutes the ultimate imprisonment of all
realities which are not expressed in word: the dumbness of their
reference to God." Ibid., p. 302. By contrast, Gerardus van der
Leeuw writes that "the word pronounces and limits; music sings
of the ineffable and undefinable." For van der Leeuw, the sacred
word is indispensable, but not superior to other forms of sacred
symbol (*Sacred and Profane Beauty*, p. 302).

33. As Rahner points out, however, this "distinction" is
unique and is ultimately constituted by God's own being.
"When we say against pantheism that God and the world are
different, this statement is radically misunderstood if it is
interpreted in a dualistic way. The difference between God and
the world is of such a nature that God establishes and is the
difference of the world from himself, and for this reason he
establishes the closest unity precisely in the differentiation."

Karl Rahner, *Foundations of Christian Faith* (New York: Crossroad, 1990), p. 62. This perspective points to a possible point of contact between the Christian idea of creation and the Vedanta school of "qualified nondualism" represented by such thinkers as Ramanuja.

34. Boris Pasternak, *Doctor Zhivago*, transl. by Max Hayward and Manya Harari (New York: New American Library, 1958), p. 44.

35. Aquinas applies the quotation from Augustine directly to the singers; but immediately after, he says, *"et eadem est ratio de audientibus"* ("and the same reasons [i.e., those that justify singing] apply to the hearers"). Thus, although the only explicit justification he gives for music with regard to the hearers is that they know the reason of the singing, we must assume that Aquinas meant the quote from Augustine to apply here as well.

36. Boris Pasternak, *Doctor Zhivago*, p. 44.

37. *Paradiso* XXXIII, 143, 145.

38. See, for example, *The Consolation of Philosophy*, book III, ch. IX.

39. Ibid., book II, ch. VIII.

40. Susanne K. Langer, *Feeling and Form* (New York: Charles Scribner's Sons, 1953), p. 27.

41. The naturalistic theory of the mechanics of aesthetic experience is explained at length in George Santayana's classic study, *The Sense of Beauty* (New York: Charles Scribner's Sons, 1896). The essential idea, however, that beauty is a matter of the correspondence of experience to the proportions inherent in our organs of sense is already found in Thomas Aquinas; see for example *Summa Theologica* I, 5, 4 ad 1.

Nicholas Wolterstorff cites several psychological studies of *synestheia* (the production of a sensation or "image" in one sensory mode through the stimulation of another) and spontaneous cross-sensory associations. These studies support the idea that there is a high degree of intercultural agreement in the association of certain sensations with particular ideas or moods. The psychologist C. E. Osgood, cited by Wolterstorff, gives an explanation similar to the naturalistic theory: that is, there is a similarity not in the qualities perceived by us but in our biological mode of perception. This similarity produces the association of affective responses. Wolterstorff himself, however, favors an objective explanation, at least for certain types of association: We directly judge the presence of similarities in the qualities themselves. See Nicholas Wolterstorff, *Art in Action. Toward a Christian Aesthetic* (Grand Rapids, Mich.: William B. Eerdmans, 1980), pp. 100–12.

42. Rudolf Otto, *The Idea of the Holy* (London: Oxford University Press, 1969).

43. "The beautiful is difficult"—the first part of a proverb quoted by Socrates in Plato's dialogue *Cratylus*. The entire proverb runs: "Whatever is beautiful [= good] to know is difficult to learn."

44. Boris Pasternak, *Doctor Zhivago*, p. 378.

45. Cf. *Summa Theologica*, Ia, q. 5, 4, ad 1am; *Commentarium in de Divinis Nominibus*, lect. VI.

46. Thomas Aquinas, *Commentarium in De Divinis Nominibus*, lect. V.

47. "*Wer das Christentum völlig verlernt hat, der hört es hier wirklich wie ein Evangelium.*" Letter to Erwin Rohde, April 30 1870. Quoted in Karl Albert, "Zur Ontologie des Sakralen in der Kunst," in Günter Pöltner and Helmth Vetter, eds., *Theologie und Ästhetik* (Wien, Freiburg, Basel: Herder, 1985), pp. 65–76, at p. 72.

48. Van der Leeuw, *Sacred and Profane Beauty*, p. 292.

49. Ibid., p. 293.

50. A propos of this point van der Leeuw points to the difference between two kinds of coloratura singing: one in which the word is indifferent, except as sound, and another in which the music attempts to reproduce the content of the word "plastically." Ibid., p. 291. The latter form is especially typical of the musical rhetoric associated with Bach and the Baroque period in general.

51. Ibid., p. 292.

52. Van der Leeuw reminds us that "music is never the servant of religion" precisely because "it is the servant of God." Ibid., p. 269f. Van der Leeuw is presuming that true music seeks beauty, which mediates God's presence, as we have discussed above.

53. Alasdair MacIntyre, *After Virtue* (Notre Dame, Ind.: University of Notre Dame Press, 1981), pp. 36–37; quoted in James Alfred Martin, *Beauty and Holiness. The Dialogue between Aesthetics and Religion* (Princeton, N.J.: Princeton University Press, 1990), p. 33.

54. See Bernard Lonergan, *Method in Theology* (New York: Herder & Herder, 1972), p. 110.

55. See s.v. "*Begierde*" in Karl Rahner and Herbert Vorgrimler, eds., *Kleines Theologisches Wörterbuch* (Basel/Wien: Herder, 1967), p. 45f.

56. Amos 6:1, 4–6.

57. Isaiah 53:2b–3.

58. See Iris Murdoch, *The Fire and the Sun. Why Plato Banished the Artists* (Oxford: Clarendon Press, 1977), p. 69.

59. We leave aside for the present the question of whether, in

the light of contemporary scientific cosmology, the biblical notion of the *eschaton* must be demythologized and theologically reconceptualized in the same way the biblical myths of the "beginning" of the world are demythologized and retrieved in the metaphysical and theological concept of "creation ex *nihilo.*"

60. I take it for granted that among these priorities for the Christian community will be not only witness to the poor, but concrete action on their behalf. See 1 Corinthians 11:17ff.; James 2:5ff., 14ff.

NOTES TO CHAPTER 2

1. The statue is now in the Accademia di Belle Arti in Florence. A reproduction stands in its place in front of the Signoria.

2. Giorgio Vasari, *The Lives of the Artists*, trans. by Julia Conaway Bondanella and Peter Bondanella (Oxford: Oxford University Press, 1991), p. 428.

3. For a brief treatment of each work in its historical and artistic context, see Howard Hibbard's studies of the two artists: *Michelangelo* (New York: Harper and Row, 1974), pp. 51–61; and *Bernini* (Harmondsworth: Penguin Books, 1965), pp. 54–65.

4. Donatello's *David* probably dates from ca. 1440 (although earlier and later dates are also given); Verrocchio's from ca. 1474. Both are now housed in the Museo del Bargello in Florence.

5. Hibbard, *Michelangelo*, p. 61. Others point out that the carved irises of the figure's eyes give the face a look of concentration and determination. Hibbard sees in the overall effect of the face a projection of Michelangelo's own "troubled ambition" (Ibid.).

6. Vasari, *Lives*, p. 427.

7. Hibbard notes that the description *manu fortis* ("strong of hand") was applied to David in the Middle Ages and sees the oversized hand of the statue as a symbolic reference to this quality. *Michelangelo*, p. 57.

8. It is entirely possible that Michelangelo, with his affinity for Platonic thought, may have had such a meaning in mind, at least in an unthematic way. But the interpretation does not depend upon this possibility.

9. For a closer analysis of what follows, in particular on the originality of Bernini's style, see Hibbard, *Bernini*, pp. 55ff.

10. Hibbard, Bernini, p. 57.
11. Ibid., p. 55.
12. Ibid.
13. See Hibbard, p. 60, for a discussion of Bernini's preoccupation with coloristic effects.
14. This is not to say that Michelangelo's David is devoid of narrative psychological interest. If we accept the common interpretation that Michelangelo has portrayed David in anticipation of the battle, then we can see here also a certain dramatic tension. But in the overall effect of the work, this element is subordinated to the iconic and symbolic meanings, and especially (in connection with the latter) to the concern for beauty of form. In Bernini's work the priorities are reversed.
15. These elements are not altogether lacking, however. Note for example David's harp and lion skin, iconographic marks of identity (1 Samuel 16:18; 17:34–36), lying at his feet.
16. Bernini is reputed to have remarked that nature is almost always weak and insignificant; for him it was the function of art to speak powerfully to the human mind and feeling.
17. Hibbard, Bernini, p. 19. Hibbard gives the following quote from the diary of Bernini's contemporary John Evelyn: "Bernini...gave a public opera wherein he painted the scenes, cut the statues, invented the engines, composed the music, writ the comedy, and built the theatre."
18. In his papal projects Bernini was in fact a major propagandist for the claims of the Roman church; the Altar of the Chair in St. Peter's Basilica is the prime example. Hibbard notes that in his personal life Bernini seems to have accepted fully the spirit of his times. He was a devout Catholic, who is said to have remarked (a propos of Borromini), "Better a poor Catholic than a good heretic" (p. 20). He was also apparently quite comfortable with absolutism both in church and state, serving not only the papacy but also Louis XIV of France.
19. This idea underlies a great deal of contemporary art history. See for example the widely used text by William Fleming, Arts and Ideas (New York: Holt, Rinehart and Winston, 1974).
20. Hans-Georg Gadamer, Truth and Method (New York: Crossroad, 1982), p. 87.
21. Ibid., pp. 87–88.
22. Thomas S. Kuhn, The Structure of Scientific Revolutions (Chicago: University of Chicago Press, 1962).

238 • Theology and the Arts

23. See especially the collection of symposium papers edited by Hans Küng and David Tracy, *Paradigm Change in Theology* (New York: Crossroad, 1984). Küng's programatic essay, "Paradigm Change in Theology: A Proposal for Discussion" also appears, with few changes, in his *Theology for the Third Millennium*, transl. by Peter Heinegg (New York: Doubleday, 1988).

24. Avery Dulles, *Models of Revelation* (Garden City, N.Y.: Doubleday, 1983); *Models of the Church* (Garden City, N.Y.: Doubleday, 1974); "The Use of Scripture in Theology," in *The Craft of Theology* (Garden City, N.Y.: Doubleday, 1992). Sallie McFague, *Metaphorical Theology. Models of God in Religious Language* (Philadelphia: Fortress Press, 1982) and *Models of God. Theology for an Ecological, Nuclear Age* (Philadelphia: Fortress Press, 1987).

25. Although the adoption of Kuhn's terminology and analysis adds a new element, the understanding of theology through paradigms is not entirely original; it has an antecedent in Lonergan's technique of "horizon analysis" and its application to the development of doctrine through various contexts of thought.

26. It should be noted that the theological use of Kuhn's thesis does not necessarily imply a total acceptance of his analysis of the process of paradigm change. Kuhn's analysis has been challenged within the philosophy of science because of its alleged consequence of axiological relativism—the contention that there is no ground for rational choice between different goals of thinking—and the related presumption that different paradigms are incommensurable and therefore that translation or communication between them is impossible. See Paul Rigby, John Van den Hengel, and Paul O'Grady, "The Nature of Doctrine and Scientific Progress," in *Theological Studies*, vol. 52, no. 4 (Dec. 1991), pp. 669–88. On the other hand, Garrett Green, while also rejecting axiological relativism, holds that this position is incorrectly attributed to Kuhn. See his *Imagining God. Theology and the Religious Imagination* (San Francisco: Harper & Row, 1989), p. 141. In any case, some theologians who use Kuhn's ideas, including Hans Küng, to whom reference will be made here, have modified them substantially in their application to theology.

27. Kuhn, op. cit., p. 175; quoted in Küng, *Theology for the Third Millennium*, p. 132.

28. Küng seems somewhat flexible in his use of these three terms; the concrete examples of each do not appear entirely consistent.

29. Sallie McFague, *Metaphorical Theology. Models of God in Religious Language* (Philadelphia: Fortress Press, 1982), pp. 25–26.

30. C. S. Lewis, "On the Reading of Old Books," in *God in the Dock. Essays on Theology and Ethics*, ed. by Walter Hooper (Grand Rapids, Mich.: Eerdmans, 1970), p. 202.

31. Küng, "Paradigm Change in Theology: A Proposal for Discussion," in Küng and Tracy, eds., op. cit., p. 24.

32. Kuhn has been criticized on precisely this point by other philosophers and historians of science. See, for example, Larry Laudan, *Science and Values* (Berkeley: University of California Press, 1984), pp. 73–75. Laudan explains that the apparent abruptness and radicality of Kuhn's paradigm shifts are due to our "telescoping" into a single moment what are actually gradual changes over a period of time. According to Laudan, individual pieces of a system frequently have been replaced without the abandonment of others, so that there is in fact more continuity and room for progress than Kuhn seems to allow. Küng, as will be seen, makes similar observations in applying the idea of paradigm changes to theology.

33. Küng, "Paradigm Changes," p. 27.

34. Ibid., p. 28.

35. A helpful diagram is given in Küng, *Theology for the Third Millennium*, p. 128.

36. Ibid.

37. For a treatment of the notion of schemata of representation, see Ernst Hans Gombrich, *Art and Illusion. A Study in the Psychology of Pictorial Representation*. The A. W. Mellon Lectures in the Fine Arts, 1956. Bollingen Series XXXV, 5. (Princeton, N.J.: Princeton University Press, 1969 <1960>).

38. José Ortega y Gasset, "Sobre el Punto de Vista en las Artes," in *La Deshumanización del Arte y Otros Ensayos Estéticos* (Madrid: Revista de Occidente, 1967), p. 187.

39. Ibid., p. 189.

40. Ibid., pp. 190–1.

41. Ibid., p. 192.

42. Ibid., p. 193.

43. Ibid., p. 194.

44. For a brief summary of the history of this analysis of Western art, which to a certain extent forms the background for Ortega's observations, see Gombrich, pp. 18–19. For Gombrich's own revised version of the progression of Western painting from "narrative" to "illusionism," see especially pp. 291–329.

45. Ortega, op. cit., pp. 194–5.

46. Leon Battista Alberti, On Painting, in Elizabeth Gilmore Holt, ed., A Documentary History of Art (Garden City, N.Y.: Doubleday and Co., 1957), vol. 1, pp. 209–11. See also Gombrich, op. cit., p. 152.

47. Ortega in his schematic overview associates this phase with Raphael, who exemplifies its high point, but—as the examples I mention show—the painting of space and the use of architecture as an organizational principle were already established by his quattrocento predecessors.

48. Ortega, op. cit., p. 199.

49. Ibid., p. 201 (my translation).

50. Ibid., pp. 201–2.

51. Ibid., pp. 202f. André Malraux makes a similar remark regarding the artist as subject: at the turn of the century, attention to the artist's act of painting began to dominate over the painting's content, rather than vice-versa. The Voices of Silence (Frogmore, Herts.: Paladin, 1974), pp. 53–54, quoted in Nicholas Wolterstorff, Art in Action. Toward a Christian Aesthetic (Grand Rapids, Mich.: William B. Eerdmans, 1980), p. 206. It is also at this time, according to Malraux, that art came to be seen as a value in itself. Wolterstorff qualifies this observation by restricting it to the institution of high art, not art in general. Ibid., p. 207f.

52. See Günter Rombold, "Transzendenz in der Malerei des 19. und 20. Jahrhunderts" in Günter Pöltner and Helmuth Vetter, eds., Theologie und Ästhetik (Wien: Herder, 1985), pp. 88–89.

53. Aiden Nichols, The Art of God Incarnate, pp. 9–11.

54. Ortega, op. cit., p. 205.

55. James Alfred Martin, Beauty and Holiness. The Dialogue Between Aesthetics and Religion (Princeton, N.J.: Princeton University Press, 1990), p. 178.

56. Wassily Kandinsky, Concerning the Spiritual in Art (New York: George Wittenborn, 1947).

57. Ibid., p. 2.

58. Ibid., p. 14.

59. Ibid., p. 47.

60. Ibid., p. 16.

61. Ibid., pp. 16, 19.

62. Ibid., p. 40.

63. Ibid., p. 73. Kandinsky explains that Cubism was merely a transitional stage to full abstraction. "Let us suppose a rhomboidal composition, made up of human figures. The artist asks himself:

Are these human figures absolutely necessary to the composition, or could they be replaced by other organic figures, without affecting the fundamental harmony of the whole?" "Cubism, as a transitory form, demonstrates how natural forms are subordinated to constructive purposes and what unessential hindrances these realistic forms are. A transition is cubism, in which natural form, by being forcibly subjected to constructional ends, becomes an impediment." Pp. 49, 73.

64. Ibid., p. 47.

65. Ibid., p. 25.

66. Ibid., p. 57. Note the parallel to the highly constructive techniques of twelve-tone music.

67. Ibid., p. 47.

68. Michael Brenson, "How the Spiritual Infused the Abstract," *The New York Times*, Sunday, Dec. 21, 1986, section 2, pp. 1, 33.

69. Kandinsky had already to some extent anticipated this move: "Consciously or unconsciously, artists are studying and investigating their material, weighing the spiritual value of those elements with which it is their privilege to work." Ibid., p. 39.

70. Cf. Ortega, op. cit., p. 206. I have obviously extended Ortega's synopsis to cover the metaphysical realism of the early Middle Ages at one end and the deconstruction of the subject in contemporary culture at the other.

71. Ibid., p. 207.

72. Ibid., p. 208.

73. Günter Rombold, "Transzendenz in der Malerei des 19. und 20. Jahrhunderts," in Günter Pöltner and Helmth Vetter, eds., *Theologie und Ästhetik* (Wien, Freiburg, Basel: Herder, 1985), pp. 77–89, at pp. 78–79.

74. Ibid., pp. 80–83. Rombold also associates the sublime with the holy as characterized by Otto: the *"mysterium tremendum et fascinans"* (although Otto himself holds that the sublime is a different, albeit analogous category).

75. Ortega, op. cit., p. 208. Cf. ibid., pp. 78–79. Rombold sees a parallel between the ongoing crisis of secularization and a crisis of metaphysical thinking that is manifested in painting's turn from spiritual meaning first to the natural world (Renaissance), then to subjective emotion (Romanticism), and finally to pure physical impressions (Impressionism).

76. Rombold, pp. 83, 84.

77. Loc. cit. Rombold sees the pursuit of transcendence as

taking a further step in Cézanne's efforts to attain by painting a "realization" of nature: Cézanne gives us a glimpse into the depths of reality by presenting the objective givenness of things, their sheer *presence*, which evokes the "ontological experience" of which Heidegger spoke: the recognition of the presence of Being (*das Sein*) in individual beings (*Seienden*) as a gift. Ibid., pp. 88–89; cf. Karl Albert, "Zur Ontologie des Sakralen in der Kunst," in Günter Pöltner and Helmth Vetter, eds., *Theologie und Ästhetik* (Wien, Freiburg, Basel: Herder, 1985), pp. 65–76, at pp. 67f.

78. As we have seen above, many painters of the modern nonrepresentational school were explicitly concerned to restore "spirituality" to art. Paul Tillich saw in "expressionism" a fruitful vehicle for spiritual meaning because in it the transcendent dimension of meaning is revealed in the dissolution of natural form. Jeremy Begbie points out that this parallels Tillich's ideal of "theonomy"; but also that Tillich's interpretation of expressionism differs from that of art historians and of the "Expressionists" themselves. See Jeremy S. Begbie, *Voicing Creation's Praise. Towards a Theology of the Arts* (Edinburgh: T&T Clark, 1991), pp. 8–9, 15, 67.

79. H. Chipp, *Theories of Modern Art* (Los Angeles: University of California Press, 1968), p. 553, quoted in Paul Crowther, *Critical Aesthetics and Postmodernism* (Oxford: Clarendon Press, 1993), p. 185.

80. For an account of varieties of postmodern architecture, see David Kolb, *Postmodern Sophistications. Philosophy, Architecture, and Tradition* (Chicago: University of Chicago Press, 1990), ch. 8.

Kolb also gives a brief but informative summary of the origins of the term *postmodern*:

> Arnold Toynbee, in 1946, seems to have been the first to use the word *postmodern* in anything like its current sense. He so named the time since the last decades of the nineteenth century, when the great modern syntheses began to break down. The word was picked up around the same time by poets (Randall Jarrell, in particular) and a bit later by literary and then architectural critics. In each case it named a breakdown of older unities and the transgression of prohibitions that had been set up by modernism. The word has come to philosophers just when the artists and

architects are getting pretty tired of it. Announcements of the imminent death of postmodernism began in 1979 and have continued ever since.

Ibid., pp. 4–5; see also p. 186, n. 9, where Kolb notes that the word was reportedly used about architecture as early as the 1950s.

81. For a more extensive discussion of postmodernism in the visual arts, see Crowther, ch. 10. Crowther centers his discussion around Arthur Danto's claim that in postmodernity art has come to an end, its internal aesthetic impetus having been replaced by economic forces:

> In response to the usurping of its mimetic functions by cinematography, Modernist art became energized by an internal "logic" necessarily progressing towards the revelation of art's real essence—an essence that would not be assimilable in terms of other forms of communication. In Warhol's Pop Art this progression issues in its logical culmination. The essence of art is, in effect, declared as institutional. This self-congruence of art with its own essence is the culmination of art history. After it there can be nothing new in a distinctively artistic sense. On these terms, in other words, postmodern art is essentially *posthistorical*. Art, in effect, has come to an end.

That is, art is now determined simply by artistic intention alone so that anything is admissible as art (p. 181f) (or, as Marshall MacLuhan put it, "Art is whatever you can get away with").

Crowther counters that the effect of photography and cinema on visual art can also be seen as a liberation (as Kandinsky held; see above): "Artists were now free to orient their work towards salutary effects that eluded more conventional techniques of representation" (183). Crowther further argues that "there are two fundamentally different aspects to Postmodernism in the visual arts" (190): one, represented by "critical" Super-Realism and Neo-Expressionism, is deconstructive and skeptical about the possibilities of high art; the other, represented by "uncritical" versions of the same styles, supports the traditional view that art is legitimized by "some kind of elevating expressive effect embodied in its creation and reception" (185,190f.). This elevation may be achieved by complexity and virtuosity (188), by deconstrutive irony itself (192), or by "affective jolts" to the perceiver (193). Even Critical Postmodernism, Crowther concludes, in spite of itself ends in the reaffirmation of art as a kind of "elevating" experience (192–6).

As the above makes clear, the meanings of postmodern in artand in other areas, including philosophy, do not entirely coincide: Much of what is generally referred to as modern (i.e., nonrepresentational) art already anticipates elements of the "post-" modern in the philosophical sense of the term—especially the latter's rejection of representation. If we list the major movements in twentieth-century art—Cubism, Dada, Surrealism, Expressionism, Abstraction, Assemblage, Pop, Minimalism, and Conceptualism—we find this rejection already at work in most of them. In his review of the New York Museum of Modern Art's exhibition, "Objects of Desire: The Modern Still Life" ("The Art World" in The New Yorker, June 9, 1997, pp. 104–6), Calvin Tomkins notes that "From 1960 on, the objects in advanced art mostly reflect the irony, ambiguity, and deadpan anomie that have come to be regarded as hallmarks of the postmodern experience" (p. 106). ("These are," Tomkins adds, "pretty depressing hallmarks…").

Postmodern as it is now commonly used indicates less a definite style or position than a plurality of movements in art, philosophy, literary criticism, linguistics, and sociology, all loosely related by their rejection of one or more aspects of modernity (an idea, however, whose content is also fluid). Other characteristics ascribed to the postmodern mentality include mistrust of the idea of "progress" and its accompanying assumption of the superiority of the modern over the pre-modern; rejection of all "meta-" narratives or systems of thought; cognitive relativism; criticism of logocentrism and rationality, and revaluation of the irrational and emotional; interdisciplinary activity; preoccupation with style and genre; emphasis on "textuality" and intertextuality; provocative means of communication. See Pauline Marie Rosenau, Postmodernism and the Social Sciences. Insights, inroads, and intrusions (Princeton: Princeton University Press, 1992), pp. 5–8, 94–96.

82. Obviously the discussion of paradigm shifts itself is an aspect of this historical consciousness.

83. It is impossible here to give a complete overview of the philosophical and theological literature that may be qualified

as postmodern or even of all the meanings given to this ambiguous category. A number of helpful surveys exist. For a sociological perspective, see for example David Lyon, *Postmodernity* (Minneapolis: University of Minnesota Press, 1994); Rosenau, pp. 14ff., where she makes a helpful (if somewhat artificial) distinction between affirmative and skeptical forms of postmodernism.

On the philosophical level, see Modernity and its Discontents, James Marsh, John Caputo, and Merold Westphal, eds. (New York: Fordham University Press, 1992); Louis Dupré, "Postmodernity or Late Modernity," in Review of Metaphysics 47 (1993), pp. 277–95. For repercussions in religion, see Religion, Ontotheology and Deconstruction, Henry Ruf, ed. (New York: Paragon House, 1989).

For a general survey of postmodern thought as it relates to Christian theology, see Paul Lakeland, Postmodernity. Christian Identity in a Fragmented Age (Minneapolis: Fortress Press, 1997); for more technical discussions, see David Tracy, "The Uneasy Alliance Reconsidered: Catholic Theological Method, Modernity, and Postmodernity," in Theological Studies 50 (1989), pp. 548–70; Jack A. Bonsor, "History, Dogma, and Nature: Further Reflections on Postmodernism and Theology," in Theological Studies 55 (1994), pp. 295–313; Thomas Guarino, "Between Foundationalism and Nihilism: Is Phronesis the Via Media for Theology," in Theological Studies 54 (1993), pp. 37–54; "Postmodernity and Five Fundamental Theological Issues," in Theological Studies 57 (1996), pp. 654–89.

It may perhaps be observed that just as England escaped the more violent manifestations of Romanticism that affected French drama and literature, precisely because English writing (due to the lasting influence of Shakespeare?) had never been so completely imbued with the values and norms of that classicism to which Romanticism was opposed, so Roman Catholic thought is perhaps less prone to be attracted by the more radical forms of postmodernity precisely because it never totally or uncritically accepted modernity—and indeed long struggled against many of its intellectual and social positions.

84. See for example Bernard Lonergan's *Insight* (New York: Philosophical Library, 1957) and *Method in Theology* (New York: Herder & Herder, 1973). For many postmodern thinkers, any such attempt is linked to a philosophical foundationalism that must be rejected.

85. For example, David Tracy in *Plurality and Ambiguity. Hermeneutics, religion, hope* (San Francisco: Harper & Row, 1987).

86. Instances might be drawn from the various forms of liberation theology. From a methodological perspective, see for example Clodovis Boff, *Theology and Praxis. Epistemological Foundations*, transl. by Robert R. Barr (Maryknoll, N.Y.: Orbis, 1987); Enrique Dussel, *Método para una filosofía de la liberación: Superación analéctica de la dialéctica hegeliana* (Salamanca: Sígueme, 1974).

87. See George Lindbeck, *The Nature of Doctrine. Religion and Theology in a post-liberal age* (Philadelphia: Westminster Press, 1984).

88. In this direction one may cite the thought of Emmanuel Levinas, for example, or that of his Latin American follower, Enrique Dussel. More classical metaphysical theology is also open to this perspective: cf. Rahner's *"reductio in mysterium,"* for example. This line of thought might also be fruitfully connected with the ideas of "non-self" and of "emptiness" (*sûnya*) in Buddhism. The "mystical" quality often noted in abstract paintings like Rothko's referred to above, consisting simply of imperfect bands of color, perhaps has a link to the Buddhist idea of the realization of the eternal in the "suchness" or "thisness" (*tathatâ*) of each finite event.

89. Lonergan does not see these as simply proceeding in linear succession; there is also dialectic. *Method in Theology*, p. 319.

90. Ibid., pp. 305–18.

91. See for example Jeremy Begbie's summary of Paul Tillich's *Masse und Geist*, in which he examines the spiritual implications of the way masses are portrayed in the history of painting. *Voicing Creation's Praise*, p. 17.

92. See Rigby et al., op. cit., pp. 673–76. As already noted (see above, n. 26), Garrett Green believes that the assertion of arbitrariness in choosing among paradigms (and the "Wittgensteinian fideism" sometimes espoused as a consequence) cannot correctly appeal to Kuhn's position for justification. Op. cit., p. 141.

93. See Green, loc. cit.; Rigby, et al., op. cit., p. 675.

94. A. J. Ayer, *Philosophy in the Twentieth Century* (New York: Random House, 1982), pp. 2–3.

95. Of course, such scientific progress, from a more comprehensive point of view, may not necessarily lead to total betterment for individuals or for the world; witness our current ecological problems resulting from poorly managed scientific technology. Nevertheless, purely within the realm of empirical knowledge,

there can be little doubt that contemporary science is an advance upon that of preceding eras.

96. Ibid.

97. Rigby et. al., loc. cit. The authors expand on Laudan's argument that even if the cognitive goals of science are themselves somewhat susceptible to change, there is a basis for judgment among the various goals in the common empirical validational process.

98. As noted above (see note 20), Gadamer presents the history of art as the principal example of the multiplicity and changeability of worldviews precisely because "this historical multiplicity cannot be resolved into the unity of a progress toward true art." *Truth and Method*, pp. 87–88.

99. No doubt such technological advances had a great deal to do with making possible the shift in "point of view" noted by Ortega. The relation of art to technology, however, lies outside the scope of the present paper's concerns.

100. Ayer, loc. cit.

101. Lonergan, *Method in Theology*, pp. 305ff.

102. Of course, one might also reject even this "quantitative" notion of progress on the grounds that it means the loss of an original undifferentiated integrity of experience. So Taoism encourages us to discard learning and return to the simplicity of the "uncarved block" (*Tao Te Ching*, 28). It also must be remarked that the sheer plurality of points of view, combined with increasing temporal distance, makes it ever more difficult to know thoroughly any one of them.

103. Lonergan, *Method in Theology*, p. 305.

104. As Edward Schillebeeckx remarks, *human* truth is only possible as remembered truth. See his *Christ: The Experience of Jesus as Lord* (New York: Seabury, 1977) p. 739. See also his comments on the humanizing effect of critical recollection of past in *Jesus: An Experiment in Christology* (New York: Seabury, 1979), p. 592.

105. To what extent art and philosophy are necessarily involved in dialogue with history seems to me a question too complex for discussion in the present context. However, it seems clear that these fields are in any case less *intrinsically* connected with history than theology is.

106. Bernard Lonergan, "Theology in Its New Context" in William F. J. Ryan, S.J., and Bernard J. Tyrrell, S.J., eds., *A Second*

Collection. Papers by Bernard J. F. Lonergan, S.J. (London: Darton, Longman & Todd, 1974), p. 55.

107. Ibid., p. 56.

108. Lonergan, "Theology in its new Context," p. 57.

109. Küng, "Paradigm Change," p. 28.

110. Ibid., p. 24.

111. Lonergan, "The Transition from a Classicist World-View to Historical Mindedness" in *A Second Collection* (London: Darton, Longman & Todd, 1974), pp. 1–9.

112. Lonergan, "Theology in its New Context," p. 58.

113. Ibid., pp. 58f.

114. It should be noted, however, that thinkers like Lonergan had already spoken of the "constitutive" dimension of meaning even before the postmodern movement brought it to prominence.

115. See above, p. 30.

116. Cf. Gen 1:28. As has frequently been pointed out, for example by Jürgen Moltmann, the use of this text to justify the exploitation of the Earth is unwarranted, nor is there evidence that such a theological use is at the root of the secular spirit of domination. Nevertheless, there is at least an indirect link between the Christian theology of creation and its secular substitutes.

117. For an overview of the meaning and development of liberation theology, see Alfred T. Hennelly, S.J., ed., *Liberation Theology: A Documentary History* (Maryknoll, N.Y.: Orbis Books, 1990).

118. Frank Burch Brown, *Religious Aesthetics. A Theological Study of Making and Meaning* (Princeton, N.J.: Princeton University Press, 1989), p. 45.

119. Ibid., pp. 178–184; see especially p. 179.

120. This is a crucial step in preparing the ground for the operation of the theological specialties that Lonergan calls "dialectics" and "foundations." See *Method in Theology*, 235–66.

121. Frank Burch Brown, *Religious Aesthetics*, p. 43.

NOTES TO CHAPTER 3

1. In recent years a number of works have appeared that manifest this tendency. Already classic are Hans Urs von Balthasar, *The Glory of the Lord. A Theological Aesthetics*, vol. 1, transl. by E. Leiva-Merikakis, ed. by Joseph Fessio and John Riches (San Francisco: Ignatius Press, 1982), and Gerardus van der Leeuw,

Sacred and Profane Beauty. The Holy in Art, transl. by David E. Green (New York: Holt, Rinehard and Winston, 1963). Among other notable works that explicitly attempt an integration of theology and aesthetics, see: Frank Burch Brown, *Religious Aesthetics. A Theological Study of Making and Meaning* (Princeton, N.J.: Princeton University Press, 1989); Jeremy S. Begbie, *Voicing Creation's Praise. Towards a Theology of the Arts* (Edinburgh: T&T Clark, 1991); Günter Pöltner and Helmuth Vetter, eds., *Theologie und Ästhetik* (Wien, Freiburg, Basel: Herder, 1985); Patrick Sherry, *Spirit and Beauty. An Introduction to Theological Aesthetics* (Oxford: Clarendon Press, 1992); J. Daniel Brown, *Masks of Mystery. Explorations in Christian Faith and the Arts* (Lanham, N.Y., London: University Press of America, 1997); Nicholas Wolterstorff, *Art in Action. Toward a Christian Aesthetic* (Grand Rapids, Mich.: William B. Eerdmans, 1980); Garrett Green, *Imagining God. Theology and the Religious Imagination* (San Francisco: Harper & Row, 1989); and my own *Theological Aesthetics. God in Imagination, Beauty, and Art* (New York: Oxford University Press, 1999).

2. John Ruskin, "Preface" to *St. Mark's Rest*, in *Ruskin Today*, chosen and annotated by Kenneth Clark (Harmondsworth: Penguin Books, 1964), p. 196.

3. The work of John and Jane Dillenberger has been influential in bringing art to prominence as a significant element in religious studies. See, among other works, Jane Dillenberger, *Image and Spirit in Sacred and Secular Art*, ed. by Diana Apostolos-Cappadona (New York: Crossroad, 1990); *Style and Content in Christian Art* (New York: Crossroad, 1986). John Dillenberger, *A Theology of Aesthetic Sensibilities. The Visual Arts and the Church* (New York: Crossroad, 1986); "Visual Arts and Religion. Modern and Contemporary Contours" in *Journal of the American Academy of Religion* LVI (Summer 1988), pp. 199–212; "Review of *Sacred Imagination: The Arts and Theological Education*" *Arts* 7, no. 1 (1994). Also important and influential is the work of Margaret Miles. See especially *Image as Insight. Visual Understanding in Western Christianity and Secular Culture* (Boston: Beacon Press, 1985).

4. John E. Cort, "Art, Religion, and Material Culture: Some Reflections on Method," in *Journal of the American Academy of Religion*, LXIV (1996), pp. 613–32, at p. 614.

5. Ibid. Cort performs the interesting experiment of examining exclusively from images a religious tradition that is also known from texts (Jainism) to demonstrate that a different view of the tradition emerges from the two approaches and thus to

support the contention that both are necessary and mutually enlightening.

6. Van der Leeuw, *Sacred and Profane Beauty*, p. 11.

7. Frank Burch Brown, *Religious Aesthetics. A Theological Study of Making and Meaning* (Princeton, N.J.: Princeton University Press, 1989), pp. 40, 165.

8. See Bernard Lonergan, *Method in Theology* (New York: Herder & Herder, 1972), pp. 160–61. David Freedberg reminds us of the limitations of a contextual approach to art history: "We have seen and learned too much; we cannot see with old eyes." David Freedberg, *The Power of Images. Studies in the History and Theory of Response* (Chicago and London: Chicago University Press, 1989), p. 431. Despite this hyperbolic assertion, Freedberg acknowledges the value of seeking historical context, both in theory and in his practice. He opposes only "a strict and unthinking contextualism." Ibid., p. 439.

9. Arthur Mirgeler, *Mutations of Western Christianity*, transl. by Dom David Knowles, O.S.B. (Notre Dame, Ind.: University of Notre Dame Press, 1968), p. 11.

10. For a theological reflection on the distinction in nature between the church and the covenanted people of Israel, see Wolfhart Pannenberg, *Systematic Theology*, transl. by Geoffrey W. Bromiley (Grand Rapids, Mich.: William B. Eerdmans and Edinburgh: T&T Clark, 1998), vol. 3, pp. 25–26, 31–32, 98, 469–78.

11. On realms and stages of meaning, see Lonergan, *Method in Theology*, pp. 81–86.

12. Ibid., p. 114.

13. Mirgeler, *Mutations of Western Christianity*, p. 17.

14. Nineteenth-century scholarship posited exactly such a gap between Christian intellectual leaders and popular religion as the explanation for the seeming contradiction between the early fathers' frequent iconoclastic pronouncements and the simultaneous emergence of Christian visual art. More recent scholarship, however, tends to see this supposed contradiction as an oversimplification. See especially Paul Corby Finney, *The Invisible God. The Earliest Christians on Art* (New York and Oxford: Oxford University Press, 1994), p. 291 and passim. See also David Freedberg, *The Power of Images. Studies in the History and Theory of Response* (Chicago and London: Chicago University Press, 1989), p. 62, and Aidan Nichols, O.P., *The Art of God Incarnate. Theology and Image in Christian Tradition* (New York: Paulist Press, 1980), pp. 21–33.

15. Mirgeler, *Mutations of Western Christianity*, pp. 19, 45.

16. Saint Bonaventura, *The Mind's Road to God*, translated, with an introduction, by George Boas (Indianapolis: Bobbs-Merrill Educational Publishing, 1953), Prologue, #4, p. 4–5.

17. On sacred orders and hierarchy in the church, see the Council of Trent's "Decree on the Sacrament of Orders" (DS 1764–1778), especially canons 6 and 7 (DS 1776–1777); on the superiority of the celibate state, "Decree on the Sacrament of Matrimony," canon 10 (DS 1810).

18. See Josef Sudbrack, *s.v.* "Spirituality" in Karl Rahner, ed., *The Concise Sacramentum Mundi* (New York: Seabury Press, 1975), pp. 1625ff., 1631.

19. Dom David Knowles, "Foreword" to Mirgeler, *Mutations of Western Christianity*, p. vi.

20. Lonergan, *Method in Theology*, pp. 235ff.

21. Margaret R. Miles, *Image as Insight. Visual Understanding in Western Christianity and Secular Culture* (Boston: Beacon Press, 1985), p. 9.

22. For expansion of the idea of picturing as a direct expression of thought, see Nadine Pence Frantz, "Material Culture, Understanding, and Meaning: Writing and Picturing" in *Journal of the American Academy of Religion*, vol. 66, no. 4 (Winter, 1998), pp. 791–816.

23. *"Nam quod legentibus scriptura, hoc idiotis praestat pictura cernentibus, quia in ipsa ignorantes vident quod sequi debeant, in ipsa legunt qui litteras nesciunt; unde praecipue gentibus pro lectione pictura est…"* Ep. *"Litterarum tuarum primordia."* DS 477.

24. See for example Bernard of Clairvaux's *"Apologia"* to William, Abbot of St.-Thierry, PL 182, 914–16. Bernard fiercely criticizes the richness of the decoration of churches, particularly those of monks who are ostensibly devoted to evangelical poverty, but he accepts the need of art in its practical pastoral function for the common people.

The Protestant Reformation saw a renewal of the iconoclast spirit. Although Luther took a positive attitude toward sacred images, Karlstadt, Zwingli, and Calvin rejected them. Calvin explicitly rejected Gregory the Great's position, arguing that it not only falsely presumes pictures to be more effective at communicating the message than narration, but also implies a kind of "class structure" among the faithful, relegating the uneducated to a secondary place in reception of God's word.

25. Guglielmus (William) Durandus, *Rationale Divinorum Officiorum*, Book I, transl. by J. M. Neale and B. Webb, in Elizabeth Gilmore Holt, ed., *A Documentary History of Art*, vol. I (Garden City, N.Y.: Doubleday and Co., 1957), p. 123. The same idea is found in Aristotle and is echoed in later writers like Erasmus and Leonardo da Vinci. See Freedberg, *The Power of Images*, p. 50.

26. Leonid Ouspensky, *Theology of the Icon*, transl. by Anthony Gythiel (Crestwood, N.Y.: St. Vladimir's Seminary Press, 1992), vol. I, pp. 138–39.

27. St. Augustine, *The Trinity*, transl. by Edmund Hill, O.P. (Brooklyn, N.Y.: New City Press, 1991), book VIII, ch. 3, p. 246.

28. Ibid., p. 247.

29. Ibid., p. 246.

30. Ibid. The verse is a slightly modified quotation of the famous lines from Horace's *Ars Poetica*, 9:

Pictoribus atque poetis
Quidlibet audendi semper fuit aequa potestas.

"Painters and poets have always had equal license for daring [to invent] anything." Durand's text has substituted *addendi* ("adding on") for *"audendi"* ("daring").

31. *The Trinity*, book VIII, ch. 6, p. 246.

32. See Bernard Lonergan, *Method in Theology* (New York: Herder & Herder, 1972), chs. 10 and 11.

33. As we have seen above, a similar idea is present in the Orthodox theology of the icon—although it should be pointed out that the Orthodox view of what constitutes valid sacred art is more restricted than the one I am presenting here, and the rationale of the theological evaluation is somewhat different.

34. Patrick Sherry, *Spirit and Beauty. An Introduction to Theological Aesthetics* (Oxford: Clarendon Press, 1992), p. 77f.

35. Ibid., p. 176.

36. On the notion of "natural" knowledge of God, see the "Constitution on Catholic Faith" of the First Vatican Council, esp. DS 3004, 3026; Vatican II, "Dogmatic Constitution on Divine Revelation," ch. I, paragraphs 3 and 6.

37. For an expanded discussion of this point, see my *Theological Aesthetics*, ch. IV.

38. For Balthasar's views, the entirety of the first volume of *The Glory of the Lord* is relevant. For Barth, see *Church Dogmatics*,

ed. by G. W. Bromiley and T. F. Torrence (Edinburgh: T&T Clark, 1970), vol. II, part 1, especially pp.641ff.

39. Balthasar tends to speak of the "form" (*Gestalt*) of the Christ event in the singular, even when referring to the scriptural accounts. I would rather say that even though the life of Christ can be spoken of as a concrete and single revelatory event, there is no single adequate categorical form corresponding to this event taken in its wholeness, that is, including the resurrected Christ and the experience of the Spirit. Rather, the event, insofar as it includes the faith response of Christ's followers, constitutes itself in a multiplicity of categorical forms "incarnating" a transcendental reality. Even the Christ event that is constituted by Jesus personally is available *to us* only through anamnesis in a plurality of scriptural and ecclesial forms. Finally, the Christ event itself is mediated to us historically through an ongoing series of categorical formulations, including not only the sacred narratives, but also the liturgical, spiritual, and communal life of the church. In the latter, sacred art has a significant, if sometimes neglected, place.

40. Julian, Anchoress at Norwich, *Revelations of Divine Love. A Version from the Manuscript in the British Museum*, ed. by Grace Warrack (London: Methuem & Co. Ltd., 1949), p. 147. This piece has been set to music by William Mathias in the anthem known by its opening words, "As truly as God is our Father." There is a recording by the Christ Church Cathedral Choir under Stephen Darlington on the compact disk *William Mathias. Church and Choral Music* (Nimbus Records, 1990; NI 5243).

41. Alternate opening prayer for the third Sunday in ordinary time; cf. the opening prayer for the twenty-seventh Sunday.

42. Alternate opening prayer for the seventeenth Sunday of ordinary time.

43. Barth, *Church Dogmatics*, vol. 1, p. 652.

44. Edward Schillebeeckx, "Living in Human Society," in *The Schillebeeckx Reader*, ed. by Robert Schreiter (New York: Crossroad, 1984), p. 55.

45. If we follow the Scholastic tradition and think of beauty as a transcendental quality, having its basis in God and participated in analogously in different degrees by creatures, then God is the source of all beauty, at whatever level. Then, as Augustine saw, God is in some way hidden in all "illusory" desires as well and is the source of whatever is good in them. In

this perspective, Paul Claudel could write: *"rien n'est illusion, tout est allusion."*

46. Joseph Campbell, "The Symbol without Meaning," in *The Flight of the Wild Gander* (Washington, D.C.: Regnery Gateway, 1969), p. 188, quoted in Joseph M. Felser, "Was Joseph Campbell a Postmodernist?" in *Journal of the American Academy of Religion,* LXIV (1996), pp. 395–418, at p. 409.

47. For a more extended treatment of this topic, see my *Theological Aesthetics. God in Imagination, Beauty, and Art* (New York: Oxford University Press, 1999), especially ch. VI.

48. David Tracy, *The Analogical Imagination. Christian Theology and the Culture of Pluralism* (New York: Crossroad, 1981), pp. 68, 108.

49. Ibid., p. 163.

50. Ibid., p. 234.

51. Ibid.

52. Ibid., p. 237.

53. Ibid., p. 249.

54. Tracy gives several concrete examples. He names Chartres cathedral as an artistic and religious classic that retains a disclosive power even when its religious character is denied; the religious art of Rubens and Bernini as embodying the dialectical character of every classic, which is intensified in the religious classic; and a number of literary works—"some of the Psalms, Job, Jeremiah, Paul's hymn to love, parts of John's gospel, the prose of Augustine, Pascal, Newman, Kierkegaard, the poetry of Dante, John of the Cross, Milton, Donne or Eliot." Ibid., pp. 172, 176, 201. Tracy notes, however, that such works are not religious and aesthetic classics for identical reasons.

55. Frank Burch Brown, *Religious Aesthetics. A Theological Study of Making and Meaning* (Princeton, N.J.: Princeton University Press, 1989), pp. 40, 165.

56. Ibid., pp. 162ff.

57. Ibid., p. 168.

58. Ibid.

59. Paul Tillich, *Systematic Theology,* vol. 1 (Chicago: University of Chicago Press, 1951), p. 8. See also pp. 59–66.

60. Ibid., pp. 12–14.

61. Various Christian theologies of a Barthian cast have rejected or minimized the place of apologetics (and therefore also the "method of correlation") in theology, arguing for a purely intratextual or hermeneutical approach. See especially

George A. Lindbeck, *The Nature of Doctrine: Religion and Theology in a Post-Liberal Age* (Philadelphia: Westminster Press, 1984). David Tracy has attempted to answer the legitimate concerns of anti-correlational theologians, while arguing for the continued need for apologetics and providing the outline of a "revised" correlational method. See his *Blessed Rage for Order* (New York: Seabury Press, 1975), pp. 43–63, 79–81; cf. *The Analogical Imagination* (New York: Crossroad, 1981), pp. 24–27, 60–61, 374–76, 405–8.

62. Paul Tillich, *The Religious Situation*, quoted in Jeremy Begbie, *Voicing Creation's Praise. Towards a Theology of the Arts* (Edinburgh: T&T Clark, 1991), p. 47.

63. Paul Tillich, *Theology of Culture*, ed. by Robert C. Kimball (New York: Oxford University Press, 1959), p. 70; quoted in Begbie, *Voicing Creation's Praise*, p. 48. It is not my intention here to endorse Tillich's theory of art in every respect. The relationship between religion, theology, and art is perhaps more complex and multidimensional than Tillich's remarks might lead one to think. Nevertheless, I believe there is a fundamental truth in Tillich's assessment of the function of art as manifesting the situation of an era.

64. Nicholas Wolterstorff, *Art in Action. Toward a Christian Aesthetic* (Grand Rapids, Mich.: William B. Eerdmans, 1980), pp. 86–89.

65. Ibid., p. 89 n.

66. On the notions of transcendental and categorical, general and special revelation, see my *Answering for Faith* (New York: Paulist Press, 1987), pp. 80–87. For a brief overview, see below, ch. 5.

67. David Tracy, *The Analogical Imagination. Christian Theology and the Culture of Pluralism* (New York: Crossroad, 1981), pp. 57, 63f.

68. See Wolfhart Pannenberg, *Systematic Theology*, transl. by Geoffrey W. Bromiley (Grand Rapids, Mich.: William B. Eerdmans, 1991, 1994, 1998), vol. 1, p. 58; vol. 3, pp. 170f, on the anticipatory and provisional character of the certitude of faith and the questioning of faith as coming from God, as an essential part of God's self-manifestation in history.

69. On the classic's demand for conversion on the part of the subject, see Lonergan, *Method in Theology*, pp. 160–1.

70. Tracy, *The Analogical Imagination*, p. 163.

71. Ibid., p. 200.

72. See Raphael Schulte, developing Karl Rahner's view, *s.v.* "Sacraments" in Karl Rahner, ed., *Encyclopedia of Theology. The Concise Sacramentum Mundi* (New York: Seabury Press, 1975), p. 1481. For a

Protestant objection to this conception of sacrament, see Wolfhart Pannenberg, *Systematic Theology*, transl. by Geoffrey W. Bromiley (Grand Rapids, Mich.: William B. Eerdmans; Edinburgh: T&T Clark, 1998), p. 342. However, Pannenberg also recognizes the ambivalence of the word and explicitly speaks of the church's "sign" character as "sacramental."

73. Robert H. Sharf, "The Scripture on the Production of Buddha Images," in Donald S. Lopez, Jr., ed., *Religions of China in Practice*. Princeton Readings in Religion (Princeton, N.J.: Princeton University Press, 1996), p. 261. One text of the kind Sharf mentions is given in Donald K. Swearer, "Consecrating the Buddha," in Donald S. Lopez, Jr., ed., *Buddhism in Practice*. Princeton Readings in Religion (Princeton, N.J.: Princeton University Press, 1995), pp. 50–58. The consecration formula explicitly intends to confer on the image the powers of Buddha himself: "May all of the transcendental states of the Blessed One...be invested in this image....May the boundless concentration and the body-of-liberation of the Buddha be invested in this image....May all of the miracles performed by the Buddha be invested in this image....May the Buddha's boundless virtue be stored in this image..." and so on (p. 57).

74. See for example the accounts in Hans Belting, *Likeness and Presence. A History of the Image before the Era of Art*, transl. by Edmund Jephcott (Chicago and London: University of Chicago Press, 1994), pp. 60, 194, 308,, 332f.

75. See the decree of the Second Council of Nicaea (787), DS 600–601.

76. See the decrees of the Council of Frankfurt (794), and those of the XXV session of the Council of Trent (1563) on the veneration of sacred images (DS 1823).

77. I believe that this statement accords with both Western theology and the Orthodox doctrine of the icon, despite the seeming ambiguity of statements like Ouspensky's that icons "contain grace" (explaining the doctrine of the Seventh Ecumenical Council [Nicaea II] in *Theology of the Icon*, vol. I, p. 130). When St. John Damascene, for example, says that the Holy Spirit lives in the images of the saints, he carefully adds that this is so "not because of their nature, but as a result of grace and divine action" (*De imaginibus oratio*, I, 19; PG 94 [I]: 1249CD; quoted in Ouspensky, *Theology of the Icon*, vol. I, p. 173).

78. Presumed here is the notion that God's self-gift as an offer is a continually present "existential," experienced as a transcendental condition of concrete existence, and realized categorically only in and through the human acts and symbolic formulations of which it is the transcendental condition of possibility. See Karl Rahner, *Foundations of Christian Faith*, transl. by William B. Dych (New York: Crossroad, 1990), pp. 126–33.

79. For a discussion of the idea of conversion, see Lonergan, *Method in Theology* (New York: Herder & Herder, 1972), especially pp. 130f., 240f.

80. I prescind here from the question of whether and to what extent this absoluteness and definitiveness also implies uniqueness. See my *Answering for Faith* (New York: Paulist Press, 1987), pp. 232–52.

81. Tracy, *The Analogical Imagination*, pp. 107–8.

82. Brown, *Religious Aesthetics*, pp. 169–78.

83. Ibid.

84. On this notion that certain pictures were directly produced by God or by Christ during his lifetime—with the implication that they are therefore of equal "authority" with the scriptures as a witness to revelation—see Belting, *Likeness and Presence*, pp. 62–69; Ouspensky, *Theology of the Icon*, vol. 1, pp. 51ff.

Notes to Chapter 4

1. Jean-Dominique Robert, O.P., *Essai d'Approches Contemporaines de Dieu en Fonction des Implications Philosophiques du Beau* (Paris: Beauchesne, 1982).

2. Boris Pasternak, *Doctor Zhivago*, transl. by Max Hayward and Manya Harari (New York: New American Library, 1958), p. 339.

3. In using the terms *heart* and *feeling* I am of course already engaging in the aesthetic, metaphorical level of discourse. For a discussion of these terms in relation to philosophical discourse, see Andrew Tallon, "The Concept of Heart in Strasser's *Phenomenology of Feeling*" in *The American Catholic Philosophical Quarterly*, vol. LXVI no. 3 (Summer 1992), pp. 341–60; "Affection, Cognition, Volition: The Triadic Meaning of Heart in Ethics," in Ibid., vol. LXVIII, no. 2 (Spring 1994), pp. 211–32. See also the treatment of *symbol* in Lonergan's *Method in Theology*, pp. 64–69.

4. See, for example, the Constitution on the Sacred Liturgy *Sacrosanctum Concilium*, #52; *General Instruction on the Roman Missal* #41.

5. The Fourth Lateran Council, in the context of its response to the Waldensian movement, restricted the office of preaching (in public or in private) to those who have an official ecclesiastical mission; the same restriction is reiterated by the Council of Trent (see DS 809, 1777). The need for a canonical "mission," however, which is intended to assure the ecclesial nature of preaching and the unity of faith, does not per se tie preaching exclusively to ordination; that is, not every ministry of the word need imply ordained sacramental ministry. On the other hand, the converse relationship—that is, an essential connection between ordained sacramental ministry and ministry of the word—seems to be theologically necessary.

6. The Second Vatican Council explicitly extends to Christian laity as a whole the responsibility for evangelization (addressed to both unbelievers and believers) not only by example, but also by the "apostolate of the word" (Vatican II, "Decree on the Apostolate of Lay People" [*Apostolicam Acuositatem*], ¶ 6 and 16). Lay people in missionary countries are specifically exhorted to "be ready to carry out the special mission of preaching the Gospel and teaching Christian doctrine" ("Decree on the Church's Missionary Activity" [*Ad Gentes Divinitus*], ¶ 21; see also ¶ 41).

7. Gerhard Von Rad, *Theology of the Old Testament* (New York: Harper & Row, 1962) vol. II, p. 378.

8. For a survey of the Old Testament language of faith, see Juan Alfaro, "Fides in terminologia Biblica" in *Gregorianum* 42 (1961).

9. On the dimension of faith as belief, see Juan Alfaro, *Fides, Spes, Caritas* (Rome: Pontificia Universitas Gregoriana, 1968), pp. 67–73.

10. For formulations of the content of the primitive kerygma, see especially the speeches of Peter and Paul in Acts: 2:14–36; 3:12–26; 4:9–12; 5:29–32; 10:34–43 (Peter); 9:20–22; 13:16–41; 17:1–3; 18:5 (Paul).

11. Alfaro notes the parallel between *belief* and *knowledge* in John's Gospel; compare for example John 11:27 with 7:26; 8:24 with 8:28; 14:12 with 14:20; 17:21 with 17:23.

12. See TDNT s.v. κηρύσσω, εὐαγγελίζομαι.

13. Other relevant New Testament terms include *discourse* (1 Cor 2:4), *consolation* or *encouragement* (1 Cor 14:3), *testimony* or *wit-*

ness (1 Cor 1:6), *exhortation* (Rom 12:8), *announcing* (Lk 9:60), and even simply *speaking* (Acts 20:7) or *telling* (Mk 2:2).

14. Humphrey Carpenter, ed., *The Letters of* J.R.R. *Tolkien* (Boston: Houghton Mifflin Company, 1981), p. 75.

15. Olivier de La Brosse, O.P., "La Prédication." In *Initiation à la pratique de la théologie. Tome* V., ed. by Bernard Lauret and François Refoulé (Paris: Les Éditions du Cerf, 1983), p. 113.

16. Bernard Lonergan, *Method in Theology* (New York: Herder & Herder, 1972), p. 4.

17. Lonergan, *Method in Theology*, p. 362.

18. This correlation is not meant to be exclusive. All three elements—insight, virtue, and art—are, of course, requisites for every form of preaching; but we may discern a particular affinity of each for the three interrelated goals.

19. See Lonergan, *Insight*, p. 210.

20. For a detailed analysis of "the biases," see Ibid., pp. 218–42; *Method in Theology*, pp. 52–55.

21. Quoted in Valentin Bulgakov: *The Last Year of Leo Tolstoi*, transl. by Ann Dunnigan (New York: The Dial Press, 1971), p. 87.

22. For an overview of the meaning and development of liberation theology, see Alfred Hennelly, S.J., ed., *Liberation Theology: A Documentary History* (Maryknoll, N.Y.: Orbis Books, 1990).

23. For an analysis of *scotosis*, or the bias that affects the subject on the level of the psyche, see Lonergan, *Insight* (New York: Philosophical Library, 1957), pp. 191–206.

24. Lonergan, *Method in Theology*, p. 130. For Lonergan's analysis of intellectual, moral, and religious conversion, see pp. 237–44.

25. On the "group bias," see Lonergan, *Insight*, pp. 222–25.

26. Cf. Lonergan, "*Existenz* and *Aggiornamento*" in *Collection*, ed. by F. E. Crowe, S.J. (New York: Herder & Herder, 1967), p. 245.

27. For the notion of conversion as a shift of horizon, see Lonergan, *Method in Theology*, pp. 235ff. For a treatment of the place of imagination in this shift, see David Tracy, *The Analogical Imagination. Christian Theology and the Culture of Pluralism* (New York: Crossroad, 1981), especially p. 562. For a parallel analysis from the point of view of liberation theology, see Enrique Dussel's treatment of the "totality" and the "other" in *Método para una filosofía de la liberacion* (Salamanca: Sígueme, 1974), pp. 188 ff.

28. See above, ch. 3, sections C.2. and C.3.; for a reference to the notion of *contrast experiences* in the theology of Schilllebeeckx, see ch. 3, note 45.

29. C. S. Lewis, *The Great Divorce* (Glasgow: William Collins Sons, 1972), p. 7.

30. "The purpose of the homily is to explain the readings and make them relevant for the present day." "Third Instruction on the Correct Implementation of the Constitution on the Sacred Liturgy, *Liturgiae Instaurationes*" (AAS 62 [1970]), #2, a.

31. Paul Tillich, *Systematic Theology*, vol. I (Chicago: University of Chicago Press, 1951), pp. 1–8.

32. David Tracy, *The Analogical Imagination* (New York: Crossroad, 1981), pp. 57, 97 n. 4.

33. Ibid., p. 57.

34. Ibid., p. 97, n. 114.

35. Ibid., p. 57.

36. Ibid., p. 97, n. 114. George Lindbeck gives a similar division: Systematic or dogmatic theology is concerned with faithfulness, practical theology with applicability, foundational theology with intelligibility. Lindbeck, *The Nature of Doctrine* (Philadelphia: The Westminster Press, 1984), p. 112.

37. See, for example, Aleksandr Solzhenitsyn, "A World Split Apart." Commencement address at Harvard University, June 8, 1978. Printed in *Vital Speeches* XLIV (Sept. 1, 1978) pp. 678–84.

38. Karl Rahner, "Observations on the Situation of Faith Today" in René Latourelle, and Gerald O'Collins, eds., *Problems and Perspectives of Fundamental Theology* (New York: Paulist Press, 1982), p. 281.

39. Loc cit.

40. Hans Urs von Balthasar, "Another Ten Years," transl. by John Saward, in John Riches, ed., *The Analogy of Beauty. The Theology of Hans Urs von Balthasar* (Edinburgh: T&T Clark, 1986), p. 227.

41. John Riches, "Balthasar and the analysis of faith" in Ibid., p. 47.

42. Lindbeck, *The Nature of Doctrine*, p. 124.

43. Cf. the postconciliar document "On Dialogue with Unbelievers" of the Secretariat for Unbelievers (*Humanae Personae Dignitatem*; AAS 60 [1968], pp. 692–704), which recommends that "Preaching and catechetical formation should take account of this new climate" of dialogue with unbelievers (#IV, D). This dialogue is not merely a "missionary" necessity, but helps the believer to increased understanding of the "truths of faith" themselves (# II, 1).

44. See the decree *Gaudium et Spes*, #22; cf. the encyclical letter of Pope John Paul II *Redemptoris Missio*, 10.

45. Tillich, *Systematic Theology*, vol. I, pp. 59–66. See also David Tracy, *Blessed Rage for Order* (New York: Seabury Press, 1975), pp. 79–80.

46. Tillich, op. cit., pp. 61–62; see also Richard Viladesau, *The Reason for Our Hope* (New York: Paulist Press, 1984), pp. 3–19.

47. Tracy, "Hermeneutical Reflections in the New Paradigm" in Hans Küng and David Tracy, eds., *Paradigm Change in Theology* (New York: Crossroad, 1989), pp. 35, 54. Tracy notes that theology is "hermeneutical" from the start, because each of the "constants" is not immediately available but is only understood through interpretation. Ibid., p. 54. Cf. Tracy, "Some Concluding Reflections," in ibid., p. 462 (here Tracy adds the note of praxis to the definition).

48. See Tracy, "The Uneasy Alliance Reconceived: Catholic Theological Method, Modernity, and Postmodernity" in *Theological Studies*, Vol. 50, no. 3 (Sept. 1989), p. 559. In Tracy's view, it is possible to integrate transcendental method with contemporary heremeneutical concerns. But see Jack A. Bonsor, "Irreducible Pluralism: The Transcendental and Hermeneutical as Theological Options" in *Horizons* (Journal of the College Theology Society) 16, no. 2 (Fall 1989), 316–28; pp. 326, 328. Bonsor's point is that the hermeneutical and transcendental approaches have mutually exclusive philosophical starting points. Thus, "one cannot be *fundamentally* both a transcendental and a hermeneutical theologian" (ibid.; my emphasis). This is true, given Bonsor's definitions of the two approaches. But it does not obviate the possibility of integrating elements of the two approaches into a theology which is not exclusively one or the other.

49. Lonergan, *Method in Theology*, p. 20.

50. Ibid., p. 14.

51. Ibid., p. 25.

52. Immanuel Kant, *Kritik der Reinen Vernunft* (Hamburg: Felix Meiner, 1956), p. 14.

53. Briefly, knowing is seen to consist in an affirmation of being; but the judgment of being depends on an anticipation of being-as-such [Lonergan's "notion" of being; Rahner's *Vorgriff* of being]; and the condition of the real intelligibility of every judgment of being is seen to be the coaffirmation of the existence of God as the absolute Act of Being or Intelligibility; a like structure can be seen in the act of valuing and choosing; hence every act of knowing or loving manifests and implicitly affirms a dynamism toward God.

54. Richard Viladesau, *Answering for Faith* (New York: Paulist Press, 1987), p. 11.

55. Vid. Lonergan, *Method in Theology*, pp. 155–62.

56. On the other hand, there is also a danger in a totally aesthetic approach to liturgy. As we have seen in the first chapter, the word should be a corrective to any tendency to merely aesthetic religion and should embody the existential challenge of the message's content. Hence, the proclamation of the word itself should not be made into simply another aesthetic moment.

NOTES TO CHAPTER 5

1. *Theological Aesthetics* (New York: Oxford University Press, 1999).

2. Augustine, *Confessions*, book I, ch. 2.

3. Ibid., book III, ch. 6.

4. Ibid., book I, ch. 1.

5. In Scholastic language, the "natural" knowledge of God is possible because the mind has an intrinsic "obediential potency" (*potentia obedientialis*) for revelation. This potency consists in the "image" of God in humanity, which makes the human person intrinsically "open" to being and goodness.

6. Vatican II, "Dogmatic Constitution on Divine Revelation" (*Dei Verbum*), ch. I, in Austin Flannery, O.P., ed., *Vatican Council II. The Conciliar and Post Conciliar Documents* (Northport, N.Y.: Costello Publishing Co., 1975), pp. 750–51.

7. See Wolfhart Pannenberg, *Systematic Theology*, vol. 1, transl. by Geoffrey W. Bromiley (Grand Rapids, Mich.: William B. Eerdmans, 1991), p. 222 and n. 70. For a summary of the development of this idea, with an emphasis on modern Protestant thinkers, see pp. 222–29.

8. For a fuller treatment of this theology of revelation, see Karl Rahner, *Foundations of Christian Faith*, transl. by William V. Dych (New York: Crossroad, 1990), pp. 116–75.

9. For a concise exposition of the understanding of the Trinity that underlies this assertion, see Karl Rahner, "Oneness and Threefoldness of God in Discussion with Islam" in *Theological Investigations*, vol. XVIII, transl. by Edward Quinn (New York, Crossroad: 1983), pp. 105–21.

10. For the use of the category "conversion" in this connec-

tion, see Bernard Lonergan, *Method in Theology* (New York: Herder & Herder, 1972), pp. 52, 130ff., 238–43.

11. See Bernard Lonergan, *Method in Theology* (New York: Herder & Herder, 1972), p. 238.

12. Ibid., p. 240.

13. See my *Theological Aesthetics*, pp. 205–7.

14. These two are not to be conceived as complementary elements in the conversion event: rather, the human reception of grace is itself wholly God's gift, although remaining a truly human achievement. That is to say that God's causality is transcendental; it is not to be thought of as being on the same level as inner-worldly events or causes. Radical dependence on God and genuine human achievement are, in Rahner's phrase, "in direct and not in inverse proportion" to one another. See Karl Rahner, *Foundations of Christian Faith*, transl. by William V. Dych (New York: Crossroad, 1990), p. 79.

15. Cf. Rom 8:29.

INDEX